Stockhausen: Life and Work

KARL H. WÖRNER

Stockhausen
LIFE AND WORK

*Introduced, translated
and edited by*
BILL HOPKINS

UNIVERSITY OF CALIFORNIA PRESS
Berkeley and Los Angeles 1973

UNIVERSITY OF CALIFORNIA PRESS
Berkeley and Los Angeles, California

ISBN: 0–520–02143–6
Library of Congress Catalog Card Number: 76–174460

Printed in Great Britain

Contents

Illustrations

Introduction

The aim of this book is to present the non-technical 'background' to Stockhausen. Background it must remain, for there can be no foreground but the music—a music whose understanding and enjoyment presupposes nothing that can be learnt through words. Yet this is by no means a monochrome or indistinct background. For one thing, the characteristic ideas expressed by the composer encompass many areas of thought, both concrete and abstract. For another thing, Stockhausen never for long remains unconscious of the need to find outlets for his creative will, and it is with such a will that he wields his words; rarely content merely to describe or merely to argue, his verbal style becomes a direct form of expression, often seeking out and exploring regions quite its own. And finally, there emerges from this 'background' a kind of spiritual biography, revealing the most striking contours in the mentality of an artist whose energetic pioneering has never blighted his musical sensitivity.

One might suspect that Stockhausen's standard procedure with ideas is to follow them up to see how far they will reasonably go, then to doggedly push them somewhat further. There are pages in this book where the reader will probably permit himself an indulgent smile as images flit across his mind—perhaps of a Beethoven dreaming of the day when his quartets could at last be realized electronically; or of such victims of 'universal mediation' as a procession of variously graded hermaphrodites arrayed in proportional rows. Then he may think twice—of Moog synthesizers, of Unisex—and time and again will realize that Stockhausen's ideas tend to relate rather closely, and often prophetically, to the realities around us, whether we like those realities or not. (Stockhausen was drawing up the BBC's plans for radio many years before they were put into practice.)

But although all possible manner of associations of ideas seem to be openly invited, we must always remember that it is in the music that Stockhausen's concepts are most fully expressed, and through the music that they will most truthfully take effect. The caution is rendered necessary by the composer's naivety, indispensable accomplice of his extraordinary vitality. For this book contains

not half so much a prospectus for a brave new world as a record of
the aspirations and inspirations that went into works as compelling
as *Gesang der Jünglinge*, as *Carré*, as *Stimmung*. Once the works are
lost sight of their motives are soon enough trivialized, and Stockhausen has been generous with ammunition for his earless critics to
seize upon.

From his 'visions' we must distinguish a great number of highly
consequential practical ideas. All, it is true, belong inextricably together within a superbly integrated mind; but on paper, fragments,
concrete proposals, are separable, and can be seen to speak with the
voice of a whole generation. Indeed many would claim, with reason,
that Stockhausen plays with unerring accuracy the role of spokes-
man for everything that marches under the New Music banner. His
direct influence has been vast; but so has his instinct for rooting out
the genuinely relevant musical issues of our time. It is certain that
many of his practical suggestions would be equally welcomed by
composers outside of his circle of influence, and even by composers antipathetic to his music and its techniques.

How many composers, for instance, have been influenced towards complexity by the assurance that the gramophone would
encourage listeners to sort it all out in repeated hearings ? (Admit-
tedly, not many of them can have been as often recorded as Stockhausen, with over thirty records at the present date.) In many
respects, the gramophone represents an ideal musical instrument of
the future—in type, if not in form. At present the user can 'perform' on little more than a single parameter—the overall dynamic
level—but already it enables him as listener to choose his music and
his occasion with complete freedom; and, crucially, a gramophone
recording is something lived with, something repeatedly confronted
and explored. These are considerations that must have been in
Stockhausen's mind while composing *Gruppen*, for it is a work he
singles out for mention in this connection. That being so, it is difficult to avoid the conclusion that the same work harbours a further
prediction—that of stereophonic gramophone recording, which in
1955 remained a thing of the future.

A possibility we have yet to see realized is that of the orchestra specializing in nineteenth-century music, suggested elsewhere in this book. In the light of recent debates about the future of the symphony orchestra, this idea is a fascinating one. In the first place it would demonstrate the absurdity of the position which holds that the symphony orchestra is moribund—for in exactly what sense are, say, our specialist medieval ensembles 'dead'? It is surely gross sentimentality to insist that 'life' depends on the infusion of new music, or rather—as is more often the case—of music by living composers, whether written to order or not. It should certainly not be seen as the responsibility of any contemporary composer to keep such existing bodies alive, or, shall we say, well fed.

Such are the more substantial thoughts to which this book can lead us. Yet at the centre of it all we must insist on placing the creative personality and work of Stockhausen. Whatever their practical consequences, the ideas are supremely validated only in the music that is in some sense contingent on them; if they stimulate our minds, they can become a 'background' shared with the composer.

Stockhausen's literary style is more vividly and variously exemplified in his collected writings (published as *Aufsätze* in three volumes) than in the more modest extracts included here, which are mainly restricted to his programme notes—forming the chapter 'Notes on the Works'—and conversational material. But the reader can still form a fair idea of the composer's range of literary expression, and may judge for himself the extent to which the style is always consciously and deliberately chosen to match as closely as possible the mood and the message of the moment. It is also relevant here to note how the author's own style has been sparked into rhetoric by a committed involvement with his subject: with a mind whose very governing principle would appear to be prolificity.

Particularly in the programme notes, though also in isolated quotations throughout the book, one can discern an evolution taking place in Stockhausen's attitude to his public. And here the style and presentation is a mirror of developments whose significance is a central one in the wider context of composition as it is practised today. What has happened is that the composer has gradually turned his attention from the specific technical problems severally described in notes on the earlier works, and has sought to confront more directly the sort of physical situation which actually exists when an audience assembles to hear new music. The performance itself assumes the principal weight—as a social event, and as a communing which seeks contact with 'higher vibrations'. The existence of composed music serves only a secondary purpose, whether as an object for contemplation through which an audience may 'tune in', or as 'found', familiar material upon which the performers are to freely exercise their current intentions. And, just as musical objects depreciate in their relative value, so will the figure of the composer diminish in stature: instead of the egocentric monster of yore, we shall see a breed of objective musical inventors and planners playing their role in the creation of a music in which every participant can truly find his own identity—a music in which the millions are not only embraced but are seen to be embraced.

Dr. Wörner rightly sees the note on '*Momente* 1965' as indicative of a turning-point. However, it reads more like the end of an old road than the beginning of a new one, and I believe it was not until he subsequently visited Japan that Stockhausen decisively struck out towards his present position. The text in question (dated 1964) gives us a candid portrait of a 'mind at the end of its tether'. We feel Stockhausen's perplexity as well as his excitement at glimpses beyond the dualistic philosophies of his youth; he has reached a cross-roads and is uncertain where to turn next, but is prepared to marshall all his intellectual forces to shake off the dust of self-consciousness gathered on the way. And we may sense that here lies a parable about the whole state of music today. However they may choose to confront it, composers are increasingly aware of a burden to be shed, the precipitate of half a century's intellectual inbreeding—of music about music, music about theories of music and music about the history of music. Cage has elected to shed the entire Western tradition, though even on him it has left ineffaceable scars; Stockhausen, more positively, has re-routed it.

These programme notes trace an evolution—and for all his innocence of the past, and of the nineteenth century in particular, Stockhausen is no denier of tradition, no revolutionary. Stockhausen's musical development, a progressive reclamation of the art of composition, has acted as a sort of blueprint for the itinerary of many a composer following in his wake: his thought is central to a proper understanding of much that is happening in music at the present time. There is great intrinsic beauty in that thought—it is continuous in its essentials and follows a route of some logical stringency. According to one report, Stockhausen's progress was planned by himself at the time of his earliest compositions—a progress towards greater indeterminacy to be followed by a return to more determinate forms of composition. If there is substance in this report, we shall see the composer, having once done his duty by 'the music of the whole world', taking up once again the detailed planning of music, seeking ways and stratagems whereby he can once again give of himself in every particular of music bearing his name, and yet again changing our whole concept of what it is to be a composer.

Such a prospect for the future cannot but awaken the keenest interest and anticipation. Under what new classical restraint will the composer feel entitled to shoulder again the whole weight of determinate composition while still scrupulously conserving the territory gained by the banishment of the ego? How will supreme talent regain its former status as a humble instrument after having been for so long viewed as a quirkish personal attribute? And how long will it take the world to prepare for such an eventuality? It is surely inevitable that an important part of the background to Stockhausen's music consists of thoughts on the subject of 'Music and Society'—for there can be no real change or development in the one without an implicit revision of the other; and it seems evident that to an inordinate extent Stockhausen has sustained his remarkable series of creations on buoyant hopes of a new society which would itself be worthy of their balance and harmony. It is for the sociologists and politicians to cavil; let us musicians and listeners be content awhile with gratitude.

When the first version of this book was published in Germany in 1963, it represented a first full-length study of Stockhausen's works and ideas; and it remained unique in its field when, five years later, Dr. Wörner added extensive new material with the present English edition in view: some forty per cent of the present book is here published for the first time in one volume. Before his death in 1969, I had not the opportunity to consult Dr. Wörner about the final form the book should take, and although he had clearly planned the new material as a simple expansion of the first published text (to the extent of indicating where it was to be inserted), there remained a number of loose ends and undesirable duplications; I also became convinced that what Dr. Wörner had now produced amounted substantially to a new book, and decided upon a form which would give this conviction some degree of expression. Some account of how the present volume differs from the script that reached me is to be found in what follows.

Originally, the book ended with a selection of press reviews of Stockhausen's works; the decision to eliminate this feature was Dr. Wörner's own. He also removed a brief section in which the doubts he had expressed have since proved largely unfounded. The cuts for which I am responsible are of a purely economic nature, primarily intended to bypass any reduplication of material. In the chapter 'Notes on the Works', I have allowed each work only one note, in the interests of convenient reference. This has involved 'telescoping' pairs (never more) of texts. I have interwoven texts in order to introduce greater continuity, and wherever it has for some reason seemed desirable to distinguish one original from another, they have been separated by spaces in the text. Dates and sources for the notes have been indicated only where they are of special relevance. My alterations in other parts of the book have been of a less sweeping nature, and I have always striven to retain every scrap of material the author wished to see published. Even where this material interrupts the continuity of the text, I have borne in mind that this is a source book as well as an introduction to Stockhausen. A few sub-heads have been added to break up the longer stretches; a revised discography is now combined with the catalogue of works.

The new form of the book is largely the result of a re-ordering of its chapters. Judging that not every reader would wish to take the book in 'moment form', I have endeavoured to construct a continuous form which could be followed from end to end without too great a feeling of *non sequitur*. Roughly speaking, the book describes an arc leading from the music to the man, and may be read through in direct or reverse order of chapters, depending upon whether the reader's interest is primarily musical or primarily biographical. It is still principally intended to serve as a work of reference, and I have furnished one or two footnotes giving cross-references that may be of use. My feeling that this book differs substantially from its German counterpart has also led me to rechristen it, the original title having been 'Karlheinz Stockhausen: his work and ideas'.

It having been Dr. Wörner's evident intention to keep the book as up-to-the-minute as possible, I have secured and added some extra material—principally the notes on *Kurzwellen mit Beethoven* and *Stimmung*, and some additions to the texts on *Gruppen, Refrain, Kontakte* and *Kurzwellen*. And of course, the biographical material and catalogue of works have both been supplemented with the latest information to hand. It is with this hindsight that I invite the reader to modify Dr. Wörner's own informative Foreword.

I should like here to express my thanks to the composer for his kindness and promptness in assisting me with extra material; to Richard Toop for a number of very helpful suggestions; and to John Thomson and Charles Ford for much valuable encouragement and advice at various stages of my work on the book.
B. H.
April 1972

Foreword

In 1960 I approached the publisher P. J. Tonger of Rodenkirchen (Cologne) to ask him if he would be interested in bringing out a book on Stockhausen in the series 'Kontrapunkte: writings on present-day German music' (edited by Heinrich Lindlar) which he was publishing. He agreed to the proposal, and the form of the book was quickly decided upon: Stockhausen consented to provide, in the form of conversations, the material on which my work was to be based. These conversations, spreading over a period of several months, were recorded on tape, and their content was transcribed into book form. The book then appeared in 1963. The text is authorized by Stockhausen, and forms an essential and not inconsiderable complement to the lectures and essays he himself has published in two volumes.

This new edition of my book is a much expanded version of the original text; the additional material was necessary in order to bring the book up to date, and deals with the works Stockhausen has written between 1962 and 1968, as well as with the most recent developments in his thinking. Once again it has been possible to refer to authentic material which Stockhausen has made available. The present version of my book, too, has been authorized by Stockhausen.

KARL H. WÖRNER
Heiligenkirchen über Detmold, January 1969

Catalogue of Stockhausen's works
Comprising discography

(Asterisks denote recordings available in Great Britain, April 1972)

1951 **Kreuzspiel** ('Cross-play') for oboe, bass clarinet, piano and percussion
First broadcast: WDR Cologne, December 1951
First public performance: Darmstadt Summer School, 21 July 1952
(Oboe: Romolo Grano; bass clarinet: Friedrich Wildgans; piano: Irmela Sand; percussion: Hans Rossmann, Bruno Maderna, Willy Trumpfheller, Paul Geppert; conductor: Karlheinz Stockhausen)

1951 **Formel** ('Formula') for orchestra

1952 **Etude.** Musique concrète

1952 **Spiel** ('Play') for orchestra
First performance: Donaueschingen Festival, 11 October 1952
(Conductor: Hans Rosbaud)
Unpublished

1952 **Schlagquartett** (Percussion quartet) for piano and 3 × 2 timpani
First broadcast: NDR Hamburg, 12 March 1953
First public performance: Musica Viva Munich, 23/24 March 1953
(Piano: Hans A. Kaul; timpani: Friedel Weber, Rudolf Bachmann, Kurt Pertkes; conductor: Wilhelm Schüchter)
Unpublished

1952 **Punkte** ('Points') for orchestra: *see* revised version, 1962

1952/53 **Kontra-Punkte** ('Counter-points') for 10 instruments
No. 1 *First performance:* Cologne Festival of New Music, 26 May 1953
(Cologne Radio Symphony Orchestra, conductor: Hermann Scherchen)
Recordings:

Bruno Maderna	*RCA Victrola VICS 1239
Pierre Boulez	Vega C 30 A 66 (France)

Klavierstücke I–IV (Piano pieces I–IV)   1952/
First performance: Darmstadt Summer School, 21 August 1954   No. 2
(Marcelle Mercenier)
Recording: Aloys Kontarsky   ★CBS 72591–2 (2-record set)

Studie I Electronic music   1953
First performance: 19 October 1954   No. 3/
Commissioned by NWDR Cologne and composed in NWDR's
Cologne studio
Recording: DGG LP 19133

Studie II Electronic music   1954
First performance: 19 October 1954   No. 3/
Commissioned by NWDR Cologne and composed in NWDR's
Cologne studio
Recording: DGG LP 19133

Klavierstücke V–X (Piano pieces V–X): *see also* revised versions of 1954/
IX & X, 1961   No. 4
First performance (**V–VIII**): Darmstadt, 1 June 1955
(Marcelle Mercenier)
Commissioned by the town of Darmstadt
Recordings:
     Aloys Kontarsky   ★CBS 72591–2 (2-record set)
     David Tudor (**VI** only)   Vega C 30 A278 (France)
     David Burge (**VIII** only)   ★Vox STGBY 637

Zeitmasze ('Tempi') for woodwind quintet   1955/
First performance: Domaine musical Paris, 15 December 1956   No. 5
(Oboe: Claude Maisonneuve; flute: Jacques Castagnier; cor ang-
lais: Paul Taillefer; clarinet: Guy Deplus; bassoon: André Rabot;
conductor: Pierre Boulez)
Recordings:
     Robert Craft   Odessey 32160154 (USA)
     Pierre Boulez   Vega C 30 A 139 (France)

55/57 Gruppen ('Groups') for three orchestras
No. 6   *First performance:* Cologne, 24 March 1958
(Cologne Radio Symphony Orchestra, conductors: Bruno Maderna,
Pierre Boulez, Karlheinz Stockhausen)
Commissioned by WDR Cologne
Recording: Stockhausen, Maderna, Gielen   *DGG 137002

1956 Klavierstück XI (Piano piece XI)
No. 7   *First performance:* Darmstadt Summer School, 28 July 1957
(Paul Jacobs)
Recordings:
Aloys Kontarsky   *CBS 72591–2 (2-record set)
Marie-Françoise Bucquet   *Philips 6500 101

55/56 Gesang der Jünglinge ('Song of the Youths'—*Benedicite*). Elec-
No. 8   tronic music with text from Daniel 3, lvii–lxv
First performance: WDR Cologne, 30 May 1956
Recordings:
monaural   DGG LP 19133
stereophonic version (1968)   *DGG 138811

1959 Zyklus ('Cycle') for one percussion player
No. 9   *First performance:* Darmstadt, 25 August 1959
(Christoph Caskel)
Composed as test piece for Kranichstein Music Prize for percus-
sion players, 1959
Recordings:
Christoph Caskel/Max Neuhaus   Heliodor Wergo 2549016
Christoph Caskel   Mainstream 5003 (USA)
Max Neuhaus   Columbia MS 7139 (USA)
Sylvio Gualda   Erato STU 70603 (France)
Yasunori Yamaguchi   Sonc 16 012 (Japan)

Carré for four orchestras and choruses   1959/
First performance: NDR Hamburg, 28 October 1960   No. 1(
(NDR Chorus: Max Thurn, Otto Franze; NDR Symphony
Orchestra, conductors: Michael Gielen, Mauricio Kagel, Andrzej
Markowski, Karlheinz Stockhausen)
Commissioned by NDR Hamburg
Recording: Kagel, Stockhausen, Markowski, Gielen *DGG 137002

Refrain for three players   1959
First performance: Berlin, 2 October 1959   No. 1
(Piano and wood blocks: David Tudor; celesta and antique cym-
bals: Cornelius Cardew; vibraphone, cowbells and glockenspiel:
Siegfried Rockstroh)
Commissioned for the Berlin Festival
Recordings:
    Aloys Kontarsky, Caskel, Stockhausen   *Vox STGBY 638
    Aloys & Bernhard
        Kontarsky, Caskel   Mainstream 5003 (USA)

Kontakte ('Contacts') for electronic sounds   1959/
Recording: *DGG 138811 No. 1

Kontakte for electronic sounds, piano and percussion
First performance: Cologne (34th ISCM Festival), 11 June 1960
(Percussion: Christoph Caskel; piano: David Tudor)
Commissioned by WDR
Recordings:
    Aloys Kontarsky, Caskel, Stockhausen   *Vox STGBY 638
    Tudor, Caskel, Stockhausen   Wergo 60009 (Germany)

Originale ('Originals'). Musical theatre   1961
12 performances between 26 October and 6 November 1961
Commissioned by the Theater am Dom, Cologne

54/61 Klavierstück IX
No. 4) *First performance:* WDR Cologne, 21 May 1962
(Aloys Kontarsky)
Recordings:
Aloys Kontarsky   *CBS 72591–2 (2-record set)
Marie-Françoise Bucquet   *Philips 6500 101

54/61 Klavierstück X
No. 4) *First performance:* Palermo Festival, 10 October 1962
(Frederic Rzewski)
Recordings:
Aloys Kontarsky   *CBS 72591–2 (2-record set)
Frederic Rzewski   Heliodor Wergo 2549016

62/64 Momente ('Moments') for soprano solo, four choral groups and
No. 13 13 instrumentalists: *see also* later version, 1963/64
First performance: WDR Cologne, 21 May 1962
(Soprano: Martina Arroyo; WDR Chorus: Helmut Franz; conductor: Karlheinz Stockhausen)

52/62 Punkte 1952/62 for orchestra (revised version)
First performance: Donaueschingen Festival, 20 October 1963
(SWDR Orchestra, conductor: Pierre Boulez)

1963 **Plus/Minus** 2 × 7 pages for elaboration
No. 14 *First performance:* Rome, 14 June 1964
(Cornelius Cardew, Frederic Rzewski)

63/64 Momente (1965 version) for soprano, four choral groups and 13
No. 13 instrumentalists
First performance: Donaueschingen, 16 October 1965
(Soprano: Martina Arroyo; Cologne Radio Chorus: Herbert Schernus; Cologne Radio Symphony Orchestra, conductor: Karlheinz Stockhausen)
Recording: Arroyo, Stockhausen   Wergo 60024 (Germany)

Mikrophonie I ('Microphony I') for tam-tam, 2 microphones, 2 1964
filters and potentiometers (6 players)   No. 1
First performance: Reconnaissance des musiques modernes Brussels, 9
February 1964
(Tam-tam: Aloys Kontarsky, Christoph Caskel; microphones:
Johannes Fritsch, Bernhard Kontarsky; filters and potentiometers:
Hugh Davies, Jaap Spek, Karlheinz Stockhausen)
Recording: Stockhausen Ensemble   *CBS 72647

Mixtur ('Mixture') for orchestra, sine-wave generators, ring 1964
modulators and loudspeakers: *see also* later version, 1967   No. 1
First performance: das neue werk NDR Hamburg, 9 November 1965
(NDR Symphony Orchestra, conductor: Michael Gielen; elec-
tronic modulation: Hugh Davies, Johannes Fritsch, Harald Bojé,
Makoto Shinohara; monitoring: Karlheinz Stockhausen, Jaap
Spek)

Mikrophonie II ('Microphony II') for chorus, Hammond organ 1965
and four ring modulators   No. 1
First performance: WDR Cologne, 11 June 1965
(Cologne Radio Chorus and Studio Chorus for New Music:
Herbert Schernus; Hammond organ: Alfons Kontarsky; co-
ordinator: Johannes Fritsch; monitoring: Jaap Spek, Karlheinz
Stockhausen)
Recording: as first performance   *CBS 72647

Stop for orchestra: *see also* Paris version, 1969   1965
                                           No. 1
Solo for melody instrument and tape recorder   1965/
First performance: Japan, 1966 (flute, trombone versions)   No. 1
                Basle, 2 May 1967 (oboe version)
(Oboe, oboe d'amore, cor anglais: Heinz Holliger)
Recording: Vinko Globokar (trombone)   *DGG 104992

1966 **Telemusik** ('Telemusic'). Electronic music: original five-track tape
No. 20 Realized in the studio for electronic music of Japanese Radio, Nippon Hoso Kyokai, Tokyo (January-April)
Recording: *DGG 137012

1966 **Adieu für Wolfgang Sebastian Mayer** ('Adieu for W.S.M.') for
No. 21 wind quintet
First broadcast: WDR Cologne, 3 February 1967
First public performance: Calcutta, 30 January 1967
(Cologne Radio Symphony Orchestra Wind Quintet)

1967 **Hymnen** ('Anthems'). Electronic music/musique concrète
No. 22 *First broadcast:* WDR Cologne, 23.00 hrs 30 November 1967
Recording: *DGG 2707039 (2 records)

No. 22½ **Hymnen** Electronic music/musique concrète with soloists: *see also* Third Region with orchestra, 1969
First performance: Apostel-Gymnasium (WDR Cologne), 20.00 hrs 30 November 1967
(Piano: Aloys Kontarsky; viola: Johannes Fritsch; electronium: Harald Bojé; percussion: Rolf Gehlhaar, David Johnson; technical assistants: David Johnson, Werner Scholz; direction and monitoring: Karlheinz Stockhausen)
Commissioned by WDR

1967 **Prozession** ('Procession') for tam-tam, viola, electronium, piano,
No. 23 microphones, filters and potentiometers
First performance: Radio Helsinki, 21 May 1967
German première: Darmstadt, 26 August 1967
(Fred Alings, Rolf Gehlhaar, Johannes Fritsch, Harald Bojé, Aloys Kontarsky, Karlheinz Stockhausen)
Recordings:
Stockhausen Ensemble *Vox STGBY 615
Stockhausen Ensemble
(different version) Fratelli Fabri mm–1098 (Italy)

Mixtur (revised version) for chamber ensemble, sine-wave genera- 1967
tors and ring modulators   No. 1
First performance: Frankfurt am Main, 23 August 1967
(Hudba Dneska Ensemble, Bratislava, conductor: Ladislav
Kupkovič; sine-wave generators: Harald Bojé, Johannes Fritsch,
David Johnson, Rolf Gehlhaar; monitoring: Karlheinz Stock-
hausen)
Recording: as first performance   *DGG 137012

Stimmung ('Attuning') for sex-tête (6 vocalists)   1968
First performance: Paris, 9 December 1968   No. 2
German première: Cologne, 13 December 1968
(Collegium Vocale der Rheinischen Musikschule—sopranos:
Dagmar Apel, Gaby Rodens; mezzo-soprano: Helga Albrecht;
tenor: Wolfgang Fromme; baritone: Georg Steinhoff; bass: Hans
Alderich Billig)
Recording: as first performance   *DGG 2543003

Kurzwellen ('Short-waves') for six players   1968
First performance: Pro musica nova Bremen, 5 May 1968   No. 2
(Fred Alings, Johannes Fritsch, Harald Bojé, Aloys Kontarsky,
Rolf Gehlhaar, Karlheinz Stockhausen)
Recording: Stockhausen
    Ensemble (2 versions)   *DGG 2707045 (2 records)

Kurzwellen mit Beethoven: Stockhoven—Beethausen Opus
1970
First performance: Düsseldorf, 17 December 1969
(Aloys Kontarsky, Johannes Fritsch, Harald Bojé, Fred Alings,
Rolf Gehlhaar, Karlheinz Stockhausen)
Recording: Stockhausen Ensemble   *DGG 139461

1968 **Aus den sieben Tagen** ('From the seven days'). 15 compositions,
No. 26 May 1968
  Recordings:
     Stockhausen Ensemble
        ('Setz die Segel zur   Harmonia Mundi MV 30795
        Sonne' & 'Verbindung')   (France)
     Stockhausen Ensemble   'Nuits de la Fondation Maeght'
        ('Unbegrenzt' & 'Es')   (St. Paul) (2 records–Belgium)

1968 **Spiral** for one soloist with short-wave receiver
No. 27 *Recordings:*
     Heinz Holliger (oboe)   DGG 2561109 (Germany)
     Michael Vetter (electric recorder)   Wergo 325 (Germany)
     Michael Vetter/Harald   'Nuits de la Fondation Maeght'
        Bojé (electronium)   (St. Paul) (Belgium)

1969 **Fresco** for four groups (Wall-sounds for meditation)
No. 28
1969 **Stop** (Paris version) for orchestra

1969 **Hymnen**—Third Region with orchestra

69/70 **Pole** for two
No. 29
69/70 **Expo** for three
No. 30
69/70 **Für kommende Zeiten** ('For times to come'). Seventeen texts for
No. 31 intuitive music

1970 **Mantra** for two pianists
No. 32 *Recording:* Aloys and Alfons Kontarsky   *DGG 2530208

1971 **Sternklang** ('Star-sound')
No. 33
1971 **Trans** for orchestra
No. 34

Stockhausen's notes on the works

Concerning my music*

The constant goal of my searches and efforts: the power of transformation—its operation in time: in music. Hence a refusal of repetition, of variation, of development, of contrast. Of all, in fact, that requires 'shapes'—themes, motives, objects, to be repeated, varied, developed, contrasted; to be dismembered, rearranged, augmented, diminished, displayed in modulation, transposition, inversion or retrograde. All this I renounced when I first began to work with 'pointillism'. Our own world—our own language—our own grammar: nothing neo- . . .! But then what? For me there followed *Kontra-Punkte*: a series of metamorphoses and renewals both deeply hidden and extremely apparent—tending to no visible end. Never is the same thing heard twice. Yet one has the clear feeling that an immutable and extremely homogeneous continuity is never abandoned. There is a hidden power of cohesion, a relatedness among the proportions: a structure. Not similar shapes in a changing light. Rather this: different shapes in a constant, all-permeating light.

Kreuzspiel

Kreuzspiel dates from Autumn 1951 and was first broadcast by WDR Cologne shortly afterwards. The first public performance at the Darmstadt Summer School in 1952 ended in an uproar. Influenced by Messiaen's *Mode de valeurs et d'intensités* and by Goeyvaerts' *Sonata for two pianos*, *Kreuzspiel* is one of the first compositions of 'pointillist music'.

The idea of an intersection (crossing) of temporal and spatial phenomena is presented in three stages. In the first stage (2′40″) the piano begins in the extreme registers and through a crossing of registers gradually brings into play six 'bottom' notes and six 'top' notes; the four middle octaves lying within the ranges of the oboe and the bass clarinet take over more and more notes, and at the moment when all the notes are equally distributed over the entire range of sound, all the duration and intensity series have crossed

* 1956, for a broadcast of *Kontra-Punkte*.

over in such a way that, from the initially wholly aperiodic series, there arises a series of regularly diminishing durations and one of regularly increasing intensities (*accelerando* and *crescendo*); a wood-block makes this still more evident. The whole phenomenon then reverses itself in mirror form, so that by the end of the first stage all the notes have arrived once again in the extreme registers of the piano; however, as a result of the intersection, the six 'top' notes have changed places with the six 'bottom' ones. The tomtoms pursue intersecting paths within opposed rhythmic and dynamic series, moving from longer and softer to louder and shorter, and vice versa. Whenever notes and noises meet in a single sound—and that is fairly often—the systematic course of the form is dislocated: a note gets into a wrong register, or its duration or intensity contradicts the series, etc. In the second stage (3'15") the entire formal phenomenon just described is turned inside out: everything starts in the middle octave with oboe and bass clarinet, then stretches out towards the extreme registers (piano) and back again; drums become cymbals; the regular pulsation of the first stage, in which the smallest given duration served to determine the tempo, is dropped. In the third stage (4') the two phenomena are combined with each other.

Kontra-Punkte

Kontra-Punkte for 10 instruments originated from the idea of re-solving the antitheses of a many-faceted musical world of individual notes and temporal relationships to the point where a situation is reached in which only the homogeneous and the immutable is audible. The work is in one movement. Six different timbres are used: flute-bassoon; clarinet-bass clarinet; trumpet-trombone; piano; harp; violin-cello (three different wind-instrument couples and three stringed instruments, struck, plucked and bowed). These six timbres merge into a single timbre: that of the piano (struck strings). In turn, trumpet, trombone, bassoon, violin, bass clarinet, harp, clarinet, cello and flute drop out. The six different degrees of volume (*ppp-sfz*) each yield in turn to *pp*. The considerable differences between very short and long are eliminated; only the medial, closely related durations remain (semiquavers, triplet semiquavers, dotted semiquavers, quintuplet semiquavers, etc.). A two-part, monochrome counterpoint is wrested from the antithesis between vertical and horizontal tonal relationships.

Klavierstücke I-IV

The _Klavierstücke_ are grouped into a series of cycles.

The first cycle, _I_ to _IV_, has been published. At present* I am at work on the second cycle, _V_ to _X_. Pieces _V_ to _VIII_ are already finished.

I wrote parts _I_ to _IV_ in Paris in 1952/53, hence before my Work No. 1, _Kontra-Punkte_ for 10 instruments.

The Belgian pianist Marcelle Mercenier gave the first performance of _I_ to _IV_ in Darmstadt.

If, after working exclusively on electronic composition for one and a half years, I have now taken to working on piano pieces at the same time, it is because the strictest forms of structural composition brought me up against essential musical phenomena that are not susceptible to measurement. This does not make them any the less palpable, detectable, imaginable and effective. I can (for the time being, at any rate) bring these things into play more clearly by using an instrument and a performer than in electronic composition. Primarily it is a matter of imparting a new way of feeling time in music, in which the infinitely subtle 'irrational' shadings and impulses and fluctuations of a good performer often produce what one wants better than any centimetre gauge. Statistical formal criteria such as these will give us a completely new and unprecedented angle on the question of instruments and their playing.

Elektronische Studie I & II

Studie I (Summer 1953) is the first composition to use sine-wave sounds (see NWDR Technical Review, February 1, 1954). The timbres for the composition were synthesized from the simplest of

* April 1955.

electro-acoustical raw material, and their subsequent combination was determined by the composer. The music is consciously organized down to the micro-acoustical level of the basic sounds.

An alternative fundamental method of producing electronic sounds is based, not on the addition of sine-wave frequencies to 'stationary sounds and note-mixtures', but instead on the separation of 'white noise' into 'coloured noise'. Here, electric filters are needed to split up the 'white noise' into bands of noise of any given breadth and density—comparable to the prismatic refraction of white light into bands of coloured light. In *Studie II*—in the absence of sufficiently varied filtering systems—a special procedure was adopted for producing non-stationary acoustical phenomena; this permitted the incorporation into the composition of the noise spectrum (see foreword to the score).

In both Studies, then, it was not the most varied and novel sounds that were sought, but rather an extreme homogeneity of the basic sounds and of their form.

Klavierstücke V-X
Instrumental Music 1954/55

We are no longer to think in terms of instrumental music *or* electronic music, but of instrumental music *and* electronic music. Each of these realms of sound has its own conditions and its own limitations.

One musical conception will demand instruments, while another will demand generators—with all the consequences they imply. Any attempt to minimize the limitations will lead to contradictions. It is as yet too early to speak of the possibility of a synthesis. Too many questions, in both domains, still await a clear answer. Only when one has once experienced and appreciated what is essential in the electronic compositions we already have—and this alone must be our concern when we speak of 'electronic music'—can one also recognize from this standpoint the necessary conditions of a new instrumental music. Rather than speak of a synthesis, it accords better with a responsible attitude to consider what we can accomplish at present and in the foreseeable future. Musicians lacking a clear perspective on current realities should keep their fanciful notions to themselves. Among those who have actually witnessed the world of electronic sound there is certainly no lack of imagination and creative ideas. The whole of a composer's abilities are evinced in the realization of music, in the discipline of his imagination, in the works he has hitherto written, and in those he is now writing; not, however, in his prognoses upon some hypothetical music of the future.

The second group of *Klavierstücke* was written after a period of exclusively electronic composition. The problem was to bring within the serial structure, as effectively as possible, the conditions peculiar to instrumental music. In this particular case the musical conception was so intimately bound up with the piano that its ensuing realization revealed the instrument and piano-writing in general in a fresh light.

Instrumental composition alongside electronic composition: what it leads to is an unsuspected new function of the instrumentalist. Those features of sound-production that are his typical criteria become serialized elements in composition. The scale of degrees of approximation, corresponding to the actual spacing of the notation, becomes one of the structural agents. The relative quality of 'precision' is controlled by new methods of notation. Experiential units of measurement—in contrast to the mechanical units of electronic composition—become serial components. Criteria of chance are guided by reference to notated signs (through the selection of different signs for the performer's various mental reactions) and are given a structural role in the elucidation of the musical context: indeterminate relationships used as formal properties!

All this requires of the performer is that he should respond to the notated signs as faithfully as possible by playing his instrument in the appropriate way. The way in which the signs are notated is a direct and graduated formulation of the bounds within which types of playing are distributed.

It is a desideratum that at the same time performing musicians, especially those of our generation, should begin to revise their present ideas about 'interpretation' and to come to grips with our music. That is to say, with a music which is written expressly for them and which presents them, in its own way, with the greatest of challenges: to transform notes into music. Prognostications about the decline of the instrumentalist, supposedly relegated to the sidelines of society by the mechanical production and reproduction of music, have had their day. But it is shaming in the extreme to behold the programmes offered by the 'great performers' of our time —and the 'greatest' offer the most insidious of all. So it is not at all hard to entertain the wish for a new type of instrumentalist. Experience and study of our music can provide a good idea of the characteristics of such a type.

Today's composer and tomorrow's instrumentalist are an inseparable partnership. Young pianists will not always at best insert Schoenberg, Webern or Messiaen into the nooks of their recitals; it will not always be only a handful of young instrumentalists who go along with us and have acquired the necessary technique, musical intelligence and experience to do so. Let us not arraign the public, but rather our own disunity: composer and instrumentalist at odds!

Klavierstück VI
Klavierstück VI is dedicated to David Tudor, and was commissioned by the town of Darmstadt; it was first performed in 1955 by Marcelle Mercenier (to the accompaniment of a cricket), the performance being discontinued because of audience disturbances. The piece develops a new temporal relationship between performer and sound: the sounds' own time—yielded by a wide variety of signs for the pianist's actions—comes increasingly markedly to the fore in place of chronometrical or metrical time; a number of new techniques (the piano's timbre-spectrum is modulated by harmonic effects, 'echoes', and many varieties of pedalling) are brought into play in order to determine the so-called 'time-fields' throughout which the performer responds to the autonomous life of the sounds and sound-figures.

Klavierstück IX

Klavierstück IX was begun in 1954 as part of my composition No. 4: *Klavierstücke V–X*; for seven years it remained incomplete and it appeared in its final form in 1961. It brings together different forms of musical time: periodicity, and a whole series of degrees of aperiodicity. Rigid, 'monotonous' events are transformed into flexible, 'polytonous' ones; sometimes the two are abruptly juxtaposed, sometimes they intermingle in constantly fresh conjunctions.

Klavierstück X

In *Klavierstück X* I set out to marry relative non-organization with organization. Using a scale of relationships between non-organization and organization I composed structures in series of different organizational degrees. The higher degrees are characterized by greater unequivocacy (absence of chance), the lower degrees by a greater dependence on probability and the levelling-out of differences (increasing interchangeability, decreasing aural transparency). Greater organization is linked with lower density and a stronger individuation of events. In the course of the piece extremes are reached: structures are crystallized in solitary individual shapes (degree of highest organization) or they are levelled out in massed complexes. In the course of the process of mediation between non-organization and organization the initial homogeneous state of advanced non-organization (undifferentiation) unfolds into increasingly numerous and concentrated shapes. The decrease in levelling-out is countered by an increasing emphasis on the individuation of shapes and the final unification of the extremely personal shapes evolved during the course of the piece into a higher, overall shape.

Klavierstücke V–X are dedicated to David Tudor.

Zeitmasze

In *Zeitmasze* temporal measurements proper to action and to sound enter into the composition on several levels. The work is articulated by a series of five different time-measures—both together and in succession: 1. Twelve tempi measured chronometrically in a chromatic scale between a given tempo and its value when doubled (MM 60→120); 2. As fast as possible; 3. Begin extremely fast and slow down to about a quarter of the speed; 4. Begin at about a quarter of the speed to accelerate to 'as fast as possible'; 5. As slow as possible (where a prescribed group is to be played in one breath).

Criteria derived from woodwind technique (taking into account the five different woodwind instruments, the prescribed registers, intensities, densities, and intervals within groups of notes) become determinants in the organization of time. The form bridges two extremes, with, at one end of the scale, everyone playing 'synchronously' in the same chronometrical tempo and, at the other end, all five playing in isolation—and turmoil—in different and mutually independent time-strata: between these extremes is a series of degrees of reciprocal dependence and individual freedom: the degrees of freedom become formal criteria. More extensive time-fields enter into the composition: structures move about between strictly regulated time-fields in which varying numbers of notes are pulverized into vibrating swarms of sound: free use is made of dynamic and static forms of time—often simultaneously.

Gruppen

Zeitmasze saw the revitalization of the internal form of my instrumental music. In *Gruppen*, a new development of the 'spatial deployment of instrumental music' was initiated. The new form in which there is a stratification of composed time between the various instruments is made clear in external form too. A number of independent orchestras—in *Gruppen* there are three—surround the listener; the orchestras—each under its own conductor—sometimes play independently and in different tempi; from time to time they meet in a common audible rhythm; they may call to and answer one another; one may echo another; for a while only music from the left, from the front or from the right may be heard; the sound may transmigrate from one orchestra to another, etc. As already happened with the distribution of the five loudspeaker groups in the electronic composition *Gesang der Jünglinge*, the spatial location from which the music is heard now becomes of importance in listening to instrumental music too: spatial deployment becomes functional. (It is difficult to mount such music in existing concert halls.) Each sound-source is now in a position to make its own temporal measures felt, and the listener finds himself in the middle of several temporal measures which combine to create a further, common time-world. Furthermore, the sources no longer produce 'points' of sound—as had been the case in the first place, when everything was at a 'contra-puntal', embryonic stage—but rather they produce 'groups': groups of sounds, of noises and of combined sound and noise, each an autonomous unit.

Groups of sounds, of noises and of combined sound and noise, are wholly autonomous units. Each group moves in its own temporal space, and above all with its own tempo.

So that they can move freely, the groups are divided among three orchestras, each having its own conductor, and all three are of equal strength, having virtually the same instruments. One orchestra to the left, one to the front, and one to the right: they form a semicircle around the audience.

From time to time two or three groups come closer and closer together until they meet in the same rhythm of sound—and become transformed. One receives the other into itself. Or plays with it. Extinguishes it. They fall apart or cling together.

Or they coalesce. Then all three orchestras become one—playing in the same tempo, the same harmony, the same hues. But the tempo starts to fluctuate, continually slowing down or speeding up, and from the one movement isolated instruments appear ever more clearly and in the end quite unequivocally: for stretches one hears only the strings, or maybe the guitar, or the drums on their own, the piano, two or three trumpets and trombones, or just the E-flat clarinet; and one thing plays on into another.

But the two (and hence all three) ensembles can never entirely coalesce, as they still remain spatially separate. They divide in new ways to give new groups their own space for movement—until the next movement begins.

Klavierstück XI

Elektronische Studien—Zeitmasze for woodwind quintet—*Gesang der Jünglinge,* electronic composition for five loudspeaker groups—*Klavierstück XI* (1956): instrumental music alongside electronic music.

Work was extremely functional in each medium so that each should be used productively: generators, tape recorder, loudspeakers should yield what no instrumentalist could ever give (compare the reporter's microphone); notation, performer, instrument should produce what no electronic apparatus could either deliver, imitate or repeat.

Composing electronic music involves describing sound in mechanical and electro-acoustical terms and thinking entirely in terms of machinery, apparatus, circuitry; reckoning with the single act of production and the unlimited repeatability of the composition thus produced.

Writing instrumental music—after this—involves unleashing the performer's activities through optical signs and making a direct approach to the musician's living organism, and to his constantly varying and unpredictable capacities for response; bestowing the possibility of multiple acts of production from performance to performance, and that of unrepeatability.

Electronic music and new instrumental music might coexist thus—always increasing and accelerating the differences between them—and only through this might arise the hope that occasionally they might genuinely meet in some future work.

Klavierstück XI: on a single sheet of paper (53 × 93 cm) 19 different note-groups are irregularly distributed. The following directions for performance appear on the reverse side of the sheet:

The player casts a random glance at the sheet of paper and

begins with whichever group he sees first; this he plays (always excepting the notes printed in small type) at any speed he chooses, at any basic dynamic level and using any mode of attack. Once the first group has come to an end, he reads the ensuing indications of speed ($T°$), basic dynamic level and mode of attack, casts a further random glance to find another of the groups, and plays this in accordance with the three indications he has found.

'Casting a further random glance from one group to another' means that the player will never link together any given two groups or leave any one group out of account.

Any group may be linked with any of the other 18 groups, so that any group may also be played using any of the six speeds, dynamic levels and modes of attack.

If a group closes with a fermata, the player should bide the length of the fermata before reading the indications and choosing the next group, thus making for a longer pause than would occur with a group not having a final fermata; if, however, a group closes with the word *binden* ('run on'), then the final note or sound is to be held until the directions have been read and the following group selected, and then the preceding group will be run onto that following.

Once a group has been reached for the second time, the indications in brackets are to be observed; these are mostly octave or two-octave transpositions (8va . . .) (2 okt . . .) upwards or downwards, affecting upper and lower staves separately; some notes are added or omitted.

Once a group has been reached for the third time, then one possible realization of the piece has come to an end. In this way it may happen that some groups are played only once or even not at all. Wherever possible, this piano piece should be played two or more times in a programme.

Gesang der Jünglinge

My work on the electronic composition *Gesang der Jünglinge* (1955/ 56) proceeded from the idea of bringing together into a single sound both sung notes and electronically produced ones: their speed, length, loudness, softness, density and complexity, the width and narrowness of pitch intervals and differentiations of timbre could all be made audible exactly as I imagined them, independent of the physical limitations of any singer. The electronic sounds that had to be composed were therefore much more variegated than hitherto, since the acoustical structure of sung words is probably more complex than any other—containing as it does a wide range of vowels (sounds) and consonants (noises)—so that a fusion of all the timbres used into a single family of sound only becomes palpable when sung sounds can appear like electronic sounds, and when electronic sounds can appear like sung sounds. At certain points in the composition the sung sounds become comprehensible words, at other times they remain pure sound values, and between these extremes there are different degrees of verbal comprehensibility. Single syllables and words are taken from the *Song of the Youths in the Burning Fiery Furnace* (Book of Daniel, Chapter 3). Thus wherever the music's audible signals momentarily become human speech, it is always in the praise of God.

This is a new way of experiencing musical speech, but another feature of the composition is equally essential: here for the first time the direction and movement of sounds in space was shaped by the composer and made available as a new dimension in musical experience. *Gesang der Jünglinge* is in fact composed for five loudspeaker groups, to be distributed in such a way as to surround the listener in space. Sound may issue from any side, from any number of loudspeakers at once, may move clockwise or anticlockwise, may be partly fixed and partly mobile: all these aspects of the spatial distribution of sounds and sound groups are of importance in this work. That the piece is now* available on a gramophone record has only been possible because the composer has prepared a special version for monophonic listening.

* 1956; a stereophonic version was later prepared for the subsequent recording. (Translator's note.)

Zyklus

In *Zyklus* (for one percussion player) the predominantly static open form of *Klavierstück XI*—where all depended on the instantaneity of random glances—is conjoined with the idea of a dynamic, closed form; the result is a circular, 'curvilinear' form. The piece is written on 16 spiral-bound sheets of paper; there is no beginning and no end; the performer may begin with any page, but must then play a cycle in the stipulated page-sequence; he stands within a ring of percussion instruments and during the performance turns a full circle—in terms of the principal positions he takes up— either clockwise or anticlockwise, according to the direction in which he is reading the score. Fields containing points and groups are distinguished by differing degrees of combinatorial potential; in the sequence as it was composed they mediate continuously between the wholly determinate and the extremely free; the structure having the greatest degree of freedom—the extreme point of 'instantaneity'—is formed in such a way that it might well be taken for the extremely determinate structure that immediately follows it. Thus a temporal circle is experienced in which one does in fact have the constant impression of moving towards greater freedom (clockwise) or greater determinacy (anticlockwise), whereas at the critical point of contact between the extremes the one breaks into the other unnoticed. Closing an open form in a circle, embodying the static in the dynamic, the purposeless in the purposive; wanting neither to exclude or demolish either the one or the other, nor to change them by synthesis into a third: it is a further attempt to remove the dualism and to reconcile factors apparently so different and incompatible.

Zyklus was composed as a test piece for the Kranichstein competition for percussion players in 1959 and is dedicated to Wolfgang Steinecke.

Carré

'For he who has once had to listen will listen always, whether he knows he will never hear anything again, or whether he does not

. . . silence once broken will never again be whole.' (Beckett: *The Unnamable*)

This piece tells no story. You can confidently stop listening for a moment if you cannot or do not want to go on listening; for each moment can stand on its own and at the same time is related to all the other moments.

The performing time is unusually long, since the work is played through in a continuous stream. If one is to absorb this music, one must take one's time: it does not carry one along with it, but leaves one in peace; most of its changes occur very discreetly in the intimacy of its notes.

The disposition of the four orchestras and choruses around the audience is unusual. One is tempted to look around a lot. At best, one closes one's eyes from time to time, so as to be able to hear better.

My heartfelt wish is that this music may afford a little inner calm, concentration and breadth; an awareness that we could have a lot of time, if we simply take it—and that it is better to come to one's self than to lose oneself; 'for things that happen must have someone to happen to, someone must stop them'.

Carré for four orchestras and choruses dates from 1959/60. The basic ideas came to me during my stay in America in November and December 1958, when I had to make hour-long flights every day. (Over the clouds I experienced the longest transformation times in my life.)

The score was written in collaboration with Cornelius Cardew. I left the independent working-out of composition plans to him. Our common experiences have shown how such collaboration might be further developed.

A large orchestra of eighty players is divided into four orchestras having roughly similar constitution. To each orchestra is also added a mixed chorus of between twelve and sixteen singers.

For the first performance in Hamburg I selected an approximately quadratic hall and had four podia erected for the ensembles: the four conductors, facing inwards from the walls, were Andrzej Markowski, Michael Gielen, Mauricio Kagel and myself.

Voices and instruments combine so as to make a homogeneous sound mixture. The text was composed according to purely musical criteria, using a scale of phonetic sound differentiations ranging from voiceless consonants to vowels, and is hence untranslatable; it was notated in phonetic script following the *Principles of the International Phonetic Association* (available from: Dept. of Phonetics, University College, London WC1).

The work was commissioned by North German Radio, Hamburg. The use of four orchestras and choruses in a quadrilateral layout resulted from the decision to include spatial direction and movement of sounds (a further development of spatial composition as it had been first realized in electronic and instrumental music with *Gesang der Jünglinge* for five loudspeaker groups and *Gruppen* for three orchestras respectively). A tape recording was made on a four-track apparatus: each orchestra on a separate channel. Reproduction on a four-track tape recorder with four groups of loudspeakers facilitates a rendering in which, compared with a concert-hall performance, all the structural details and spatial separations can be more clearly appreciated. The present four-track recording permitted the preparation of a single-channel broadcasting version of particular quality, since during the monitoring work it was possible to obtain regulated dynamics and effects of spatial perspective between the ensembles. This work indicates the aesthetic necessity of a further development of the practice of multi-channel broadcasting.

Refrain

A quiet and spaciously composed continuity of sounds is disturbed six times by a short refrain. This refrain contains glissandi and clusters, trills, bass notes (in the piano) and brief snatches of melody, elements which are absent from the first form. The points at which the refrain is played are chosen by the players themselves and can change from one performance to the next; once they are fixed, however, the final shape of the refrain will be influenced by its immediate context (thus trills, glissandi and melody should be based on notes of the chord standing before or after the refrain in the text); conversely, every time it has sounded, the refrain exerts a modifying influence on the music which follows it: the characteristics of piano, celesta and vibraphone sounds are altered by the intervention of 'colouring' percussion instruments, this happening in increasing or decreasing degrees depending on the points chosen for the refrain's entry. Thus, within a static condition, a dynamic formal process is awoken by unforeseen disturbances; and the one influences and leaves its mark on the other without any conflict arising.

Those who want to understand what I have written in *Refrain* for three performers will need to read the score.

Those who want to understand how the performers interpret my score will need to know the score and compare it with performances.

Those who simply want to hear a piece of music (and not understand it) need only listen.

What else remains to be said?

The work was commissioned by Dr. G. von Westerman for the Berlin Festival and was written in June and July 1959; it is dedicated to my friend Ernst Brücher. The first performance took place in Berlin on 2 October 1959; the performers were David Tudor (piano and wood blocks), Cornelius Cardew (celesta and antique cymbals) and Siegfried Rockstroh (vibraphone, cowbells and glockenspiel). Since then *Refrain* has had frequent performances in different versions and with different instruments.

On the recording made by Time Records Incorporated, Aloys Kontarsky plays the piano and wood blocks, Bernhard Kontarsky the celesta and antique cymbals, and Christoph Caskel the vibraphone, cowbells and glockenspiel.

Kontakte

The electronic part was realized in the electronic music studio of West German Radio, Cologne, in 1958–60.

The first performance took place on 11 June 1960 at the 34th World Music Festival in the concert hall of Cologne Radio.

Since then *Kontakte* has been performed thirty times,* in every European country, with Christoph Caskel (percussion) and David Tudor (piano and percussion). The Paris performance was prepared afresh with Aloys Kontarsky (piano and percussion) and Christoph Caskel (percussion).

The work was composed for four loudspeaker groups with four-channel tape; for the Paris performance a two-channel version was made.

A series of forms of contact brings together electronic music and instrumental music. The electronic music is heard through loudspeakers; at the same time a percussionist and a pianist are playing, the former producing six types of timbre: metal sound, metal noise; skin sound, skin noise; wood sound, wood noise.

The piano's role is to unite or to separate these categories. The electronic sound categories establish relationships and transitions between the instrumental timbres, fusing with them and departing from them towards hitherto unknown regions of sound.

Whereas in the electronic music five forms of movement in space interact in a constantly fresh way with differing rapidity and spatial direction (rotation, looping movements, alternation, separation of fixed sources—different sounds from each, linking of fixed sources —identical sounds from each, isolation of points in space), the instrumentalists represent spatially rigid sources of sound.

The work is composed in 'moment form'. Each moment, whether a state or a process, is individual and self-regulated, and able to sustain an independent existence. The musical events do not take a fixed course between a determined beginning and an inevitable ending, and the moments are not merely consequents of what precedes them and antecedents of what follows; rather the

* Written in 1961.

concentration on the Now—on every Now—as if it were a vertical slice dominating over any horizontal conception of time and reaching into timelessness, which I call eternity: an eternity which does not begin at the end of time, but is attainable at every *moment*.

The work is one of the longest in new music to be played without a break, and lasts for $34\frac{1}{2}$ minutes.

Momente

Momente for soprano, four choral groups and thirteen instrumentalists dates from 1961/62 and was commissioned by West German Radio. This is no self-contained work with unequivocally fixed beginning, formal structure and ending, but a polyvalent composition containing independent events. Unity and continuity are less the outcome of obvious similarities than of an immanent concentration on the present, as uninterrupted as possible.

Any given performance will be of a version in which given moment-groups are combined; these will depend on the available programme-length and resources. The comprehensiveness of resources for any given performance will thus be proportionate to the duration of that performance. At the performance of 21 May 1962, not all the sections written for soprano, four choral groups and thirteen instrumentalists and conceived as an interrelated sequence of moments had yet been rehearsed.

In the writing for speaking and singing voices there is a continuation of what was begun in *Gesang der Jünglinge* and in *Carré* for four orchestras and choruses: an 'abolition' of the dualism between vocal music and instrumental music, between notes and silence, between sound and noise—combined with the attempt to integrate and mediate between extremely different possibilities of articulation.

Punkte

Punkte 1952/62 for orchestra is a 'pointillist' score of 1952 which I rewrote in 1962.

In the new version the 'points' of the title are but seldom simple note-points. To differentiate the original points I used four formal types: a point becoming increasingly broad on top (•⊏⊐) or underneath (•⊏⊐); or a note mixture becoming increasingly narrow until it reaches a point, either from above (⊏⊐•) or from beneath (⊏⊐•). Both broadening and narrowing have typical textures (sustained notes, tremolo, trill; staccato, portato, legato; glissandi, chromatic melodies, etc.), typical colours and typical degrees of intensity.

During composition so many sound-strata sometimes became superimposed that more mass was produced than there was enough room left for. (Why do we still think of music simply as note-structures in empty space, instead of beginning with a homogene-ously filled acoustical space and *hollowing out* the music—rubbing out, as it were, the musical figures and forms ?)

Then I composed negative forms, corresponding to the positive forms already mentioned, whose edges were marked more or less distinctly by notes.

In the further course of composition I switched between one and the other sometimes carving out forms from the acoustical surfaces, sometimes projecting sound into empty spaces. At the extreme points there is an equipoise between positive and negative forms. At transitions the form becomes ambiguous.

Momente (1965 version)

Right up to the end of my time as a student my thoughts were so chockfull of dualistic pairs of concepts, such as object–subject, intellect–emotion, being–meaning, material–ideal, thematic–athe-matic, tonal–atonal, periodic–aperiodic, homophonic–polyphonic, sound–noise, note–silence, and so on and so forth, that a latent dubiousness about all merely bipolar values spread in all directions in my mind. In my first works I withdrew into an extremely mon-istic way of thinking. I then slowly extended this into trivalent and polyvalent thought.

Vertical and horizontal and vertical and diagonal and vertical and spatial and curvilinear.

Homo and poly and homo and hetero and homo and mono and homo and. And and either and or and and.

AND.

When I put down a note and allow it to stand, still leaving it standing after some years—I know at precisely what instant to finally abandon it—then it will remain standing.

To date I have completed the works: *Kreuzspiel, Punkte, Kontra-Punkte, Klavierstücke I–XI, Zeitmasze, Gruppen, Gesang der Jünglinge, Zyklus, Carré, Refrain, Kontakte, Plus /Minus.* They are complete. Each work must endure a time in which I go with it, following it up: being at performances, conducting it, playing, testing and constantly re-hearing it.

Then comes the time when I have to let it go. For *Momente,* the two *Mikrophonie* works, *Mixtur* and *Solo,* this time has not yet* elapsed. Thus between the ages of twenty-three and thirty-seven I composed on average one work per year. In each work everything is at stake, however limited my capacities may be. I am no disciple, wishing to improve on the work of his predecessor. Anyone who has scored a bullseye has scored a bullseye, whatever happens, no matter when, how or where. And when one has scored a bullseye, the whole shooting booth is filled with ringing and all the lights go on—for an instant. Everything else is practice, discipline, endurance, industry, patience.

One can form an alliance only with the future.

etc. ─────────────────────────────────────

His work and your work and my work play a TRIO, their works accompany.

Your work and my work play a DUO, his work accompanies.

Your work plays a SOLO, my work accompanies.

My work plays a SOLO, your work accompanies.

My work and I play a DUO, the second I accompanies.

My work and I and the second I play a TRIO, the third I accompanies.

etc. ─────────────────────────────────────

* 1964.

'Reflection is repetition'

Monism — Dualism — Trialism — Quatralism — Quintalism — Sexualism—

Materially suitable form and formally suitable material and suitably formed material and

Experience and invention and discovery

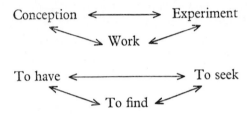

To seek or to find?

To seek AND to find.

Many artists used to say of themselves that they did not seek, they found. By this they meant to say that they felt superior to those who had to seek. Every artist seeks; in other words, he proceeds more attentively than others, opening wide his eyes and his ears and wholly concentrating himself so as to miss as little as possible. He cannot say in words what it is he seeks; yet he leaves untouched nearly everything he sees; and—if fortune smiles—he will suddenly stop and take up something that seems to him more precious than everything else. Then it is that he finds, and provided he harbours no doubt he is certain of his find.

Of course one can go about it inattentively—'I had no thought of seeking'—and still find something. But more adventurous are the great expeditions—with divining rods, sonic depth-finders, compasses, astronomical charts, tuning-forks (oxygen cylinders for high altitudes), tape recorders, provisions for months, time and still more time—where one's sixth sense is one's guide. The 'lucky finder' always knows what to do with what he has found. It is as though he has always been seeking the thing he finds. It is the key to something new, something his being had lacked. How much he lacked it he can only say when he has found it.

My reflection is altered by Webern's music.
Webern's music is transformed by my reflection.
My reflection is altered by my reflection on Webern's music.

It is confusing that notes should express something. The vibrations of notes are transferred to people, and how they describe their own sympathetic vibrations in words and gestures is quite another matter. If notes are organized in a certain way, then people on the same or a similar 'wavelength' are also moved in the same, or similar, way. Much music resonates long in the listener, much only briefly, and much not at all. Reflection and sympathy, discussion and silence are signs of 'sympathetic vibration'. After a longer time everything becomes a memory, and one has to hear once again if one wishes to vibrate. Many people oscillate violently at single strange-sounding notes; others need more complicated sound-images, being more selective—the connoisseurs. Obtrusive music can act as a drug, while other music may act like a great thought, leaving its mark on one's whole mentality and morality. Thus every medium and every combination of media has its own effect, and one's choice must be cautious. If, however, the user does not know the general effect of the medium—if it is itself new to him—he must have complete confidence in his own response to the new medium and must bear the responsibility for the decision to use one medium rather than another.

Theory of the oscillating universe having the frequency (from ylem to ylem) of 80,000,000,000 years, after which a periodic cleansing of the cosmos by fire takes place, in which the waste products are molten down and the universe is reborn, pure (hydrogen) and fresh.

Germany's a lousy little hole again.

'Feeling', 'intuiting', always penetrates through the process of thinking-out to the process of composing, in which one has to formulate what will sound, or how something will be made to sound; it makes no difference what is given as the basis from which the 'meaning' of what is composed can be deduced. That even applies where musical thought is denied—as many composers claim to do—on the grounds that the 'irrational' is thereby given more of a chance.

Today's antithetical positions are no longer truly antithetical, but are twists around which thought turns, becomes heated and tightens in order to facilitate sharper formulations. Yet as soon as such a position is taken up momentarily, another is broached in order to bring further forces into play. This is no dialectic, restricted to two positions, but a trialectic, a quartalectic, etc. The dodecaphonists made only one mistake, and that was to omit all the intermediate stages between the diatonicists and themselves, failing to see the figure twelve itself as a transitional stage.

But one must still understand the business of 'fulness–emptiness', of 'note-silence', of 'sound–noise', etc. One must ask oneself, after what and before what and with what, and 'how empty', 'how silent', 'how noise-ful' something is.

To compose the act of composing.

This is the formal scheme of *Momente* for solo soprano, four choral groups and thirteen instrumentalists, as it was projected in 1961:

M moments are concentrated particularly on melodic composition (monody–heterophony), K moments on the composition of the sound (homophony), D moments on that of duration (polyphony).

Around the 'pure' moments M, K and D, which are self-reflecting, are grouped others which reflect both themselves and one or both of the others. When, in one of these double reflections, the reflection of the other component is weak, the latter is indicated in lower case; if it is almost as strong, then two capitals are used together. M(m) is a moment with 'feed-back' self-reflection; so is

D(d–m), but this time having a transition of the self-reflection into a reflection of M; at DK(d) and DK(k) the feed-back reinforces one component of the double reflection. Furthermore to each moment is added a different number of so-called inserts from neighbouring moments—depending on the context—to 'recall' what has gone before or to 'announce' what is to come. I moments ('informal', or possibly 'indeterminate') neutralize the three groups of moments.

Between January and April 1962 all the K moments, I, I(m) and I(d), as well as M(m) and MK(d) were worked out and—except for I—were first performed on 20 May 1962 as a commission of West German Radio in Cologne, the composer conducting.

The remaining M and D moments were worked out in Summer 1963 and early 1964.

On a tour in October 1965 with the West German Radio ensemble with Martina Arroyo as soloist again, seven M moments were inserted into those that had already been performed on earlier occasions and the I moment was introduced as the conclusion of the K moments. For various reasons of practicality it was not possible to rehearse all the D moments for this tour. The texts used in the different moments are from various sources: verses from the Song of Songs; passages from letters, and from books that I was reading at the time; Christian names, nicknames, pet names; onomatopoeic sound-structures; public reactions heard at performances of my works, etc. These are supported rhythmically by clickings, clapping, stamping and so on, and small percussion instruments used by the chorus.

Mikrophonie I & II

After the composition of *Kontakte* for electronic sounds, piano and percussion, in which the electronic music preserved on tape is reproduced through loudspeakers simultaneously as two instrumentalists perform, I searched for closer conjunctions between electronic and instrumental music. In 1964 I wrote *Mixtur* for orchestra, four sine-wave generators and four ring modulators, and immediately afterwards *Mikrophonie I* for tam-tam, two microphones, two filters and potentiometers. In 1965 followed *Mikrophonie II* for chorus, Hammond organ and ring modulators.

In *Mikrophonie I* performers use a wide variety of materials to bring a large tam-tam into vibration; two performers pass hand microphones over the surface of the tam-tam; a third group of performers uses electronic filters and potentiometers to transform the vibrations picked up, which are played through loudspeakers at the same time as the original sounds of the tam-tam. The separation of the musical process into three independent areas (production, presentation and transformation of sounds) makes possible a continuous combination of all the experience of instrumental practice with that of the techniques of electronic sound. Thereby any sound-source whatsoever (traditional instruments, acoustical events of any type) can be integrated in a composition which tends towards coherence, and the dualism between instrumental and electronic music is dissolved. The title 'Mikrophonie' also points to the fact that vibrations that are normally inaudible (in this case those of a tam-tam) can be made audible by means of an active process of auscultation with microphones (in much the same way as a doctor uses a stethoscope); in contrast to its previous passive function as an extremely faithful recorder of sounds, the microphone is used actively, as a musical instrument. The procedures of working on the sound and of monitoring it, which hitherto occurred only during protracted programmes of work in the electronic music studio, are carried out in *Mikrophonie I* in virtually no time at all, hence simultaneously with the production of the original sounds, and the result is made audible immediately. It goes without saying that now we must develop processes of electronic sound transformation that are automatic and can be controlled in an extremely short time.

In *Mikrophonie II* the very different sounds of choral singers are picked up by microphones and are mixed in multiplication with the electrically generated sounds of a Hammond organ in a specially constructed ring modulator. There arises hereby a closed circle, a so-called feed-back, in which the notes of the Hammond organ and the choral sounds reciprocally modulate each other. The result is played through loudspeakers simultaneously with the original sounds. I have used Helmut Heisenbüttel's *Simple Grammatical Meditations* as the text.

There are many reasons, difficult to put into words, for this new procedure for composing sounds; one may be that in the experience of hitherto unknown and unadumbrated procedures of sound composition composer and listener have a new sort of experience of themselves and of their world, and for a moment become—ideally —speechless.

Mikrophonie I was first performed on 9 December 1964 at the music festival 'Reconnaissance des musiques modernes' in Brussels. The work is dedicated to Alexander Schlee. *Mikrophonie II* is dedicated to the American, Judith Blinken. I should like to express my special gratitude to my co-worker Jaap Spek, who has given me tireless help in experiments and in the realization of both works.

Mixtur

In my composition *Kontakte* for electronic sounds, piano and percussion (1959/60) I prepared electronic music in the studio and recorded it on a four-track tape to be replayed through loudspeakers, with a pianist as well as a percussionist performing simultaneously. After this composition I looked for possibilities of combining immediately and flexibly the instrumental production of sounds with their electronically effectuated transformation. I made experiments in this field. The first result was *Mikrophonie I*: a tam-tam is set in vibration by two performers using a wide variety of materials; at the same time two other performers pick up the tam-tam's vibrations with hand microphones; these vibrations are transformed by means of electro-acoustical filters by two further performers and are channelled directly through loudspeakers.

In *Mixtur* (composed in 1964) the notes of a woodwind group, a brass group, a *pizzicato* and an *arco* group—kept as separate as possible—are picked up by microphones while they are actually being played; four groups of microphones lead to four mixing desks where acoustical engineers control the balance between each input and the sum of each group. (At a performance in Stockholm, in October 1966, 36 microphones were used—one for every two musicians.)

The outputs of the four mixing desks are connected to four ring modulators. Four musicians 'play' oscillators, whose sine-waves modulate the instrumental notes in the ring modulators. The results of this modulation are simultaneously mixed with the orchestral sounds through four loudspeaker groups. Thus there will result from each instrumental sound, according to measurements given in the score, a mixture sound. ('Mixture', usually in organ registration but also in choral and orchestral writing, is the name given to a mixing of parallel pitches—often a coupling of the basic notes with octaves and fifths; it also refers to the colouring of timbre by harmonic, subharmonic or chromatic parallel intervals.)

In a fifth group three percussionists each play one cymbal and one tam-tam, which are furnished with contact microphones and connected to three separate loudspeakers.

In this way it becomes possible to obtain in conjunction with the use of instruments a differentiated composition of timbres such as I had hitherto only been able to achieve in the realm of electronic music.

In addition to the transformation of timbres, it also becomes possible to compose as fine pitch differentiations as one needs, beyond the hitherto customary division of the octave into twelve equal degrees. A rhythmical transformation of the sounds is effected by modulation with very low sine-wave frequencies, under about 16 Hz.

The way now seems to me completely open for a further development of instrumental music, since its irreplaceable qualities—above all its constant versatility, its 'living' quality—can now be combined with the acquisitions of electronic music to make up a new unity, which is incomparably more mobile and flexible than the additive conjunction of tape music with instrumental music we have seen in recent years. That such a process demands a completely different kind of compositional method, of formal presentation, of notation, etc., provided me with a welcome inducement to open myself constantly to the unsuspected and the unprecedented during the conception of *Mixtur*. I wrote the score fairly rapidly and without interruption during the summer of 1964, obeying only my inspiration, since experience in the field was lacking; and I hope that this music has kept something of the freshness and well-being I felt at that adventurous time. After a number of performances with the usual orchestral distribution, I prepared a new version for an extremely small ensemble in 1967. The original score already had directions to the effect that the conductor can vary the number of players as he likes.

Solo

Solo (for melody instrument and tape recorder) was written in 1966 as a commission from Japanese Radio, NHK, who broadcast the first performances of the versions for flute and for trombone.

    Solo is a composition for one player and can be interpreted on any melody instrument(s). The soloist's playing is picked up in part by microphone(s) during the performance. The recorded parts are superimposed in greater or lesser degrees of density (and possibly transformed) and at a varying interval of time are mixed with the soloist's playing through two-channel loudspeakers.

Telemusik

During my first eight or nine days in Tokyo I could not sleep. I was pleased about this, since as I lay awake my head was constantly full of sound-visions, ideas, movement. After four sleepless nights and four days working in the electronic music studio for eight or nine hours without anything usable to show for it (not only did I have to assimilate the new language, food, water, air and the yes–no confusion, but also a completely different system of technical management in the studio) a vision kept recurring with increasing frequency: it was what I was after: a vision of sounds, new technical processes, formal relationships, images of notations, of human relationships, etc.—everything at once and in a single network that was too entangled to be represented in one process: this was going to need a lot of my time. On top of all this I wanted to come closer to an old and ever-recurrent dream: to go a step further towards writing, not 'my' music, but a music of the whole world, of all lands and races. I am sure you will hear it all in *Telemusik*—the gagaku player, that mysterious familiar of the Japanese Imperial court, music from the happy island of Bali, from the southern Sahara, from a Spanish village festival, from Hungary, the Shipibos of the Amazon River, the Omizutori ceremony in Nara, in which I took part for three whole days and nights, the fantastic virtuosity of the Chinese, music of the Kojasan temple, of the highland dwellers in Vietnam, whence the horrific and distorted news reached me every morning in my hotel between the lines of an American/ Japanese newspaper, more music from Vietnam, and yet more marvels from Vietnam (a wonderful people!)—(I disembarked at Saigon and saw the clouds of smoke rising right next to the aerodrome—the soldiers and bombers and the terrified eyes)—and music of the Buddhist priests of the Jakushiji temple, music from the Nō drama *Hó Sho Riu* and from goodness knows where else too. They all wanted to take part in *Telemusik*, often simultaneously and overlapping. I had my hands full keeping open the new and unknown world of electronic sound for such guests: I wanted them to feel 'at home' and not 'integrated' by some administrative act, but rather, genuinely engaged in an untrammelled spiritual encounter.

Hymnen

For several years I had planned to compose a large-scale work of electronic, vocal and instrumental music involving the national anthems of all countries. In 1966 I started on the realization of the work in the electronic music studio of WDR. To date four regions are complete, having a total duration of about two hours. Each region has certain anthems as its centre, towards which many other nations—each with its characteristic ideas—are drawn. The first region has two centres: the *Internationale* and the *Marseillaise*. It develops as a strict, organized form from out of an international gibberish of short-wave broadcasts. I have dedicated it to Pierre Boulez.

The first and the second regions interpenetrate. The bridge passage is the sharp, flooding sound that previously hissed forth—moving from a deep, distorted note up into the higher registers—before the *Marseillaise*, and then hovered over the region until the end, where it stands on its own for a long time; after traversing nine columns of sound (with which the second region begins) it then swoops down and becomes recognizable as a human cry before further developing into bird calls—marsh ducks quacking—and human yelling, right up to the deep black recollection of the *Marseillaise* at one eighth of its speed.

The second region has four more centres: the hymn of the *German Federal Republic*, a group of intermingling *African* national hymns, alternating with the beginning of the *Russian* anthem; and at the end of the completely continuous transition between the German and the African hymns, an *individual centre* immediately appears which parts the curtain of time and, as a reflection on a second German hymn from the past, discloses the whole process of composition: it is the original recording of a moment from the actual work in the studio, and here a second present, the past and the ulterior past all become simultaneous. This second region is dedicated to Henri Pousseur. Together, the two regions last about 56 minutes.

Between the second and the third regions there should be a fairly long pause.

The third region has three centres. It begins with the slow, and now unmixed, continuation of the *Russian* anthem, which is for once constituted entirely of electronic sounds, having the greatest harmonic and rhythmic expansion of anything I have composed to date. The *American* anthem follows as a second centre, having the most colourful relationships—in fleeting collages and pluralistic mixtures—to all the other anthems. The last short-wave sound whistles 'in a few seconds across the ocean' and heralds in the exalted centre of the *Spanish* anthem. The third region lasts about 24 minutes. It is dedicated to John Cage. It is followed by a brief break.

The fourth region has a double centre: the *Swiss* anthem and a hymn associated with the Utopian realm of *Hymunion* in *Harmondie unter Pluramon*,* which is the longest and most penetrating of them all: the final chord of the Swiss anthem is shaped into a calmly pulsating bass *ostinato*, over which are heaped gigantic blocks, surfaces and highways, in whose clefts the calling of names, with their many echoes, is heard. The fourth region lasts about $32\frac{1}{2}$ minutes and is dedicated to Luciano Berio.

Hymnen for four loudspeakers and soloists: *Hymnen* for radio, television, opera, ballet, concert hall, church, open air.

The work is composed in such a way that different libretti or scenarios for films, operas and ballets can be compiled for this music. The arrangement of the individual parts and the total duration are variable. Regions can be interchanged—depending on dramatic requirements—extended or omitted. It is equally possible to play it through loudspeakers only, without instrumentalists.

I should like to thank my co-worker David Johnson for his help in the preparation of the tape.

Prozession

I composed *Prozession* in May 1967 for the ensemble with which I make regular concert tours: Fred Alings and Rolf Gehlhaar (tam-tam), Johannes Fritsch (viola), Harald Bojé (electronium) and Aloys Kontarsky (piano). The tam-tam sounds—as in my composition *Mikrophonie I*—are picked up by a microphone, and a contact microphone is attached to the viola. These two microphones are connected to two electronic filters and potentiometers, which I preside over during performance. The relationship between direct sound and filtered sounds and the movements of these sounds in space should be differentiated *ad libitum*. In playing these sounds over loudspeakers, two electronic filters can also be connected up

---

* See page 145 for an explanation of these names. (Translator's note.)

and, as in *Mikrophonie I*, used in free variation. A suitable distribution of the loudspeakers for diagonal movement of the sound between the four corners of the hall is as follows:

II ⟍ III   (tam-tam on I & III, viola on II & IV,
I ⟋ IV   with four potentiometers)

In place of the electronium an electronic organ may be used.

The score formulates a musical process that makes use of the same methods that I have already employed in *Plus/Minus*, *Mikrophonie I* and *Mikrophonie II*. The musical events are not individually notated, but are variants of parts of my earlier compositions played from memory by the performers. To be precise, the tam-tam players and the microphonist allude to *Mikrophonie I*, the viola player to *Gesang der Jünglinge*, *Kontakte* and *Momente*, the electronium player to *Telemusik* and *Solo* and the pianist to *Klavierstücke I–XI* and *Kontakte*. At the monitoring desk I use a technique similar to that in *Mikrophonie I*. In its register, volume, duration, timbre (or, with the piano, 'mode of attack') and number of components (subdivision of duration by a rhythm having a given number of attacks), each event will be determined in relation either to the last event a player has himself played or to that which another has played. Thus an 'oral tradition' is established, both between my earlier music and *Prozession* and between each player in the moment of performance.

Each instrument has a part consisting of a series of +, − and = signs. These signs indicate:

+ : higher or louder or longer or more components;
− : lower or softer or shorter or fewer components;
= : identical (or similar) register and volume and duration and timbre and number of components.

Each player begins with an event when he wishes. As soon as a player finishes an event, he reacts in accordance with the sign in his part either to the event he himself has just played (either immediately or after a pause), or else to the event of another player that is starting next, which he must hear out before reacting to it (hence trios, duos and solos are formed). Any sign (or vertical combination of signs) holds good for one event.

If a + or a — sign is applied to one parameter, then the other parameters remain as they were in the relevant previous event. A vertical combination will apply to as many parameters as there are superimposed signs. If + and — are superimposed they may also be applied to one and the same parameter.

If a player reacts to his own previous event, then he can choose his timbre as he wishes (this is not subject to the + — alterations); if he reacts to someone else's event, then he should imitate the other's timbre. The piano can do this with only relative success by means of variations of touch. The tam-tam, viola and electronium should use all their resources of timbre-production and all their varieties of noise in responding to each relevant previous event. In determining the register, the predominant and highest notes of an event are decisive.

Volume refers to maximum loudness as well as to characteristic articulation of the attack–decay phenomenon.

Lengthening and shortening of the duration should be clearly perceptible. Each player should at least once play a duration which is longer than a minute. A duration can be divided into as many components as the player wishes. Whenever a sign is applied to this number, at + the number of components increases (for an equal duration the rhythm becomes faster), at = it remains constant, and at — it decreases. Moreover at + rhythmic and melodic articulation should be more complex, at — simpler, and at = it should remain approximately identical (or similar). The rhythmical relationship of the components will normally be free (corresponding to the 'variants' of an event from the earlier compositions mentioned); however, at the sign P it should be expressly periodic.

For determining registers the tam-tam player should make use of all the materials for producing sound that were used in *Mikrophonie I* (and possibly others as well), so as to have at his disposal a correspondingly differentiated range from very high, bright sounds and noises to very deep, dark sounds and noises.

If a player reaches his minimum register (extremely low) and volume (extremely soft) and duration (extremely short) and number of components (only one attack for the whole event), and is still confronted by further — signs, then he must wait until another player's event makes further — operations possible.

Some signs are provided with enclosed directions which concern all the others. If a player reaches a direction, he makes a signal inviting the others to follow him. R means: all play in the same register; I means: all play at the same intensity (and with the same attack–decay); D means: all play the same duration (only in this case do the other players break off and begin and finish together with the event or within the duration of the player who gives the signal); *Glieder* ('components') means: all play the same rhythmic subdivisions of the duration synchronously, led by the player giving the signal. (The rhythms should either be prepared during rehearsal or else kept together by agreed optical signs.)

The number behind R or I or D or *Glieder* or a combination of these gives the number of events for which all the players are to follow the player giving the signal (in combinations these numbers often differ).

To begin: If, once everyone has started playing, a player finds that the beginning sounds similar to the beginning of a previous performance, he makes a stop signal, and a fresh start must be made. This can happen as often as any player breaks off.

To finish: A performance can be ended at any point after a playing time longer than about 23 minutes. However if one of the players finds that the end sounded similar in a previous performance, he plays a further event and everyone starts again, taking their bearings from this event. The attempt to finish can be repeated any number of times.

Thus it is possible to break off earlier than the last of the signs for events in the parts. Equally one can start again from the beginning of individual parts.

In order to terminate the duration of any tam-tam event distinctly,

an assistant should damp the sound after each event at a sign from
the tam-tam player.

Whereas in the first rehearsals each player for the most part
reacted only to himself and constantly brought new events into
play, now—after several performances—we have achieved an ensemble in which the players react very markedly to each other, with
single events going through chain reactions of imitation, transformation and mutation, and all the players often combine for long
periods in single networks of feed-backs.

   The first performance was on 21 May 1967 in Helsinki. Further
performances followed on the 24th in Stockholm, the 26th in Oslo,
the 29th at the Bergen Festival, 1st June in Copenhagen and the
3rd in London. The recording made for the gramophone record by
Vox Productions, New York, took place at Darmstadt in conjunction with the following performance there at the International
Summer School for New Music on 2 September.

Prozession is dedicated to my friends Fred Alings, Johannes Fritsch,
Harald Bojé and Rolf Gehlhaar.

Stimmung

Stimmung for six vocalists was the fruit of a commission from the
'collegium vocale' of Rhenish Music Schools in Cologne. The score
was written during February and March 1968 at a house on Long
Island Sound in Madison, Connecticut (USA). I used texts which
I had written in love-bitten times during April 1967 in Sausalito,
San Francisco, and on the sea-board between San Francisco and
Carmel. The Magic Names were collected for me by the young
American anthropologist Nancy Wyle.

   Once the musical draft was complete, I chose the title 'Stimmung', which bears many meanings: true *intonation*, for the vocalists have to sing the 2nd, 3rd, 4th, 5th, 7th and 9th harmonics of a
low B flat fundamental, and after these have become false they must
constantly be found again (with the aid of a very softly reproduced

pure harmonic sound from a tape-recorder used for tuning); the *tuning up* with which a vocalist always begins when he contributes a new 'model' of sound to the context *during the performance*; the *tuning in*, or *attuning*, of rhythm, dynamics and timbre while a Magic Name which has been freely added to the context is being integrated into it; and—not least of all—there is in the German word 'Stimmung' the connotation of 'atmosphere', 'ethos', *'spiritual harmony'* (for instance the word can often be translated as 'humour' in such phrases as 'good humour' or 'bad humour', referring to the harmoniousness or otherwise of the vibrations existing in man and his environment); moreover, in the word 'Stimmung' is hidden 'Stimme'—'voice'!

In several months, the singers—sometimes taking each other's parts in the course of long rehearsals—learnt an entirely new vocal technique. The notes actually sung must be as soft as possible, and specific *overtones*—indicated by a series of numbers from 2 to 24 and by series of voice sounds taken from the phonetic alphabet—must emerge as strongly as possible: without vibrato, resonating only in the forehead and other cranial cavities; and with deep, calm, measured breaths. If need be, each voice should be amplified by a microphone and loudspeaker so as to make every nuance of the individual singer audible. Each singer has 8 or 9 *models* and 11 *Magic Names* which—in accordance with a *'formal plan'*—he can bring into play *freely* as the context may suggest, and to which the others respond with 'transformations', 'varied deviations', 'pulsations' and 'assimilation'. Nothing is conducted. In any given combination of voices, the singer of the model always takes the lead, passing it on to another singer when he feels that the right moment has come. After a singer has 'called' a *Magic Name*, it is periodically repeated in the same tempo and with approximately the same articulation as the *model* until it is finally *assimilated*, and thus integrated into the *model* prevailing at the time. In this process, the model's lip- and mouth-positions are retained as far as possible, so that the name comes out in a more or less distorted way. A *Magic Name* will bring about a reaction in which there is a clearly

perceptible *change of atmosphere,* evoked by the character and meaning of the name. *Stimmung* is indeed meditative music. Time is
suspended. One listens to the inner self of the sound, the inner self
of the harmonic spectrum, the inner self of a vowel, *the inner self.*

The subtlest oscillations—barely a ripple—*all the senses* are alert
and restful. In the beauty of things sensual shines the beauty of
things eternal.

The first performances took place on the 9th and 10th December
1968 in Foyer B of the Maison de la Radio, ORTF Paris, in a concert promoted jointly by the Centre Culturel Allemand, the Goethe
Institute and the Groupe de Recherches Musicales de la ORTF
Paris.

Max Ernst and his womenfolk were sitting in the front row,
Pierre Souvtchinsky with Marianne in the seventh, and all in all, the
hall was filled with marvellous people on both evenings.

The performance was described in the newspapers as a 'hippies'
camp fire', probably because of the gaily coloured shirts and em-
broidered dresses sported by bare-footed singers who sat cross-
legged in a circle on the floor for 75 minutes, almost motionless in
their absorption, a dim circle of light in their midst; each held a
microphone, and six spherical loudspeakers were placed in a circle
round them, with diaphragms pointing towards the ceiling.

To begin with, we 'tuned in' by playing *Telemusik* in complete
darkness.

Since then the same group has sung *Stimmung* many times in
different European towns, and at the 1970 World Fair in Osaka this
music was performed 72 times in the spherical auditorium of the
German Pavilion.

There has also been one ill-fated performance. At the 1969
Holland Festival in Amsterdam, the performance of *Stimmung* to a
packed Concertgebouw—a performance that had started particularly well—was so severely interrupted after about twenty minutes
by caterwaulings from some dozen 'Provos' (so-called 'students of
the radical left') that we had to abandon it. According to newspaper reports, the agitators included some 'modern' Dutch

composers; and in a subsequent manifesto-like public discussion some of them explained that they had wanted to 'join in', and that if this music excluded that possibility then it must be 'authoritarian'. The incident was the subject of such distorted and blown-up publicity that in the end the German Radio was broadcasting the news that this work was 'lacking in social necessity'.

In such an atmosphere *Stimmung* cannot live, let alone be that winged vehicle voyaging to the cosmic and the divine, whose passengers possess the *inner composure* that was undoubtedly present at the three Paris performances—of which the most perfect took place on 2 June 1969 at the Théâtre National Populaire in the Palais Chaillot.

Stimmung will yet reduce even the howling wolves to silence.

Kurzwellen

Like *Prozession*, *Kurzwellen* was composed for the ensemble with which I have toured since 1964. The instruments are piano, electronium, large tam-tam (about 155 cm in diameter) with microphone, viola with contact microphone, two filters with four potentiometers, and four short-wave receivers. The work can also be played by another combination of instruments, of corresponding potential to those mentioned (although the tam-tam is difficult to replace by substitution).

It began with *Gesang der Jünglinge*: a sung syllable, a word, from the 'Song of the three youths in the burning fiery furnace'—who was the author of those biblical words that we all know?—a boy's voice in the unknown world of electronic sounds. Imagine finding an apple, perhaps even an ash-tray, on a distant star. Here, it would be so banal: there, a marvel of magic.

In *Kontakte*, sounds and noises of metal, wood and skin, and the sound of the piano were the familiar landmarks in the virgin territories of sound.

In *Momente* they were 'found objects' in sound: fragments from a dear friend's letters; William Blake's 'he who kisses the joy as it flies lives in eternity's sunrise'; audience reactions—the whispers, cries, clappings and snappings that the chorus performs; the 'Kala Kasesa Ba-u' from *The Sexual Life of Savages*; the age-old anonymous love poetry of the Song of Songs.

In *Telemusik* they were fragments of the communal folk heritage of many lands and races: from Africa, the Amazon, Japan, Hungary, China, Spain, Vietnam, Bali: modulated, transformed, harmonized and incorporated into the world of newly discovered electronic music; truly integrated so that neither music should suffer reduction to conformity or loss of identity.

In *Hymnen* there appeared the national anthems of all peoples, joined by musical scenes from shopping stores, state receptions, school classes, student strikes, shipyard launchings, studio conversations, military parades, avian paradises, short-wave transmissions.

In *Prozession* the musicians transformed events from my earlier compositions so that they became new events—often unidentifiable or genuinely unknown.

And now, in *Kurzwellen*, it is the utterly unpredictable sounds received on short-wave radios to which the six players react on the spur of the moment of performance. What I have composed is the process of transforming: *how* they react to what they hear on the radio; *how* they imitate it and then modulate or transpose it in time —longer or shorter, with greater or lesser rhythmic articulation— and in space—higher or lower, louder or softer; *when* and *how* and *how often* they are to play together or alternately in duos, trios or quartets; *how* they call out to each other, issue invitations, so that together they can observe a single event passing amongst them for a stretch of time, letting it shrink and grow, bundling it up and spreading it out, darkening it and brightening it, condensing it and losing it in embellishments.

What can be more world-wide, more ego-transcending, more all-embracing, more universal and more momentaneous than the broadcasts which in *Kurzwellen* take on the guise of musical material? How can we break through the closed world of radio waves which spread as it were a cutaneous network of music around the globe ? Does it not already hold many sounds to be picked up by our short-wave receivers that seem to come from utterly different worlds—worlds beyond speech, beyond reportage, beyond 'music', beyond morse signals ?

Kurzwellen is at one and the same time the summary of a long development and the opening up of a new consciousness. What happens consists only of what the world is broadcasting *now*; it issues from the human spirit, is further moulded and continually transformed by the mutual interference to which all emissions are subject; and finally it is brought to a higher unity by our musicians in their performance. The earlier antitheses between old and new, between far and near, between known and unknown, are resolved. *Everything* is *simultaneously* the *whole*. The notion of time is swallowed into the mind's past.

And now ? We have come to the edge of a world which offers us the limits of the accessible, of the unpredictable; it must be possible for something not of this world to find a way through, something that hitherto could not be found by any radio station on this earth. Let us set out to look for it!

The six performers in *Kurzwellen* are as follows: four instrumentalists, one microphonist (tam-tam player's assistant), one player for the filters and potentiometers (the microphones of the tam-tam and the viola are each connected to one filter and the filter outputs each to two potentiometers, which lead to four loudspeakers in the corners of the hall; the filters and potentiometers are operated from the middle of the hall).

The microphonist should perform in the manner of *Mikrophonie I*, damping the tam-tam where necessary, and perhaps joining in the playing of some events; or he may only play a short-wave receiver, following the tam-tam player's part and coming in with him; in this event the microphone can be laid down near the tam-tam frame.

The filtering, dynamic control and spatial movement between the two (or possibly even more) loudspeakers, following the example of *Mikrophonie I* and of the spatial composition of *Kontakte*, should be differentiated *ad libitum*. Suitable possibilities for the distribution of loudspeakers—depending very much on the acoustical properties (susceptibility to feed-back, etc.) of the hall—are, for example:

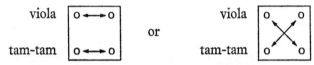

Directions for performance: In addition to his instrument, each instrumentalist has a short-wave receiver. Each plays a succession of events, separated by pauses of greater or lesser duration. Events are played either with the short-wave receiver or with the instrument. In special cases a short-wave receiver may be supported by an instrument, as closely synchronized as possible. In its register, volume, duration and number of components (subdivision of the duration by a rhythm having a given number of attacks) an event will be determined in relation to the last event that either the player himself or another player has played.

There are four parts, labelled I, II, III and IV. Each instrumentalist is given one part. It contains a series of plus-, minus- and equals-signs. At each change from one event to another, the player consults a sign or a vertical combination of signs in the sequence given in his part.

+ : higher or louder or longer or more components;

— : lower or softer or shorter or fewer components;

= : identical register and volume and duration and number of
    components.

If + or — signs apply to one parameter, the other parameters remain as they were in the relevant previous event. A vertical combination will apply to as many parameters as there are signs superimposed. ± can apply to one and the same parameter—for instance, simultaneously higher and lower, or longer and shorter (an event with sound-duration plus 'echo', or several strata with different durations) etc. ⌐ ¬ or ⌐_ or ⌐_⌐ means: the signs must be applied to the same parameter up to the end of the bracket; where there are superimposed series of signs, each bracketed series will apply to a different parameter. In determining the register, the predominant notes as well as the highest and lowest in an event are decisive; the tam-tam player should use all the materials for producing sounds that are used in *Mikrophonie I* (and others too), so as to have at his disposal a correspondingly differentiated range from very high and bright to very low and dark sounds and noises.

Volume refers to maximum loudness as well as to a characteristic articulation of attack–decay. Lengthening or shortening of the duration should be clearly perceptible. Duration expressly means the duration of the event, rather than that of any single component. Each player should play, at least once, a duration that is longer than a minute; this duration is best played at a place where a $+$ and a $-$ sign immediately follow each other, so that one can proceed to the longer duration and then change back to a relatively short duration without a transitional break. A duration can be subdivided into any number of components. In a case where a sign applies to the number of components, this will increase at $+$ (the rhythm for a constant duration becoming faster), will remain constant at $=$, and decrease at $-$.

In the case of a short-wave event the rhythm (number of components with the given points of entry) will be regulated by the volume control knob when the receiver is constantly tuned to a single transmission, for example ♪. ♪♪ ♪ o ; the timbre and attack-decay form can in this way be varied by slight alterations in the tuning. In order to find a required register (whether higher, lower or similar), the player should first softly seek out a transmission yielding the appropriate register, and then begin on the event.

One can also articulate a rhythm by alternating between transmissions on closely neighbouring wavebands.

Unmodulated realistic short-wave events (music, speech etc.) should be avoided.

The search carried on softly from one transmission to another until the player decides on a particular short-wave event should itself be communicated as a characteristic feature and consequently should be carefully, and always musically, shaped; rejected transmissions too should be attended to as moments with distinct durations and attack–decay before going on to alter the tuning.

Each player begins with an event when he wishes. Whoever begins first must play a short-wave event, *ad libitum*. As soon as a player finishes an event, he reacts, consulting the sequence of signs (and vertical sign-combinations) in his part, either to the event he himself has just played or else to the event of another player that is starting next, which he must hear out before reacting to it.

Thus anyone not beginning as the first may either enter with any short-wave event or wait until the first event of another player has finished and then react to it.

In the instrumental playing, the rhythm, timbre, melodic contour and attack–decay of that event to which the player is referring should be imitated as closely as possible and transformed according to the prescribed degree of alteration. Above all, in instrumental imitations of short-wave events the players should make use of the entire acoustical potential of their instruments. The chief concern for the individual practice of each player is to grasp the characteristic properties of a short-wave event quickly and to imitate it unmistakably with his instrument, remaining free to transpose it in respect of the four parameters. If the player reacts with one short-wave event to another short-wave event, then register, volume, duration and number of components can certainly be controlled according to the player's part; however rhythm (which, depending on the type of short-wave reception, may possibly arise within the planned components), timbre, melodic contour and attack–decay can be altered at will; but, on most occasions at least, the player should try to find similar events even when using the short-wave receiver. When and how often each individual player alternates between short-wave and instrumental events is for himself to decide.

If a player reaches his minimum register (extremely low) and volume (extremely soft) and duration (extremely short) and number of components (only one attack for the whole event), and is still confronted by further — signs, then he must wait until another player's event makes further — operations possible.

Each player takes a name in the form of a musical signal. With this name he can be invited by another player to join in a duo, a trio or a quartet. If a player is following another and is invited by a third player, he himself can decide whether he remains committed or responds immediately to the new invitation. A player who is not already committed must accept an invitation.

In the parts there are six different signs which call forth the issuing of an invitation from one player to the others. They are placed in boxes over the system and should be used in the region where they appear (possibly earlier or later).

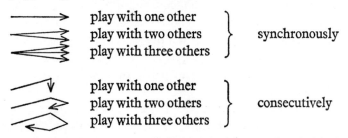

. . . as many events as are indicated by the number behind the sign.

According to the sign he has, the player invites one, two or three others to follow him by playing their names, and continuing to do so until they give him their attention (variations of the names in dynamics, duration, tempo, inner sequence etc., also by repeated playing of one name among several).

When a 'guest' player has become attentive, he plays an event through to its end and waits. Once the 'host' player has ascertained that the 'guest' player has understood him, he performs an event (either with the short-wave receiver or with his instrument). If his sign indicates synchronicity (⟶ ⟨ ⟨), then he repeats the event with his instrument continuously for as often as the

number prescribes, each time consulting his part. He gives the
entries. The others should play synchronously with him, while consulting the signs in their own parts. On this account the rhythm
should be preserved; added components in a constant duration
should be inserted into the rhythm and subtracted components
played as ties (eg., given ♩. ♪♩ ♩, ± for components might be read
as ♩. ♪♪♩♩.. ♩) ; where the components and duration are altered,
further components may be appended to the rhythm.

If his sign indicates alternation, for instance ∧ ∧ , then he first
performs an event, then the 'guest' player answers, whereupon the
'host' player reacts further to this answer. With two, three, four or
five events, the alternation to and fro occurs as often as is prescribed
by the number. Thus the 'host' player is always the last to react.

At the signs ⟋⟍ and ⟍⟋ the sequence of players reacting to the
event the first time round should be retained. The first sequence
will best be decided by signs from the player giving the invitation.
If at ⟋⟍ or ⟍⟋ two or more events per player are to be played,
then the consecutive events can partly overlap from the second
circuit onwards.

Once the prescribed number of events has been played, either
synchronously or consecutively, the 'host' player must next play a
short-wave event, which will be a sign to the others that he is no
longer to be followed and that each of them can again play on for
himself. If at the alternation sign the 'host' player has continued his
events with the short-wave receiver, then he must make an agreed
sign when he is no longer to be followed. If a player invites another
to follow him, and the latter is already committed and on this
account does not wish to follow, then the player issuing the invitation either waits until the other is free, to invite him again, or he
picks another player who is free.

If someone is invited simultaneously, or nearly simultaneously,
by more than one player, then he himself decides who to follow.

The invitations a player can expect at any approximate time are
given in the parts, enclosed within dotted lines under the system;

for instance, II $\diamondsuit$ 5 means that player II will issue an invitation for an alternating quartet for 5 events per player, plus his own final one.

Since the players' parts can be dislocated by different event-durations and pauses—sometimes conflicting between parts—and since moreover duos, trios and quartets have to be postponed if the invited players are not free, the invitations to and from others indicated in the parts can become correspondingly displaced. Each player must realize every invitation. However if a player has had to defer one invitation sign until he has arrived at the next, then he may drop the missed invitation.

There are four thickly marked bar-lines with the sign $\boxed{\text{W}}$. Anyone coming to one of these bar-lines must repeat the event he last played and apply the last alteration sign (or vertical combination of signs) before the bar-line as many times as necessary for everyone to arrive at this bar-line. When all the players have arrived, then the player who has to give an immediate invitation to a synchronous quartet plays the event to which the quartet will relate.

If the 'host' player is the first to reach $\boxed{\text{W}}$, then he repeats the names of the others until they have all arrived.

The final vertical stroke is to be treated like a bar-line with $\boxed{\text{W}}$, but without any invitation to play further.

A performance should not last substantially longer than about 45–50 minutes.

Only in the rarest cases does one know who has composed or produced the sounds emitting from the short-wavebands, how they came into being or whence they came—all possible manner of acoustical phenomena might crop up in their midst; through the concentration of all the players on such unpredictable events, an unexpected intensity of hearing and intuitive playing is achieved and conveyed to each performer and listener.

From the very first performance we thus had the direct experience of a *lasting* meta-personal inspiration, expanses of calm, dimensional plurality, freedom, spaciousness, and of a *medial self-*

renunciation transcending all our previous experiences and heralding something decisively new in musical interpretation.

At the moment I can report no more about *Kurzwellen* than that
the times and spaces in which we were hitherto accustomed to
make music have been suspended and the possibility of registering
a conjunction of strata of consciousness which were hitherto closed
to us or only available in extremely brief moments of intuitive
inspiration has become clear.

Kurzwellen was performed for the first time on 5 May 1968 as a
commission of Radio Bremen during the 'Pro musica nova' Festival
in the Radio Bremen television studio, and is dedicated to the ini-
tiator of the Cologne Course for New Music, Hugo Wolfram
Schmidt.

The performers were: Aloys Kontarsky (piano and short-wave
set), Alfred Alings (tam-tam and short-wave set), Johannes Fritsch
(viola and short-wave set), Harald Bojé (electronium and short-
wave set) and Karlheinz Stockhausen (filters and potentiometers).

Kurzwellen mit Beethoven
(Stockhoven-Beethausen Opus 1970)

When requested to give a 'lecture' on Beethoven for the Bicen-
tenary Year, my spontaneous reaction was to propose an evening of
meditating on Beethoven's music in a performance with the musicians Aloys Kontarsky (piano), Johannes Fritsch (electric viola),
Alfred Alings and Rolf Gehlhaar (tam-tam with microphone) and
Harald Bojé (electronium).

The starting-point is my composition *Kurzwellen*, which,
without mediation, uses unpredictable musical events received on
short-wave radios as material for *development*—transposition,
modulation, spreading, bunching, lengthening, shortening, increased articulation, decreased articulation, colouration, multiplication and synchronization.

Now I propose to simulate the improbable 'special case' in
which, wherever we tune, Beethoven's music is playing from all
the short-wave receivers, interspersed with passages from his

letters. Instead of short-wave receivers, the four players each have a tape-recorder with which, by switching on a loudspeaker, they can play a continuous stream of recorded fragments on Beethoven's music. I myself concocted the tapes and prepared them in such a way that they display the characteristic qualities of short-waves.

Under these special conditions too, we had to be in a position to *intuitively* transform 'found' music into *new music*.

Our aim is not to 'interpret', but—as in *Gesang der Jünglinge, Kontakte, Momente, Hymnen, Prozession* and *Telemusik*—to hear with fresh ears musical material that is familiar, 'old', preformed; and to penetrate and transform it with a contemporary musical consciousness.

What will be decisive in this performance is whether we are sufficiently inspired to lift the artificial barrier between the past and the present, and to make manifest the intuitive power of transformation as the first principle of creation: whether in fact we can put all our experience of playing together for the last five years into this version of *Kurzwellen mit Beethoven*.

It is certainly in keeping with the spirit of Beethoven—that timelessly universal spirit—that we should use the whole of his music (and not merely a 'theme' from it) as the material for a *development without mediation*, in which not merely sections, but *even the single notes and sounds are spontaneously 'developed' the moment they are heard*. For this music is not fenced off and dead, but is rather a living generative force: an immediate cause and pretext for the new and the unknown.

New forms in music

Paths of development

It was in 1950, his last year as a student in Cologne, that Stockhausen first got to know a work by Webern—the *Five Movements* for string quartet, Op.5, of 1909. Until then, he had studied as much of Schoenberg's and of Berg's music as was available at the time, but had had no knowledge of Webern's scores; then at Darmstadt in 1951, Karel Goeyvaerts, a pupil of Messiaen, gave him his first real idea of Webern, pointing out the differences between Webern's music and that of Schoenberg and Berg. Looking back on the impression made on him by performances of Webern, Stockhausen has recently said: 'It is almost impossible to describe the sheer excitement of the musical experience. I only know that from that time on I felt a deep desire to hear more of this music, to know how it was created and what manner of man it was who wrote it.' An utterance such as this must be seized upon; it shows the emotive impulse of almost elemental force underlying the key position Webern's music came to occupy in Stockhausen's mind.

Such an insight yields interesting perspectives. The concept that Messiaen had formulated in his own utterly personal way, namely that of the unification of all the properties of sound under a single principle of organization, had already been taken a long way by Webern, as Stockhausen points out. Messiaen himself, he continues, must have known his way about Webern's works in great detail, for on the basis of a few analyses Messiaen demonstrated as early as 1952 that Webern was seeking not only a greater complexity of the serial principle as applied to melody and harmony, but also an actual unification of the sort he had found in his studies in musical history. Webern was a pupil of Guido Adler and for his doctorate had submitted a thesis on Heinrich Isaac; he was an expert on Ars Nova and the Netherlands composers, and would thus be familiar with the principle of *talea* and *color*, that organization of form by means of interlaced techniques involving both the rhythmic-metrical and the melodic-harmonic aspects of music. To the question of where Webern's artistic development would have led had his life not been tragically cut short, Stockhausen replies with the greatest confidence: Webern would have achieved complete structural integration.

In the decisive step taken by Messiaen, Stockhausen sees a direct parallel with Webern's conception. The first attempts to formulate the musical realms of agogics, rhythm and melody by means of a connecting principle already make their appearance in earlier works of Messiaen—the song cycle *Harawi* and the piano works *Visions de l'Amen* and *Vingt Regards sur l'Enfant Jésus*. The principle is realized for the first time in the piano study *Mode de valeurs et d'intensités*, composed in 1949. In Messiaen this principle centres on the concept of the mode. He discovered it in three precedents: Gregorian chant, Hindu rhythm, and the isorhythm of late medieval music. In Indian music he found predetermined sequences of rhythmic elements, combined with accents, over which new melodic formulations were constantly improvised. Something similar can be observed in Gregorian chant; Messiaen interprets such signs as the *torculus, clavis, podatus* and *porrectus* not simply as melodic formulae alone, but also as indications of rhythmic duration and schemes of dynamic accentuation. In this way, wholly determinate pitch formulations are inseparably combined with relationships of intensity and duration, and by using these formulae largish sections can be composed by piecing the various elements together. The isorhythm of 14th-century music, which can still be found partially adhered to in the motets of the 16th century, brings rhythmic sequences into conjunction with the melodic line in a way that is strictly governed by an abstract principle.

Stockhausen tells how he had always asked himself, and others, why it should be that the music of Mozart exercised such a peculiar fascination, but the answers he was given were never anything more than the usual reference to Mozart's inventive genius or to that boundless prolixity by which everything is correlated in a way that is almost covertly polyvalent. Since these particulars did not satisfy Stockhausen, he made a special study over a number of years, preparing one analysis after another. They provided evidence that in Mozart a synthesis is achieved of harmonic and rhythmical regularities, which are accorded equal validity and are strictly formulated; in this synthesis sixteen rhythmic forms of cadential opening and cadential close (excluding exceptions and hybrid forms) are combined with the harmonic cadential openings and cadential closes (see Stockhausen's article, 'Die Kadenzrhythmik Mozarts'). The hidden principle in Mozart is to be found in the fact that the rhythm becomes emancipated and can take a direction other than that of the harmony. In Beethoven, on the other hand, the rhythm becomes involved in certain clichés of expression and thereby loses this independent formal function. (In late Beethoven it is different again as a result of his retrospective deliberation on polyphonic forms. Over and above the individualistic expressive gestures a general principle comes into effect: universal variability —variation as the reclamation of the figurative by means of melodic-rhythmic formulae.)

Here then is another pointer towards Anton Webern. In Webern Stockhausen finds this same feeling for the universality of an abstract principle. From a historical point of view it can be said that Webern himself prophetically put into practice what we now call the principle of serialism.

To resume our narrative: In the summer of 1951 Stockhausen learnt from Antoine Goléa* in Darmstadt of the multidimensional, modal work of Messiaen, in which all the components of music with the exception of timbre (in other words, melody, harmony, rhythm, dynamics and mode of attack) are organized by means of modes. It was at that time that Goléa brought with him to Darmstadt Messiaen's 4th *Etude*, which Stockhausen listened to over and over again: he was fascinated by this music of Messiaen's, emotionally overwhelmed exactly as he was by the music of Webern. At the time Stockhausen used a phrase that is still bandied

---

* In the original: 'Karel Goeyvaerts'; however, Goléa's own account of the encounter appears in his *20 ans de la musique contemporaine*, and in a private communication to Mr. Richard Toop, Goeyvaerts confirms that the text is here in error. (Translator's note.)

Three early pictures of Karlheinz Stockhausen

Stockhausen and Varèse, Hamburg 1954

about by the dilettantes of today: 'fantastic music of the stars'. He played the record to Dr. Herbert Eimert in Cologne, and in conversation Eimert hit upon the word *punktuell* ('pointillist'), which was subsequently used to describe music of this kind. Remembering this experience today, Stockhausen says: 'Pointillist—Why? Because we hear only single notes, which might almost exist for themselves alone, in a mosaic of sound; they exist among others in configurations which no longer destine them to become components of shapes which intermix and fuse in the traditional way; rather they are points amongst others, existing for themselves in complete freedom, and formulated individually and in considerable isolation from each other. Each note has a fixed register, and allows no other note within its preserve; each note has its own duration, its own pitch and its own accentuation, and in Messiaen's piece every time a note recurs after an interval one already knows it a little better. This music won me over without any difficulty; it was very charming and there was something of a floating quality about it, something that was worlds apart from any sort of dramatic music. I made up my mind to study with Messiaen in Paris. There I could find out how much Messiaen had learnt from others and how much was his own contribution.'

Messiaen is a musician who is deeply attached to tradition. Like most of the great French composers he has a special feeling for the descriptive, less in the sense of realistic programme music than of music that is visually imagined by the composer. He combines this graphic trait with the horizons of the Catholic faith, whose antitheses and whose tendencies towards both abstraction and sensual vividness are entirely Latin characteristics. Hence his music is steeped in symbolism. In point of fact the fusion of exotic and naturalistic elements in Messiaen's music is simply a direct continuation of a characteristic line of thought within the French tradition. Messiaen would be unthinkable without Debussy—in Stockhausen's opinion the greatest genius to have appeared in the history of French music.

What is particularly evident in Debussy is the 'modern' way in which formal thinking is transformed. Classical thought attempts to show the same things—objects, shapes and motives—in a constantly changing light, doing this with the aid of a highly developed technique of modification, transformation, disintegration, variation and modulation. On the other hand, it was possible for Debussy—in Stockhausen's words—by reason of an 'inner principle, held in suspension, to constantly add new ideas to each other in sequence'. It may perhaps be no more than a few successions of whole-tone and semitone steps that are at the root of all these new ideas; one has the impression of always hearing something similar, yet in fact one is hearing something new. The new principle is that of repeating oneself as little as possible. Unity is created by means of relationships between proportion and mass. The proportion existing between given elements placed in conjunction may remain identical while what is actually placed in conjunction may be constantly changing. This is a new approach. A fundamental principle governing ratios and proportions constantly creates new shapes; in the end, there will no longer be any formal repetition at all. To this extent we may trace back to Debussy those aspects of large-scale forms which, after further development by Webern and Messiaen, came to be known by the general term of 'serial form'.

Serial thought

Serial music demands serial thought.

Serial thought—the term is deliberately chosen, rather than 'serial technique'—sets out to mediate between any given extremes. What is new about it is that this mediation between two extremes is to be established through at least two intermediate stages. Without first putting this idea in musical terms let us take the extremes of black and white. Here serial thought would be nothing more than setting up between black and white, according to the complexity of the proposed form, a scale having a sufficiently large number of degrees of grey, so that black appears not simply as an antithesis is direct contrast to white, but also as a degree of white itself, by virtue of the different values of grey in between. Now the transition from the one extreme to the other may be made either continuously or discontinuously: in the first case as a *glissando* from black to white—a transformation completely free of hiatuses—and in the second case as a scale of equidistant degrees (a scale in equal intervals, such as might correspond to the chromatic scale on the piano). If, given a specific number of equidistant degrees in such a scale, we now permutate the succession of degrees in the series so as to bring them into a new order, no longer having a regular sequence of intervals, then we no longer have a scale but a 'row', or 'series'. Hence the musical definition of 'series' (not to be confused with the term's mathematical definition).

To retain the example of contrasts and transitions between black and white, let us suppose that between a given black and a given white five intermediate degrees are interposed at perceptibly equal intervals. A 'series' might, for instance, be formed as follows: contrasting black and white together, followed by the central grey tone as the first mediating degree; then might follow a light grey, so that the emphasis would shift back towards white; after that might follow a dark grey, and then the second light grey tone followed by the second dark grey tone, completing the series and with it this particular mediation between the extremes: black and white will have lost their antithetical character. By this means anything that is seemingly insusceptible to mediation in life, in nature, in art, or anywhere else, may be mediated. And in Stockhausen's view this concept, undermining as it does the dualism at the very fount of classical form, is a specifically modern idea. It entails a different attitude to life, bringing with it a new kind of formal thinking, whose beginnings were already present in instances as early as the work of Kandinsky, Klee, Joyce, Musil, Debussy, Schoenberg and Webern, amongst others.

The resulting consequences are of the utmost importance. Once this idea of mediation has been grasped, then nothing should be excluded from its scope. Its conceptual principle is a principle of organization: to establish a scale between extremes and then to construct a series having determinate proportions. These proportions are to be observed throughout a work's entirety, and will give the work its character and its structure.

Universal mediation constitutes the first basic idea of serialism, but there is also a further idea: everything connected with a structure and requiring formulation should be included in the form on a basis of equal participation. This principle too is related to a general principle in modern thinking (Webern: 'Everything is a principal idea'). But equality in this sense does not mean levelling-out; on the contrary, it is necessary to give every single structure its due wherever it appears.

These two principal ideas, universal mediation and equal participation, have their technical correlatives in processes which one can invent in order to build musical forms. The question arises of how, in any composition, the organization of time can be brought into a lasting balance with the organization of pitches—in other words rhythm and metre on the one hand with melody and harmony on the other—in such a way that each aspect can be deployed effectively yet without either one coming to predominate at the expense of the other. This can only be achieved by means of different shifts of emphasis within the forces in operation, so that they will only reach a perfect equilibrium once the whole composition has taken its course. This principle has led to a whole series of formal discoveries and to new combinatorial forms which mediate between, for instance, extremes of the static and the dynamic, or of open and closed composition, in works such as *Zyklus*, *Gruppen* and *Klavierstück X*.

Before we come to explain serial form, there is a further comment to be made on the concept of the scale. We know today that Western music progressed from monody to an ever more differentiated harmonic polyphony, and that in the countries to the north of the Alps this monody came to us in church music by way of Gregorian chant. Gregorian chant has its roots in the music of the Mediterranean countries, and is intimately related to the music of the Near East. In consequence it once used to possess (for how long, we do not know) a number of this music's peculiarities, including *inter alia* many intervals that are smaller than would be possible in our own semitone scale, and continuous transitions between every degree. With the development of harmonic polyphony during the European Middle Ages, intervallic degrees had to be subjected to an increasingly meticulous control, and it has been our finding in modern times that the chromatic semitonal scale is the best for the multilayered techniques of harmony and, above all, polyphony. Various paths of investigation lead to evidence for this, and practical experience provides confirmation of it. On the other hand, the twentieth century has seen attempts to break through into the realm of quarter-, third- and sixth-tones, by means of systematized extensions of the scale principle. In actual fact, these systems did not result from any new way of conceiving melodic invention but rather were imposed on the existing harmonic structure of music as an attempted refinement. The scope of electronic music now admits of scalic divisions which could never have been achieved by pursuing instrumental means alone. *Gesang der Jünglinge* and *Kontakte* confront us with new yields. Stockhausen's experiences can be summarized thus: the more vertical and harmonic the music, the greater will be the intervals between neighbouring degrees of the scale; the more monodic, linear and horizontal the music, the smaller the intervallic degrees. Here again, series of structures may be set up between the extremes of horizontal and vertical. The scale having the smallest intervals will correspond to the purely monodic structure, and the scale with the widest intervals will correspond to the most harmonic, vertical structure.

Special and general serial formation

In the following pages the concepts of form and formation (in other words, the process of becoming form) are frequently used. Form is always used in the sense of *a* form (rather than form in general), which is the state of a process of formation at any given moment of observation, hence a momentaneous crystallization of form as a sample taken from a continuous process of becoming. If the emphasis is rather on a specific genetical principle of forming, then the concept of formation is referred to. Stockhausen has indicated that the modern study of form has increasingly to do with the discovery and assessment of such principles of formation, within which individual partial forms or the forms of single works are only limited and variant phenomena.

Basically the idea of serial formation is today understood as covering not only the melodic and the harmonic aspects but all the elements that are to be submitted to general organization. These elements include all the properties of any sound: its duration, the particular frequency it has, its loudness or softness, the specific way in which it is 'coloured' (whether presented by an instrument or electronically produced), the particular position and direction in space from which it issues. We now give the name of special serial formation to the formulation of each individual aspect—also called 'parameter'—of a composition that is to be organized within the form according to its own directives, its own principle of organization. For instance, thanks to the possibility we have of tuning instruments in a 'chromatic scale' one can construct certain pitch series, such as twelve-note rows. If one subsequently wishes to organize dynamics, there is no chromatic scale ready to hand, since dynamics are controlled by finger pressure, breath pressure, and so on, rather than by any ready-made mechanism in the instrument itself. In music of the past, pitches have been specified very precisely; this is a feature of the one-sided development of 'pitch music' in the realms of melody and harmony. Rhythm is much less differentiated. As against about 90 notatable pitches there are about 40 durations that can be notated in the traditional symbols. Added to this, if we take the orchestral timbres hitherto in use, there are about 20 unmixed and clearly identifiable timbres at any given pitch (for example, at C') and six or seven notatable dynamic degrees. Thus the determinability of the four aspects constantly decreases in the order described. Finally there is only a single platform, hence just the one specification of spatial position, and it is unimportant for the understanding of classical music to know whether the sound is coming from the right or from the left.

It is quite possible—not only in theory but in practice as well—to train the ear to perceive a vast number of fine dynamic gradations, and on the other hand to teach the performer how to bring out various subtle dynamic differentiations. It is only a question of time and of evolution before chromatic scales, so to speak, are established for durations, intensities and timbres. It is logical that all these endeavours to introduce a chromaticization of the 'parameters' should lead into the domain of electronic music, for here scalic definitions can be changed at will. It is not possible for us simply and without further ado to build new mechanical instruments. However, we can build electrical instruments whose capabilities far exceed those of mechanical ones. If all the aspects of music are to participate in its formation on an equal footing and are to be structured in similar ways, then one must have just such corresponding scales, divided with equal exactitude and having equal numbers of degrees (or else one must have an equivalent continuum for every parameter). Special serial formation as we now know it involves the formulation for each of these aspects of its own series.

At first Stockhausen's procedure in any composition was to invent for the pitches a row that was completely different from that used for the durations, with yet another row again for intensity (as in *Kreuzspiel*). But these rows had basically nothing in common with each other. Although Stockhausen tried to adhere to the number twelve each time so as to find a more or less common regulator for use in composition, he was still conscious of using virtually separate categories of measurement. The same was true in regard to form. 'Densities' have quite different characteristics from 'degrees of brightness' or 'registers' or 'degrees of connexivity' (the latter being the unit of definition by which the juxtaposition of related and unrelated material can be controlled). At first Stockhausen thought it impossible to use the same proportions throughout—to establish a scale between extremes and then to construct a series with determinate proportions to be observed throughout a work's entirety. Then he found ways of interpreting more comprehensively all the individual parameters with the help of adequate flexibility in the serial process of composition. This idea can best be realized in electronic composition, where all those boundaries fixed by the instrumental tradition can be overcome, and the 'parameters' can be organized through one and the same principle, using a single series of proportions. This kind of composition befits Stockhausen's concept of 'general serial formation'.

Though at first sight this principle might appear likely to yield unification and simplification, it in fact produces diversification and affluence. Unexpected results present themselves during the process of composition as a result of the fact that a series which is at first developed independently of the special aspect for which it is to be used then acquires further uses for different aspects—pitch, timbre, duration, intensity, spatial location etc.—thus opening up at any given point in the material complexes produced in a synthetic way and impossible to imagine in the first place; these in turn present themselves to the composer's musical discretion for correction, enriching the musical experiences available to him.

A version of this idea that is even more crucial for Stockhausen consists in working with a transformation-potential series in which a single potential can be simultaneously composed of several degrees of transformation within the various parameters. Thus, for instance, the transformation potential of a sequence of events can remain constant even though transformations may be taking place in a constant interchange between one region and another.

If, for example, we wish to establish a constant potential in a sequence of three events, we may do this as follows:

1st potential: transformation-degree 6 in pitch parameter,
                 all other parameters remain constant.
2nd potential: transformation-degree 3 in duration parameter,
                 transformation-degree 2 in intensity parameter,
                 transformation-degree 1 in timbre parameter,
                 pitch and spatial location remain constant.

3rd potential: transformation-degree 4 in timbre parameter,
      transformation-degree 2 in intensity parameter,
      all other parameters remain constant.

The figures refer to degrees of scales which Stockhausen would set up specially for each work.

Not only the development of this concept but even the idea itself at first seemed quite impossible. Stockhausen ran into contradictions everywhere and he recalled the objection expressed by Fortner in 1951, namely that one could not count pears as apples. A year later Stockhausen wrote *Kontra-Punkte*, the first piece in which the same principle and the same set of proportions were used for all the parameters. At the root of all these explorations lies the selfsame problem that has engaged scientists since the beginning of the century, that of reducing different types of phenomenon to a general law that is not at first evident. In the first place, in fact, nature appears to us only in its multiplicity; unity is nowhere in evidence. It is by virtue of our thinking that we can create unity. The fact that we conceive of the idea of multiplicity as arising out of unity is a symptom of that central consciousness existing within us which invariably conceives of multiplicity by way of unity. Since the latter is not visible, we must imagine it. In terms of music, Stockhausen formulates it in this way: The idea of a work comes from a basic consciousness of the organization of a community of notes. A work requires a homogeneity of elements and represents a form in which something happens between the elements, between the groups, between the complexes and between the shapes and structures, which can again be seen and heard as a whole, in a higher unity. Yet the problem is always that we are representing and shaping quite new forms of thought and of life. This is what the artist accomplishes, as opposed to the natural scientist or the philosopher. The artist is in a position to externalize his conception, to make it accessible to others in a form open to the perceptions of the senses. Musical form is life-form, thought-form, made audible. To that extent the search for a 'general serial formation' was, at least at its beginnings just after 1950, the only justification for the use of electronic means, which in turn made possible forms which could not otherwise have been realized and which could never have been worked out at an earlier stage in musical history.

Thus 'general serial formation' respects a law that applies not in the realm of music alone.

It is entirely the composer's task to imbue a work with integrity through his choice of a proportional series. The contrast of extremes may, for instance, appear at the beginning, in the middle or at the end of a series; in terms of large-scale forms this will in each case give quite distinctive tendencies to the musical sequence. Series may be bound together by means of an overall series. All the techniques that have hitherto had a part to play in music (augmentation, diminution, transformation, adaptation, substitution etc.) can likewise be applied to series. Serial formation offers the opportunity to symbolize any form of life and to mediate between anything and everything.

Point–field

A note can be precisely 'pitched' by stating its frequency. We would call this a pointillist specification. However, instead of the 'point' there may be a 'field'—for instance, a note may fall at any point between a' and e'. This gives limiting values within which something can occur, and relationships between preceding and subsequent events can be specified with varying precision.

Form arises only by virtue of differentiations between degrees. What then do we mean by form among notes? It is not only single notes that are used: two notes together make up an interval, and three constitute a short melodic figure or a chord; and already we find that here the first note will be related to the third, as well as to the second and the second to the third. And since these relationships are co-ordinates, the density of notes occurring in a given unit of time will be decisive. This may be very small (in other words, with few events occurring in a long time) or very great (in other words, with many events occurring in a short time). Between these extremes lie different degrees of density, so that here again a scale (and a series) of densities will ensue. Correspondingly one creates a scale (and a series) of registers (very high or low; or: high and low; or: two octaves, three octaves, four octaves wide; or: only within the compass of a second, third, fourth etc.). Similarly overall formal categories can be submitted to mediation—for instance, static and dynamic form would be subject to mediation between states and processes.

In 1949 Olivier Messiaen composed his *4th Etude* at Darmstadt. After this classic there appeared the *Sonata for two pianos* by Goeyvaerts, *Kreuzspiel* by Stockhausen and *Structures I* by Boulez. As an extension of melodic and harmonic twelve-tone technique, the durations in these works (in the Stockhausen the relationship between 'duration' and 'interval of entry'), as well as their intensities and modes of attack, are all organized by the use of series. In the course of a work, higher formal unities result from the greater or lesser densities arising by virtue of the distribution of the durations in the series or by virtue of the number of layers that are superimposed on each other. There will then result moments of greater concentration and of greater dispersion: fields in which softer intensities predominate, or else louder ones, and fields in which a staccato mode of attack predominates, or else a legato articulation. These large-scale formal differentiations are neither structures nor formal sections in the same sense as were the stretches of motivic–thematic work of former times. There are often predominating intervals in specific areas of a piece, termed 'interval fields' (as for example in Stockhausen's *Kontra-Punkte* and *Klavierstück VI*: here there will be a predominance of, say, thirds, there of fourths, etc.); however, all this arises more or less from the simultaneous superposition of different series and serial segments.

Groups

The next step now was to create formal units that were one degree larger than the isolated single note. Stockhausen calls these 'groups'. They entail the bringing together of several notes by means of overall characteristic properties, the serial principle being applied not only to the properties of the individual notes but also to the relationships of the groups with each other. To give a simple example, we might take groups of 3 notes, 2 notes, 4 notes, 1 note, 5 notes and 6 notes. Thus we will have six groups which will be characterized as such by, for instance, the fact that the first group is identified as *piano*, the second as *forte*, the third as *mezzoforte*, etc. Or the groups may be distinguished by register, which might give 3 notes in the upper register, then 2 very low, 4 in the middle register, etc. In this way the note-groups can once again be understood as single units. There are now a great number of possible ways of differentiating between groups. The relationships between the groups can once again be defined by means of the general application of a proportional series.

Groups can be differentiated in quantitative terms, for example, by the number of notes they have, by the measure of their duration, etc. In this case a number or a duration will remain typical for a group, whose other properties can then become subject to variability. In this way, then, all the characteristic properties that had been used in order to differentiate between individual notes are again applied in order to differentiate between individual groups.

In addition to these possibilities, groups may also be differentiated in qualitative terms. One group out of several may be very predominant. How does this come about? It depends on the context. A second group may perhaps be less dominant, a third still less so, until finally one finds groups that are completely insignificant. In this way there arises a hierarchy of group differentiation which is not susceptible to quantitative measurement and can only be assessed qualitatively. 'Equal participation of groups' now demands that, for instance, side by side with a very loud group there is room for a very soft one to subsist as well. And here there is a need for further qualitative differentiations which cannot be grasped in simple numerical terms. The question at issue might be expressed thus: How must one provide for a soft group in such a way that it can subsist in its own right side by side with a loud one?

(For instance, could one not allow a longer time for the soft one ?) The outcome of considerations of this kind must rest with the composer's musical sensibility and his compositional experience. To compose does not simply mean to juxtapose and to compare, but entails putting things in relationships with each other. It involves the qualitative assessment of such quantities as intensity, duration, register, interval preponderance, and timbre preponderance: all these entail relationships which the composer has to weigh against each other.

Structure and shape

Composition of groups provides a mediation between the two concepts of structure and shape. A structure represents a certain measure of conformity and homogeneity while shape implies a measure of non-conformity and heterogeneity. And Stockhausen also quotes Paul Klee's *Bildnerisches Denken* in this connection: 'Shape is individual, indivisible; a structuration is dividual, reposing on division and repetition.' In general, where a principle of repetition can be identified the problems before us are ones of structure. And in general, where we encounter something unchangeable, presenting itself without repetition, we are in the presence of a shape. In the first serial compositions, where series were interwoven like threads, tied end to end in long chains, and constantly combined in new permutations, nothing in the order of a shape—except perhaps the odd accidental one—was formed by such procedures. Stockhausen makes a distinction between motive (or theme) and shape. He only speaks of a musical motive when it actually motivates something—when it leads to something, whether to variations, to transformations, to disintegrations, or anything else of the sort. When this does not happen, there will be no 'motive' but rather a unique shape, isolated and without any motivic character. The same will also be true of the concept of theme.

As far as shapes and structures go, the particulars of the composer's invention will be the result of the conjunction of proportions and elements. In this way the invention of configurations is firmly moored to a principle which the composer will have set up for any given work and to which he will adhere—and which will indeed constantly provide him with the basic stimuli for his invention. 'I see myself as no longer in the position of using just any musical language that happens to be at hand, and still less just any grammatical rules; rather, I invent the forms within a given piece as well as the grammatical rules of combination for that piece once and for all.'

Let us now, with the aid of Stockhausen's *Klavierstück X*, start to consider how a work is constructed. In this work an attempt is made to mediate between relative lack of organization (relative, that is, in comparison with other degrees of organization) and organization. Stockhausen's aim was to establish relationships between different degrees of organization and to that end he drew up a scale of degrees of organization and non-organization. Using this scale he composed structures in series of distinguishable degrees of organization. The higher degrees of organization are identifiable by their greater unequivocacy—in fact, their absence of chance—whilst lesser degrees of organization can be identified through their higher probability factor and their greater levelling-out of differences, constituting a tendency towards entropy. Our present-day thinking is somewhat inclined to accept the opposite view and to seek order only where things are brought into 'rank and file': where everything is treated alike instead of being distinguished and grouped according to special qualities. In actual fact, the highest degree of organization entails the maximum of differentiation. Greater organization is associated with a lower density and a stronger isolation of individual events. The greater the degree of organization there is to be in a composition, the more must that which belongs to a higher degree of organization be brought out individually, and it will become the more individual for being dissociated from its context. Now in the course of this piece extremes are reached; structures may be crystallized into unique, individual shapes corresponding to the highest degree of organization, or else they may be levelled out into vast complexes. In the course of the process of mediation— and here, as we have seen, Stockhausen is mediating between

extremes of organization and non-organization—an initial homogeneous state of considerable non-organization forms a 'background'
of extreme equalization and very little differentiation from out of
which are expounded more and more and increasingly sizable
shapes. These shapes take up more and more room. The phenomenon may be regarded as similar to a genetic process. The way in
which increasing individuation confronts Stockhausen in this piece
is through the increasing emphasis on isolated shapes. The most
personal shapes that have kept their identity through the course of
the piece are made subordinate to a higher, unifying shape. Thus
the basic problem is to mediate between what is wholly quantitative—the wholly equalized complexes of extreme non-organization
—and the extremely highly developed individual: not to see them
as opposites, but to represent the so-called non-organization as a
degree of organization and vice versa. For where does organization
stop and non-organization begin? It would be to fall into dualistic
thinking to conceive of organization and non-organization as mere
opposites, having nothing to do with one another; quite clearly, the
one passes continuously into the other.

Let us take an example that is apposite to the appraisal of
organization. If we see a tree, its shape will appear to us as a unitary
arrangement of trunk, branches and corona. The nearer we approach
the tree, the more will that which had at first appeared as a shape
break up into countless structural particulars, with branches and
leaves appearing as at a lower degree of organization. When finally
we are confronted only by a single leaf, we shall again see a simple
organization of stems and panicles; and the deeper we penetrate
into the structure of the leaf, right down to the multitude of cells
and molecules, the more will the degree of organization appear to
diminish once again. If we go still further and observe the individual
molecules, we will discover a higher organization . . . etc. It is
thus by observation that we distinguish the degrees of organization.
The next step is to put the perspectives of organization into musical
forms in such a way that—for instance—one will no longer be able
to 'hear through' the individual notes once they crystallize into an

overall complex. Thus the organizing principle that lies at the basis of a composition can be applied to any elements whatsoever—to notes, to stones, to trees, or to persons. The idea behind a work is like a formula which has an essential place in our thought and life. This attitude leads to the achievement of a higher penetration of the human spirit into musical form.

To sum up: The concept of the group mediates between structure and shape. As soon as a group approaches the state of a structure it becomes unsynoptical and the segregation of the elements in the group is strong enough to give it a great similarity to other groups in its environment. And conversely, the more a group becomes concentrated—in other words the fewer the elements it conjoins in a simple order and the less repetitions it contains—the more it approaches the state of a unique and unrepeatable shape. Thus one can establish a series of groups. Finally an entire form may be a group—as a group of groups. The largest group would then embrace the whole work. Thus after pointillist form the next step to be taken was that of group form in which partial forms that were more synoptical, clearer, more contrasted and more sharply formulated were brought together in a relationship allowing for the articulation and sub-articulation of large formal organisms as well as for greater concentration on the qualitative aspect of composing. The characterization of all the properties of groups is particularly clearly demonstrated in the composition that Stockhausen called simply *Gruppen* ('Groups'). 'Composition with groups' really began as early as the first *Klavierstück* of 1952, and is subsequently very much in evidence in *Zeitmasze*.

Blocks: statistical formation

At the same time there appeared in these works what Stockhausen has described as a development towards statistical formation. The concept of statistics is taken from mathematics and is used in a sense analogous to the statistical surveys that give the average values present in any given complex. In musical terms this means that from the listener's point of view there will be elements, partial forms and

Igor Stravinsky and Karlheinz Stockhausen and his wife,
Donaueschingen 1958

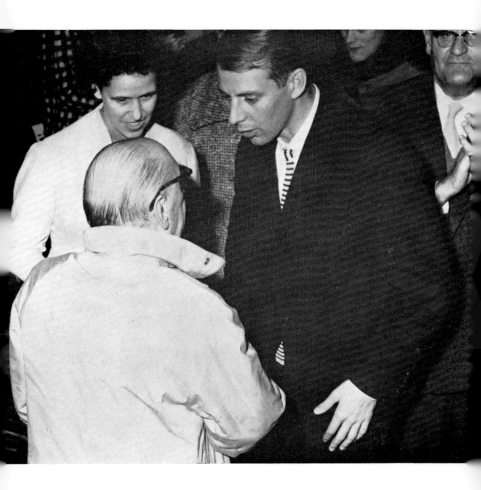

Karlheinz Stockhausen, Bruno Maderna, Pierre Boulez, Darmstadt 1956

individual groups which fuse into a whole from which they can no longer be disentangled. He may for example ascertain that in a certain complex the predominant dynamic level is *forte*; yet this does not mean that each single note must be *forte*, but that *forte* represents an average value (of most frequent occurrence). The composer establishes such statistical criteria beforehand and proceeds to work with them; thus he does not regard the form as a mere aggregation of the individual elements with all their properties, but rather he proceeds from the organizing principle itself—from statistical criteria.

There is another angle too from which it can be explained what is here meant by statistical form: that of structural analysis. Analysis and descriptive presentation of detail is quite a different matter from confirmatory listening, even if this is constantly and concentratedly fastened onto the context. The ear will comprehend the overall shapes and processes, whereas the eye, in reading a score, can pick out intellectual connections, details, combinations and relationships which can only be learnt from the score. The ear alone, even if it is intellectually guided through the written score, will only be in a position to recapitulate the results of the analysis to a limited extent, if at all. It is not just that here we have to do with two quite different forms of human perception; there is also the fact that the accumulative activity of understanding often jibs at the rate at which music penetrates the ear.

In dealing with statistical formation we speak of average speed, average intensity and so on, wherein still more precise distinctions may be found—as, for instance, where loud might be related to soft as a single to a double entity. Still further experiential results can be produced: if one oversteps a certain boundary of perceptibility in one parameter, many different elements will again crystallize into a conglomeration. This effect can already be found in Debussy: in *Jeux*, for instance, a crowd of notes rushes from the highest to the lowest register in a few seconds in the form of a shooting cascade. The ear grasps the complex as something that cannot be unravelled, whereas the eye discovers in the score that harmonic relationships exist within all the individual intervallic steps. In this instance analysis should proceed not from the single note but from the overall impression; here is where statistical analysis will pick out the essential. Understood in this way, statistical formation in composition is something quite new in comparison with traditional music as a whole, for hitherto the question has always been basically to understand each note in its context and each duration in its rhythm, and to pursue such a procedure as if one were listening to the music from one note to the next all along. In a kind of music in which the individual note plays a subordinate part in a conglomeration or pile-up of notes, something which in itself may be very complicated becomes a matter of simplicity. (It is to be noted that events that are heard as complex have always hitherto been composed additively from individual elements.)

In forms resulting from statistical formation—structures, as we have seen, whose density increases towards complexity—a certain interchangeability of notes plays some part. Within a complex it is quite possible for a note to be exchanged with its neighbour without altering anything essential, provided that the sequence is composed fairly densely. This may be compared to the difference between a linear and a vertical arrangement of notes: if I hear notes not as a melody but as a sound, then their order of succession is interchangeable without altering the impression. In a melody this is not possible, since here the order of succession plays a definitive part. Thus the essential factors in statistical composition are how densely a given number of notes is presented, and whether the permutability relates to a very small area or to a large one. If the complex is so dense as to have the appearance of a vibrating mass, then there will be a very high degree of interchangeability between its elements. The criteria of statistical composition are determined by the boundaries of the clouds of density and by their proportional frequency of occurrence. There will be continuous transitions and sudden changes. One cannot account for the whole on the basis of the individual part, for the whole is conceived as the probable result of many components. For the present we lack many of the words we would need in order to describe formal criteria. In electronic music we speak of spiral, centrifugal, perforated and exploding complexes. A complex is put together from many particulars, just as a note will comprise many partials; yet what we hear is sound-'colour'. And correspondingly we also hear typical rhythm-'colours' and form-'colours'.

The application we have just made of the concept of colour to the areas of rhythm and form merely goes to show how confusing this concept is when it is used in the conventional way to refer to a property of 'sound'.

The concept of colour is supposed to serve as a kind of short-hand for a complex of superimposed rhythmic periods. The areas of sound, rhythm and form are simply three different 'slices' of musical perception. Sound occurs wherever we perceive fast periods (between about $1/16000$ and $1/16$ of a second long), rhythm wherever we perceive moderate periods (between about $1/16$ and 8 seconds long), and form wherever we perceive slow periods (between about 4 seconds and 15 minutes long). Stockhausen advocates the point of view which holds that the time-threshold for form is just as psycho-physiologically conditioned as is that dividing sound from rhythm. He points to the singular fact that all three regions have approximately the same range of 7–8 time octaves—in other words can be divided into a progression of lengths whose ratios are 7–8 times greater than a ratio of one to two (2^7–2^8).

From all this we can see that it is possible to regard the pointillist and the statistical as two extremes. The more transparent the musical context, the more individuated will the notes seem to the ear, the more one will pay attention to the intervals and to the 'pointillist' characteristics, and the more one will differentiate between one note and the next. On the other hand, the more a musical context crystallizes into a unitary complex, the less important will characteristics such as interval, pitch, intensity and duration become, and the more important will the statistical criteria of form become—such as pitch direction (eg. high to low), rhythmical direction (eg. fast to slow), density direction (eg. very thick to very thin), timbre direction (eg. very bright to very dark), intensity direction (eg. very loud to very soft) etc.

Now relationships can be established between different degrees of statistical and pointillist form. To this end once again scales can be set up to mediate between the complete transparency of unitary shapes and the obscured transparency of unitary complexes. The 'group' will then stand in the middle of such a scale—to be precise, at the point where single notes are brought together into a higher unity in which the particular remains perceptible and not yet blended into a complex. Scales of this sort are used in *Gruppen*. In this work there are transitions from wholly statistical complexes to structures in which one hears single notes and instruments in isolation, and there are many degrees between these extremes. In *Zeitmasze* too we can hear, for example, wholly confused block-like structures side by side with moments in which every single note can be distinguished. Corresponding features are to be found in *Klavierstücke V–X*. Here statistical complexes are composed as aggregates of 'small notes' (grace notes), which are to be played as fast as possible so as to direct the ear to a principal note which is then established and can be clearly recognized as the core of the complex.

Stockhausen's earlier works were all still written under the influence of European musical determinacy. In the more recent history of European music, its characteristic properties had been worked out to an increasing extent, had been established with more and more precision, and had then been committed to notation. This tendency is an exact parallel of the fixing of locations for pieces of music in certain given environments—for instance in the concert hall. The means used in setting up these structures in sound included tempo indications (either in Italian or in the composer's vernacular tongue), the working out of instrumentation, the refinement of directives for dynamics, reference to metronome settings, and so forth. One might say that these precise expressions of the composer's will—probably reaching their climax in the scores of Mahler—parallel the increasing categorical distinctions which spread in the scientific thinking of the nineteenth century until finally, at the beginning of the twentieth, a crisis point was reached which only the introduction of the theory of relativity was to resolve. In music this tendency towards increased determinacy is to be found in compositions right up to the early 1950s. Even today —and to a certain extent particularly today—this determinacy is in evidence in many forms of society; in a totally determinate system, the human individual's activity and form of life are clearly laid down for him. However, even in these early works by Stockhausen the imminent break with systems of determinacy is clearly foreshadowed in the piling up of note groups and note blocks.

Variable formation

Proceeding from statistical formation it can be shown that within an aggregate of elements a certain variability may occur, expressed either as an interchangeability of the elements within prescribed densities or as a distinct mode of realization—as, for instance, when one directs a performer to play a group of notes 'as fast as possible', or when one admits the relativity of the traditional notation of intensities: pp, p, mf, f, ff. In the matter of dynamics the performer has a certain amount of scope—a field—for each indication, in contrast to the 'pointillist' specification of pitches. This variability of precise specification, above all in the case of dynamics and tempi, has until now been the servant of so-called interpretation. Now Stockhausen goes so far as to say that such nuances of interpretation are irrelevant to the composition insomuch as the composer notates what he considers to be important, always taking into account the nuances of interpretation. The new constructive principle of relative variability consists in the fact that now the former scope of the interpreter is to be 'composed out'; in this way a decisive gain has been made. The composer may, for example, stipulate that in a larger or smaller space of time a given note or group of notes should be played. In this way an increased and varied scope is produced as opposed to what has hitherto been understood as interpretation; and it is the composer who defines

the scope of this variability. This idea can be fully exploited in the
course of composition. The same principle, if transferred to pitches,
would mean that within a stipulated interval the performer is to
play a note or group of notes, to be chosen at will. The greater the
space of time (or space of pitch, or space of intensity, or space of
timbre) made available by the composer for variability, the less
determinate will be the musical text. A composition may be constructed on the principle whereby a more or less unequivocally
established scheme is used in order to create relationships between
completely outlined and unambiguously specified events and those
whose degree of variability makes them indeterminate. Thus, by
using degrees of determinacy as criteria, one can establish relationships between 'non-organization' and 'organization'; one need only
allot different sizes to the fields available for the player's free choice.

The new territory this opened up is related first and foremost to
instrumentalists and not to electronic equipment.

To give an example, in *Klavierstücke V–X* there appear many
modes of attack that depend on the context. Perhaps a key is to be
struck sharply and then immediately depressed silently, so that the
note is still heard sustained softly as an 'echo'. This action takes up
a certain amount of time. One is to continue playing only once the
soft echo has been heard. Regardless of the fact that the time taken
by this sound depends on the instrument used and on the individual
player, the mode of attack already to some extent determines the
duration in a relative way—relative to, say, another note that is to
be played *staccato*; or to a note that is struck sharply and is then
immediately sustained by means of the right-hand pedal; or to an
attack in which a few lower keys are silently depressed and then
higher keys in relatively simple harmonic ratios (up to about the
tenth harmonic) are struck so as to bring out the 'sympathetic'
resonances of the lower notes. In an example from *Zeitmasze*, a
group of notes is to be played 'as slowly as possible' (within a single
breath); the tempo is in fact dictated by the length of the player's
breath, but this in turn depends on the register of what he has to
play (high notes requiring more breath than those in the middle

register), and also on the prescribed intensity and number of notes.

Likewise, by determining duration within a 'field' the composer can create another scale of differentiations. Naturally, the variability which can be distributed among the individual instruments, individual notes, individual durations and individual intensities or groups, can also control partial forms, larger formal structures and the total form itself.

In Stockhausen's first cycle of piano pieces (*Klavierstücke I–IV*), he touches the extreme point in what a performer can be asked to calculate quantitatively, to consider and to mechanically perform. In around 1950 there was a predominating tendency in instrumental music to define everything in the most determinate way possible. This is why scores dating from that time have such complicated notation. It was soon realized that the existing ways in which one could notate durations were no longer adequate. As always with such phenomena, the development started in a new type of music, namely, electronic music. Here one could achieve a degree of differentiation that performers would find impossible. But would not the performer now become redundant as a result? Was there now to be no more interpreted music? And would it all have to be machine-made?

These are just the questions which Stockhausen, one of the first to give his attention to electronic music, confronted again and again. And he thought long about what were the typical characteristics of instrumental playing and how these might be utilized in the process of composition. Obviously these characteristics are the outcome of a direct transference of sensibility onto the instrument; they can be described in terms of the sensibility itself—in terms of approximate values as opposed to quantitative values, and of empirical as opposed to numerical measures. As to the consequences of this, Stockhausen believes that one should now create compositions with a particular regard to this aspect, not just bringing it into relation with one's work as a natural subsidiary phenomenon, but making of it a compositional parameter to which access may be had through these empirical measures. In this way, of course, it will mean that less precise specifications have to be given; but they will be organized by a whole scale of degrees indicating how specifications of empirical measures are to be differentiated. There is an example in *Refrain*, where the durations are measured as follows: notes are struck at a given intensity, and after each note the performers wait until it has died down by a relatively determinate amount; then they resume playing. Thus the duration is dependent on the intensity. For long stretches in *Carré* there is no metrically fixed structure. The empirical measures for relative durations are dependent on the decision of the conductors, who listen to the duration in which, say, a given *crescendo* is performed, and then give the next signal for something new to begin. All temporal events are indicated in proportional notation. With pitches this is possible to only a limited extent—in fact, only for such instruments as can produce a continuous *glissando*. One can thus also organize pitch fields in this way.

Applied to large-scale forms, we find an instance of variable formation *par excellence* in *Klavierstück XI*. Here the overall form is split up into 19 groups which are spread out irregularly on a large page in such a way that as far as possible no group predominates over the others to distract the eye. The directions for playing instruct the pianist to begin with any group and link it up to any other group that happens to take his eye. The overall form that emerges in an interpretation is genuinely the result of momentary decisions. Stockhausen has here devised regulations to control the linking of groups, consisting in indications after each group as to how the next is to be played. The first group is to be played freely—with free choice of intensity, speed and mode of attack (*staccato*, *legato*, *portato* and so on). But the following group chosen by the player (any one that may happen to catch his eye) must then be played according to the directions printed after the first group. Following this, the procedure is repeated in a similar way. When the performer comes to a group for the second time he is to respect the indications given in parentheses; this will give the group a new aspect. When he comes to the same group for the third time, he then plays no more; for this would constitute the first repetition.

At this point his version will be ended. Thus the total duration of the performance is indeterminate; it depends on the particular version—on the selection that the performer has made. Hence the same variability that can regulate the individual durations is transferred to the overall form. In each group in *Klavierstück XI* the sequences and constellations of notes are fixed, as are the sequences of durations and the relative durations of the groups. But these specifications too could have been made variable. Stockhausen united all the aspects of variability for the first time in *Zyklus*, which he composed in 1959; this is the first example of a polyvalent form in the true sense of the term.

Indeterminate formation (polyvalent formation)

Indeterminate formation is alternatively designated by Stockhausen as polyvalent formation. With the concept of indeterminate formation there is always the proviso that the limits within which the indeterminacy holds good are more or less broadly conceived and are specified by the composer from one instance to the next. Absolute determinacy, just like absolute indeterminacy, is a recent product of speculative thought. On more than one occasion, Stockhausen has pointed out that it is simply a matter of perspective whether one sees in a tree the relatively indeterminate number and distribution of the leaves or the form that determines the character of a single leaf, and whether one observes through a microscope the determinate appearance of the distribution of that leaf's cells or only the single cells themselves. This striking effect of changing perspective, the interchangeability of the concepts of determinacy and indeterminacy, does not just exist in the realm of musical composition alone, but has become evident above all in recent developments in the natural sciences. Since a long tradition of musical commentary and analysis has already concerned itself exclusively with factors of determinant formation, there is no need to say any more about it here. It is interesting to note that the first symptoms of variable formation made their appearance not only in music, but again in painting, sculpture, architecture (the *Modulor* of Le Corbusier), and finally even in the planning of the modern industrial environment.

Since he started using composed degrees of variability, Stockhausen has used the concept of indeterminate or polyvalent formation for all the aspects of musical form. What this means is that for all the moments occurring in the course of a musical context he fixes not only a single possible solution (whether determinate or variable) but different numbers of solutions which are of equal validity. The performer's decision which 'version' to choose for a performance is taken into consideration as part of the composition itself.

Between completely fixed and extremely polyvalent formation there are in *Zyklus* nine different degrees of polyvalence. Hence whatever is unequivocally fixed is structured with corresponding regularity: for example, sequences of attacks consisting of a regular *accelerando* or a regular *ritardando* or containing simple rhythms which can be grasped as such. At the same time whatever becomes increasingly polyvalent gives the aural impression of increasing indeterminacy and irregularity, and, seen as a whole, increasing interchangeability and lack of direction.

A further example in polyvalent formation is *Refrain*. Here Stockhausen has turned his attention to the old refrain principle and taken up its fundamental idea. He has constructed a through-composed form in which the individual durations are dependent on intensity, itself depending on pitch. Over the six lines of music on the first page is placed a transparent band containing relative directions for each line. What appears on the band only takes on its final significance when it is related to the context by the selection of its position on the page, which must be chosen afresh for each performance. The band may, for example, direct that a five-note melody is to be played using the notes of the following chord. Only once a position has been chosen for the band to be fixed in can one then look up the next chord in question and make a five-note melody out of it. What is indicated, then, is the number of notes, and their intensities (by means of the thickness of the notes); only pitch is variable, and this will depend on the context. Or, for instance, the band may direct that a *glissando* is to be made between the outer notes of the preceding chord (the steeper the *glissando* is made—by virtue of the position of the band—the louder should it be played). Thus the so-called refrains that appear on the band will take their final form only in the context into which they are placed. In this consists the polyvalence of the refrain. Characteristics that appear on the band do not appear in the main text; these include short melodies, *glissandi* (or clusters), trills, bass notes (on the piano), use of the soft pedal and arpeggiated chords.

Furthermore, we have already said above that new instrumental music has also been influenced by reflections about electronic music. The latter is a music having unequivocally fixed material, whereas instrumental music brings into play variable and polyvalent characteristics both in its elements and in their formation. Whilst electronic music, when it is played back on tape, is always repeated as something precisely fixed, instrumental music of the new kind will undergo a greater or lesser degree of change from one performance to another. In this sense it is unrepeatable—just as the musician who plays it, being tied to the moment of performance, is never quite the same person each time. (Moreover, neither will the listener be.) A single composition can occupy various places on the scale between the extremes of complete determinacy and extreme indeterminacy. As we have already mentioned, these aesthetic forms seem to Stockhausen to be at the same time forms of thought. A further task is to set up relationships between these forms. The essential thing for an artist is always to set up relationships within the range of his intellectual imagination and thereby to bring into a higher unity those distinctions that the natural scientist can only grasp by means of observation and description, and can likewise only relate to each other in an abstract and theoretical way. The artist attempts to give to general forms of thought a specific life.

Moment formation

If we think for a while about 'open' forms—forms, that is, which have always already begun and are always ready to continue further

—then it will become obvious that they must imply as a consequence the composition of works which have unending duration. Stockhausen calls such forms 'moment forms', or 'now forms', or—having regard to their duration—'unending forms'. It might be imagined that such works could be played at a particular location over periods of time, either through loudspeakers or by live performers: listeners could come and go at will. Insofar as the place is fixed—let us say in an urban 'music building' having one or even several performance halls, after the manner of picture galleries—individual works could be performed at given hours of the day for periods of a week or even longer. There ought to be no fixed seating arrangements in the halls, so that there would be no permanent rows of seats but rather variable seating possibilities. In order to avoid any distracting noises the floor could be laid with some suitable material and curtains could be placed in the doorways as in recital rooms. The halls should be provided with all the necessary facilities for reproduction through loudspeakers and for the adjusting of all the spatial and acoustical aspects of instrumental music, so that the requirements of any work could be met.*

Broadcasts of music on the radio are nowadays planned in much the same way as are traditional concert-hall programmes; the programme planners insert such broadcasts very abruptly into sequences of other programmes, compelling the listener either to consume the menu without any choice as it is presented or to switch on and off at prescribed times which again lie beyond his choosing. It would be much more sensible to have broadcasts of a given character on one and the same waveband so that everyone who is interested can know that he will find what he is looking for at any time at a given place. Consequently this will mean having concert music on one wavelength, light music on another and speech broadcasts on a third. This is the sort of broadcasting that would best suit unending forms of music, in which one could freely switch on and listen for as long as one wished. It is clear that within the foreseeable future there will be a number of composers engaged in

* See also pp. 160-2. (Translator's note.)

the creation of works of 'unending' duration. The problem of performing such works is one that can be dealt with by technical means. A continuously changing number of players—with variable changes of shift—could (with the simultaneous use of loudspeakers) share in the performance of a work of unending duration and from time to time—either in accordance with a planned periodicity or at the behest of public interest—the work being played could be exchanged for another, or else a different work could be selected from a group of works (for performances covering longer periods of time). A parallel that comes to mind is that of continuous cinema shows. The only thing that is new is the conception of the unending form which would become necessary and meaningful in the context of such a performing practice.

Complementarity and interpenetration of loudspeaker music with instrumental performance has already been attempted in several compositions—as it has been in the case of *Kontakte* too—and it is just this type of work, by virtue of its simultaneous and alternating combination of both media, that would be especially suited to unending forms and to the performing requirements they pose.

When Stockhausen speaks of unending form he should not be taken to mean that performances are intended not to come to an end. He makes a strict distinction between 'start' and 'beginning', 'finish' and 'end'. When he refers to 'beginning' he is thinking of a phenomenon in which something commences and starts to play; when he refers to 'end' he is thinking of something reaching a conclusion, ceasing to sound, and being extinguished. On the other hand he associates the words 'start' and 'finish' with the notion of caesurae which bound a duration whose character is that of an excerpt from a continuum. Accordingly, 'beginning' and 'end' are appropriate to closed developmental forms and dramatic forms; 'start' and 'finish' are appropriate to open forms—moment forms. It is for this reason that he can speak of an 'unending form' even though a performance is finite in its duration from the point of view of performing practice. The distinction between a 'finish' and an 'end' becomes clear immediately if one thinks of certain parties at which a finish is made even though they are not at an end (following the convention whereby a finish should be made at the point when the party is at its best); and conversely one can think of parties which have long been at an end before a finish was made.

Stockhausen abruptly broke off his work on the compositions *Gesang der Jünglinge* and *Kontakte*; he would probably still be working on *Kontakte* today had he not brought it to a finish with a decision as to a definite performance date. He tells how the moment with which—a week before its performance—he closed the work had already been conceived, with increasing exactitude, some time beforehand. Listening to these last minutes now, one feels that this awareness must indeed have found its way into the composition. Many listeners have told him that they experienced an irrevocable end and that the piece seemed to expire, or to dissolve. All he can say about this is that he did indeed make a finish but he was not by any means at an end—neither in the sense of having exhausted the material nor with regard to any possible deterioration in the invention of new moments and relationships within the scope of his chosen principles of conjunction and formal structuration, and of the work's proportions. The present finish seems to him very much like a dummy ending; it is only pretending that it cannot continue. He could in fact have continued with the invention of new moments to add to those he had already composed for an unlimited time to come.

There is yet another aspect to the questions about unending form. Stockhausen has said: 'In all these considerations about unending form one notices a peculiar tendency to overcome the time that "ends"—death; I have already spoken once of the explosion of the concept of duration. Composers who are preoccupied with suchlike ideas have to be prepared for the pejoratively intended reproach of romanticism. For me, every attempt to bring a work to a close after a certain time becomes more and more forced and ridiculous. I am looking for ways or renouncing the composition of single works and—if possible—of working only forwards, and of working so "openly" that everything can now be included in the task in hand, at once transforming and being transformed by it; and the questing of others for autonomous works just seems to me so much clamour and vapour.'

To summarize, let us repeat that, after elucidating the concept of serial formation, we have been discussing new criteria. We distinguish between:

1. pointillist formation
2. group formation
3. mass formation

Each of these can be used in compositions of:

A. determinate form
B. variable form
C. polyvalent form

And all these forms can appear in:

I. development form
II. sequential form (such as the classical suite)
III. moment form

(Categories A, I and II are not dealt with here as they should be sufficiently familiar from traditional music.)

Stockhausen has thus found concepts that are not simply derived from his own works but can apply to works by other composers as well. Using the formal criteria listed above, whole works or sections within a work can be very clearly distinguished. One might say, for instance, that this section is pointillistically formed, that one statistically; this polyvalently, that in moment form. Or perhaps there may be question in a work of some more determinate form or else of a form conceived according to the principles of articulated probability mediating between determinacy and indeterminacy. Equally well, these different forms may also be perceived in simultaneous operation. We may say that one level of a work is very transparent and pointillist, having been composed with particular attention to details, whilst another level, running simultaneously, is composed in groups in which there is a complex to be heard in a completely statistical way, with particularity totally disappearing into an over-all form of movement, and so on. Concerning the total layout of a work, it can now be said of one work that it is composed with a distinct beginning and end and of another that it simply starts and finishes; the distinction can be made between an ending form and an unending form (beginning, un-beginning) which will be of the utmost consequence for the detail of a work inasmuch as that detail is in accord with the total layout of the work. And with the aid of such formal criteria we can recognize a work's basic idea as well as the personal stylistic differences in the ways of thinking of various composers. Thus the erection of these formal categories provides the possibility of a better appraisal and understanding of many of the works written in the most recent past.

Process planning

As far as I can ascertain, it is to the musicologist Rudolph Réti, an alumnus of the Adler School in Vienna, that the credit belongs for first having introduced into the systematic observation of the mus-ical work of art the concept of the process. Réti's principal achieve-ment in his book *The Thematic Process in Music* (1951) consists in having discovered ramifications which had to a large extent hitherto remained unknown in the thematic cohesion of works in several movements—above all in those dating from the 18th and 19th centuries. Thus Réti relates the concept of the process to that of the theme and hence to a quite specific manifestation of the musical shape which, from a strictly historical point of view, first took on its definitive form in the late baroque era and was then to dominate music decisively throughout a whole epoch. In one of its most recent definitions, what a theme actually is has been outlined thus (Riemann, *Lexikon*, 1967): 'Since classical times the most import-ant thematic type has consisted of pregnant and often diametrically conflicting motives which, placed in symmetrical relation with each other, strive to expound themselves independently. Besides this type must be mentioned the melodic, *cantabile* type of theme which exhibits more static properties, is to be found preponderantly in slow movements and in rondos, and generally comes more to the fore in the Romantic composers.' Proceeding from the studies of Réti I then came to see the thematic phenomenon on a fundamental level as a process, and came to the conclusion that the period from Vivaldi and Bach up to 1950 represented a closed epoch, predominantly governed by the thematic concept and according a central importance to the theme as a factor capable of transformation, besides, in many cases, virtually inventing it as such. In particular I drew up distinctions between the following typical processes: separation processes, model-variant processes, evolution processes, assimilation processes, addition processes and reduction processes. In 1950 the period of the thematic process comes to an end; in place of the theme, whose essential features we have just sketched out, new musical shapes appear; and it is with the nature of these—as far as it is yet possible to make any definitive assertions about them today —that the present book is constantly concerned, with especial reference to the works of Stockhausen.

Stockhausen has often spoken of processes; naturally he has never associated the concept of the process with the traditional theme, since in his music he certainly neither thinks nor invents thematically in the conventional sense of the term; it is rather a further conception that he has contributed to the notion of the process. This conception became particularly clear in a work bearing the title *Ensemble*, whose first public performance took place on 29 August 1967 at the International Summer School in Darmstadt. Here, first, is the announcement in the programme.

Ensemble
For any one instrumentalist and tape or short-wave receiver
Process planning: Karlheinz Stockhausen
Compositional working-out: Participants of the composition studio

	Composer	*Instrumentalist*
Flute	Tomás Marco	Ladislav Soka
Oboe	Avo Somer	Milan Jezo

Clarinet	Nicolaus A. Huber	Juraj Bures
Bassoon	Robert Wittinger	Jan Martanovic
Horn	John McGuire	Jozej Svenk
Trumpet	Peter R. Farmer	Vladimir Jurca
Trombone	Gregory Biss	Frantisek Hudecek
Violin	Jürgen Beurle	Viliam Farkas
Violoncello	Mesias Maiguashca	Frantisek Tannenberger
Double bass	Jorge Peixinho	Karol Illek
Percussion	Rolf Gehlhaar	Frantisek Rek
Hammond organ	Johannes G. Fritsch	Aloys Kontarsky

Harald Bojé, Alden Jenks, David Johnson, Petr Kotik (potentiometers)

This is in fact a collective composition, the realization of a project that Stockhausen had long harboured: he had already expressed this intention on many occasions and over many years. The piece is made up of twelve layers, composed by the participants in the course according to a plan worked out by Stockhausen which provided for four hours' music; each of the participants was to compose the part of one of the twelve nominated instrumentalists with tape or short-wave receiver. It was ensured that each of the composers would have some scope for his own creative blossoming by providing that in every case there would be a solo section in the central part of his contribution. Variation within the composition was guaranteed by the fact that Stockhausen himself had composed extended tutti segments for use as intercalated sections with which to synchronize the ensemble from time to time; other instrumental combinations were also envisaged (in duos and trios) as well as the inclusion of electronic music played back on a tape. At the performance the twelve instrumentalists were spaced out over all the available room (the first performance was in the Ludwig-Georgs-Gymnasium, Darmstadt); directly to one side of them was the composer, giving the signals and with a tape which he had worked out and which, as we have said, was switched on from time to time;

in addition the instrumental sounds were submitted to selective amplification through loudspeakers which, in turn, were likewise distributed over the performing area.

Here a new possibility has been added to the traditional forms of concert activity. As a rule the programme of a conventional concert consists of a number of works by one or more composers; one is thus quite deliberately invited to make a double comparison—between the works themselves and between their interpretations. In the composition *Ensemble*, 'pieces' of twelve compositions (by twelve composers) are performed simultaneously. Meanwhile, these 'pieces' are not finally worked-out musical objects (or 'works') but sound structures (which are in part produced on tape or with short-wave receivers); furthermore, in addition to being notated 'events', they are individual events in the sense of being forms of action and reaction, and are brought into the playing of the ensemble by the individual composers in the context of the total performance—which is then the process itself.

The principle of collective working that underpins this process is the result of previous long daily discussions, in which the twelve systems and their co-ordination were formulated and worked out. The planning of the process was in Stockhausen's charge.

The result is a process of altogether four hours' duration, and it is in fact not simply a 'sum' of all the individual 'pieces' but a great deal more besides. It is a composition of compositions, a composition mediating and oscillating between the complete isolation of single events and the total interdependence of all the layers; moreover it mediates between the greatest determinacy in planning and the imprevisibility of its course in performance.

In the collaboration between the composer and whichever instrumentalist is allotted to him one can already imagine a kind of duo; there are, as we have already indicated, twelve players in all, distributed over the whole performing area. Four further musicians have the job of amplifying and spatially directing specific details and moments of the process; they operate from mixing desks linking microphones to eight loudspeakers distributed round the hall.

In addition there is a further factor. Even the position of the listener is included in the process as an individual feature. The listener can if he wishes move quite freely about the hall among the instruments and the loudspeakers. At any time during the process he may freely choose his position and hence also his acoustical perspective. The principle of moment form is here extended in a perfectly logical way down to its ultimate consequences from the points of view of both the composition itself and the listener.

So much for the typical process found in this work, *Ensemble*. The composition *Prozession* actually has a title that is derived from the very word 'process'. Naturally it here refers only to a process brought into play and realized in performance, and has no connotation with the procession that is a religious ceremony—a cortège accompanied by the appropriate sacred emblems.

The fundamental information about *Prozession* is given in the short note that Stockhausen provided for the work's recording by Vox of New York (see pp. 60–1, 64). This text provides documentary evidence as to the strength with which the impulse of music-making and of sheer play is allowed to imprint the typical processes with which Stockhausen is concerned. Play has ever been a part of music and of music-making, and it is of the essence of play, too, to react to one's partners and for them to react among themselves.

Typical processes of this kind are extremely polymorphic. The layout of the composition *Ensemble* is in itself already one concept of the process, collaboration in the 'duo' is another which is added to the whole, though without disrupting the proceedings;* the inclusion of the possibilities for relaying the 'duos' through microphones to loudspeakers is another phenomenon to be understood as a process.

It is notably clear that typical processes form an important part of the score of *Momente* (1962/65). The concept of the process was still further intensified in 1964, first in *Mixtur*, where five instrumental groups from a normal orchestra are each fed individually

* Wörner at this point refers to the sense of *Prozess* as 'legal proceedings'. (Translator's note.)

into microphones during the performance, these microphones being connected to ring modulators; here the sounds are modulated with impulses from sine-wave generators operated by five musicians in accordance with directions in the score, so as to modify their timbre, rhythm, intensity and pitch; and finally these sounds are played through five groups of loudspeakers simultaneously with the live orchestral sounds.

The next work to appear, also in 1964, was *Mikrophonie I*. Here Stockhausen sought possibilities of giving a flexible contour to the process of microphone positioning too; in other words, after the hitherto rigid experience of picking up sounds by microphone in which the microphones in use, as well as the musical instruments and voices that served as sound sources, were all related to each other in a totally stationary, fixed way, there was to come a further process phenomenon. The microphone itself became a portable musical instrument; moreover its use was to influence all the properties of sound: harmonic and melodic pitches, rhythm, dynamics, timbre and the spatial projection of the sound were all to be given an independent profile according to composed directions.

Theoretical considerations and experiences in the experimental field both made their contribution to the realization of this creative idea. A few years earlier, Stockhausen had bought himself a large tam-tam for use in composing *Momente* and had set up this instrument in the garden of his home. In 1965 Stockhausen reported the following: 'Last summer I made a few experiments by activating the tam-tam with the most disparate collection of materials I could find about the house—glass, metal, wood, rubber, synthetic materials—at the same time linking up a hand-held microphone (highly directional) to an electric filter and connecting the filter output to an amplifier unit whose output was audible through loudspeakers. Meanwhile my colleague Jaap Spek altered the settings of the filter and volume controls in an improvisatory way. At the same time we recorded the results on tape. This tape-recording of our first experiment in "microphony" was a discovery of the greatest importance for me. We had come to no sort of prior agreement: I used such of the materials I had collected as I thought best and listened-in to the tam-tam surface with the microphone just as a doctor might listen-in to a body with his stethoscope; Spek reacted equally spontaneously to what he heard as the product of our joint activity.'

The words of this report read as a frankly classic description of how, in the discovery of new possibilities for the artistic (and technical) world we live in, an intellectual basic conception goes hand in hand with practical research that could almost be called playful: a preconceived complex of ideas is worked out with the aid of purely empirical experiments.

Electronic music

Basic terms

In 1954 Herbert Eimert wrote that there lacked 'the broad basis of experience with which one could be fruitfully conversant'. He was referring to the question of electronic music and not for the last time, in order to stimulate 'a more widespread serious preoccupation with the issues of electronic music', he devoted a special issue of the *Technische Hausmitteilungen des Nordwestdeutschen Rundfunks* (Vol. 6, Nos. 1/2, Hamburg, 1954) exclusively to this theme.

Today we have progressed far enough to be proceeding through quite different 'bases of experience', but they are always founded first and foremost on a technical basis. Their other aspect, the aesthetic, is still the focus of utterly contradictory opinions. For this reason we must first go thoroughly into the way in which terminology and technique are organized. The basic work on terminological elucidation is due to Werner Meyer-Eppler, the late professor at the Institute of Phonetics and Communications Research at Bonn University. Meyer-Eppler made a preliminary distinction between acoustical instruments and electrical instruments. Acoustical instruments are those used for the direct production of sound in the absence of any previous stage of electrical oscillation. Electrical means of control (for instance, electrical filters) will make no essential difference to the acoustical character of these instruments. All traditional musical instruments belong to this class, as do such unusual ways of producing sound and noise as, for example, wind machines and steam organs, as well as the human and animal voice.

Electrical instruments are those used for the indirect production of sound with the aid of an electro-acoustical transformer (preferably a loudspeaker) as the sound-producing organ. (Thus acoustical instruments which are fitted with electrical drive are not electrical instruments proper.) The oscillation that is to be transformed into sound is always present in its electrical form. It is produced by an electrical wave-generator. Depending on the degree in which electrical components are used, instruments are classified in three groups; electro-acoustical, electronic–mechanical, and purely electronic instruments.

Electro-acoustical instruments are in fact constructed like conventional musical instruments, but possess free-standing or contact microphones with amplifiers and loudspeakers in order to increase the volume of sound or to enrich the sound. To this category also belongs the transformation of the human voice, picked up by microphone or throat microphone and passed through a vocoder or through electrical synchronized oscillators.

With electronic–mechanical instruments it is the motion of mechanical vibrating parts (strings, tongues, membranes) or of rotating elements (disc-sections or cogwheels) that is converted into electrical impulses by means of the electrostatic, electromagnetic or photoelectrical extraction of sound (in, for instance, the Wurlitzer and Hammond organs).

In electronic instruments electronic components alone are used for the production of impulses (thermionic valves, transistors, etc.). Hence in electronic instruments no mechanically operated parts are necessary for the production of electrical oscillation.

Those instruments which house both acoustical and electrical instruments in a common apparatus, or at least bring them together in a sufficiently small space for them to be spoken of as single instruments, Meyer-Eppler called 'compound instruments'.

Among electrical instruments Meyer-Eppler distinguished between three groups: electrical imitators, electrical performing instruments and electrical generators.

Electrical imitators attempt to 'replace' conventional instruments, whereas electrical performing instruments pursue acoustical possibilities of their own kind. According to the manner in which their sounds are generated, we can classify the following:

1. Electro-acoustical performing instruments (eg. Abbé Pujet's radio organ),
2. Electronic–mechanical performing instruments (eg. Hammond organ),
3. Purely electronic performing instruments (eg. Trautonium and Mixtur-Trautonium, Melochord, ondes Martenot).

Under the heading of 'electrical generators' Meyer-Eppler classified all the instruments, appliances and equipment that are not used in concerts or as solo instruments, but are used in the preparation of a composition with the aid of an acoustical accumulator (sound equipment using needles, light, or magnetic tape; computer tape, etc.). Electrical generators are used to enable the composer and his assistants to make a direct recording of the composition on tape, film, etc. Instead of concert performance, the sounds are replayed through reproducing equipment.

Meyer-Eppler also systematically described the range of uses to which electronic instruments might be put ('Technique of Electronic Composition' in *Melos*, January 1953). He distinguished between five categories:

Electronic instruments can be used in imitating the sound of conventional instruments. As instances he named electronic church organs and carillons, which can be used as substitutes for the traditional instruments themselves.

The second category of uses for electronic instruments concerns those designed so as to be characteristic and individual-sounding instruments for use in conjunction with traditional instruments. This is the case when Messiaen includes the ondes Martenot as a concertante orchestral instrument in his *Turangalîla Symphony*, or when Harald Genzmer writes concertos for Trautonium and orchestra.

Electronic instruments might also assume solo status whether in serious and light music or as an expedient to serve as background music in broadcasting (radio plays), stage works or films.

A fourth possibility consists in the combination of several electronic instruments in an ensemble. Works of this kind have been essayed by Edgard Varèse (*Equatorial* for two Theremin instruments, 1934) and Olivier Messiaen (*Fêtes des belles eaux* for six ondes Martenot, 1937).

The fifth possibility is the autonomous use of electronic instruments.

The basic concepts for the theoretical study of music containing

electronic acoustical phenomena were given by Herbert Eimert in
his classification of notes, sounds, note mixtures, noises and sound
complexes:

1. Note—the pure tone (sine-wave tone), free of overtones,
which never appears in traditional music (or in nature). It issues
from the electronic production of sound. 'The sinusoidal tone
system must therefore simply be a system of virtual relationships,
from which the composer can create structures in the form of series,
relationships, rows and other forms of organization.'

2. Sound—constituted of a succession of harmonic partials
(sine-wave oscillations). In electronic music the components of
partials can be varied.

3. Note mixture—frequencies of partials not harmonically related to the fundamental. Mixtures are always mixtures of sine-
wave tones (hence not the same things as chords); they have a
higher degree of fusion than do sound complexes and can become
'sounds' in a far more unified way than instrumentally produced
chords. Stationary note mixtures can be realized effortlessly in
electronic music.

4. Noise—determined by its specific character and the breadth
of its frequency range. The pitches of coloured noises are, in musical terms, the equivalent of approximately defined registers. Only
'white noise', filling the whole audible frequency range (comparable
to white light), lacks any definition in terms of register.

5. Sound complex—two simultaneous different sounds (where
more than two, there will be a chord). Between the sound and the
sound complex comes the note mixture with its degrees of fusion—
a novel feature. Sounds and mixtures can be electronically 'composed' in accordance with a predetermined compositional plan of
organization.

In this context Eimert touches on the fundamental question of
what music is. 'The work of composition begins first with the mastering of the "material", in other words, the given material itself
must suggest a suitable and direct method of erecting and working on
it.' The composer, in view of the 'fact that he is no longer operating

within a strictly ordained tonal system, finds himself confronting a completely new situation. He sees himself commanding a realm of sound in which the musical material appears for the first time as a malleable continuum of every known and unknown, every conceivable and possible sound. This demands a way of thinking in new dimensions, a kind of mental adjustment to the thinking proper to the materials of electronic sound . . . All acoustical material is necessarily devoid of history and tradition. Only he who uses it will have his place in history. And for him the only important question is whether the electronic sound materials contain those orderable constituents that might be claimed as elements of music in the traditional sense.'

All the formulations and conceptualizations we have been considering here originated in the early years of electronic composition, the years 1953 and 1954. The electronic studio at West German Radio was set up in 1953. Twelve years after its opening, Stockhausen appeared in Cologne with a series of—at first—six public radio lectures, in which he presented a kind of report, though not in the sense of a reckoning, for this had already long ceased to be necessary: electronic sound, whether as a feature of musical composition, or for experiments in acoustical research, or again in its practical uses, had already long been a literally world-wide preoccupation; the nature of Stockhausen's lectures was simply informative. The series was extended from 1964 right into 1966, the number of lectures grew to thirteen, and with the aid of numerous carefully selected musical illustrations Stockhausen reported on the impressions he had formed—mostly from a personal viewpoint—of a number of studios, including studios in Paris, Milan, Brussels, Ghent, Utrecht, at the Philips plant, in Warsaw, Stockholm, Copenhagen, Helsinki, Reykjavik, Toronto, and at various places in the United States, as well as in Tokyo. Unfortunately these talks have not been published either in print or as a gramophone record;* they represent an invaluable document, and give the point of view

* Now printed in Vol. III of *Aufsätze*, Dumont Schauberg 1971. (Translator's note.)

of an individual who has taken the initiative in this field in a way
that no other artists or researchers have. The two books by Werner
Kaegi and L. M. Cross that have since been published on electronic
music are no substitute at all for Stockhausen's talks.

Stockhausen gave his lectures the overall title 'Do you know a
music that can only be heard over loudspeakers?'. And this title
already contains a new basis from which to view this subject, for in
his first talk Stockhausen proceeds from a distinction between
'electronic music' and *'musique concrète'*. He gives the reasons for
using these two already well-known terms, but concludes that in the
course of the last few years people have in fact begun to use the
name *'musique concrète'* less and less; instead they tend to describe
as 'electronic music' any music that exists only on tape and whose
sound has been produced or controlled with the aid of electronic
equipment—and hence is also a music that can only be heard over
loudspeakers.

Right at the beginning of his series of talks Stockhausen likens
electronic music to a discovery, and takes the comparison so far
that he lists this discovery of new regions of sound in the same
breath as the discoveries of new chemical compounds, new ways of
life, new stars, and new sources of energy in our world. Without
question the accent here lies on the word discovery—on that un-
covering activity of the human mind as it reasons and quests in the
realms of what is present at hand, where things that have remained
so long unknown have now to be uncovered. And for this reason
Stockhausen declares that in the first place he would wish only to
bring the listener towards this desire: to discover electronic music,
to search it out, to puzzle it out. This should be a new country in
which the listener too is making an expedition, and not just the
specialist; his destination will be new landscapes of sound, where
he will gradually learn to give names to the various acoustical
regions and their landmarks.

The road to electronic music

Of his work in Paris with the *musique concrète* group, Stockhausen relates that he mainly made acoustical analyses of recorded sounds —sounds of wood, of metal, of speech, in fact any kind of noise that was available as a recording on tape; he also made recordings of exotic instruments in the Musée de l'homme, and analysed these too. What interested him was to know how sounds were constituted acoustically—always with the end in view of one day being able himself to build up sounds in a synthetic way using modern electro-acoustical equipment. The basic idea right from the start, then as now, has been to create for any composition one is planning to realize a sound world which is to act as a regulator for the one composition and for that alone. In previous instrumental music each composer had the same access to instrumental timbres, but now composition began to be centred on the unrepeatability of the sounds used in any specific work. This development did not come about by chance, but was foreshadowed by a general tendency for more and more properties of sound to have a functional role in compositions, in other words to become subject to the unique formal laws governing individual works. At first—in the music of the early middle ages—harmonic and melodic regularities had been typical and unique for single works; then the rhythmic dimension was added as a fixed aspect that was distinct and characteristic in individual works and parts of works; this was followed by the dynamic dimension and finally, at the beginning of our own century, that of timbre, or sound-colour, as Schoenberg called it. If, however, this idea is taken to its logical conclusion, it means that the selection of specific sounds should be just as unique as was that of the other elements in earlier times. The differentiation of sonorities has been approached from two angles, one of them being that of expressive characteristics, in evidence in as early a work as Monteverdi's *Orfeo* (1607), whilst the other is that of refinements in the actual production of the notes and in tonal quality, for instance in string-playing. Not until the advent of electronics was it possible to build up timbres oneself and to 'compose' them in the literal sense of the word (*componere*), in order to give them the unique place in a work that its proportions may require. One can

examine the basic relationships of sounds and organize them by
means of technical procedures.

This fundamental idea first cropped up in conversation between
Stockhausen and the Belgian composer Karel Goeyvaerts, and it
paved the way for the work with electrical generators that was
another of Stockhausen's activities during his stay in Paris. For
some while after he returned to Cologne in 1953 there were countless discussions—with Boulez and Pousseur among others—particularly after the appearance of *Studie I*, Stockhausen's first essay
in composing timbres, and at the same time the first electronic
composition to use series for the organization of properties constituting sound-spectra. Reflecting on this first work, making
experiments and applying them in practice, Stockhausen found the
essential difference between sounds and so-called noises becoming
increasingly clear. The idea of incorporating noises as part and
parcel of musical compositions is not something that electronic
music alone brought to light; the 20th century had already seen a
branch of instrumental music developing in parallel to music of
determinate pitch, a development primarily associated with the
names of Edgard Varèse and John Cage. Varèse, born in 1885, but
resident in America after 1915 and a naturalized American citizen,
wrote several compositions for instruments of only approximate
pitch, as has Cage too. Examples include Cage's *Construction in
metal* and Varèse's *Ionisation*. During these early years in Cologne
Stockhausen set about combining sine-wave oscillations so as to
compose noises constituted of both sounds (using harmonically
related partials) and note mixtures (using harmonically unrelated
partials). The chief characteristic of a noise will always be its
frequency range and the density of the individual oscillations superimposed in it. If sine-wave oscillations are superimposed in such a
way that their frequencies are so tightly adjacent as to render the
separation too small for our ears to be able to isolate the individual
oscillations, then the resultant impression will be that of what we
call 'noise'. And conversely, if these intervals are made so large
that one can perceive the individual partial oscillations as separate,

then they result in a 'note mixture'. Now if these intervals are adjusted in relationships of simple integral proportions, as in the harmonic spectrum, then a common fundamental oscillation will be heard—the so-called principal note, or root, deriving its colour from the composition of the partials. Thus at first the question was to establish a continuum between on the one hand the note and on the other hand, passing through the sound and the note mixture, the noise. In such a completely continuous transition between note and noise, the more densely the oscillations are superimposed, the more noise will the spectrum contain.

As Stockhausen has reported, a technique which has proved to hold great possibilities (already tried to some extent in *Studie II*, but more thoroughly worked out in *Gesang der Jünglinge*) consists in proceeding directly from noise spectra, by taking, for instance, so-called white noise—a phenomenon in which the entire range of frequencies is produced by noise generators—and filtering it into different noise bands, which can be further filtered very finely until a single note is reached once more. In this way one produces filtered noise from which one can compose further spectra, superimposing several bands, so as to discover still more new sound complexes.

Thus Stockhausen's first electronic compositions, *Studie I* and *Studie II*, were preceded by experiments undertaken in order to study once and for all how sounds can be put together. From a technical point of view, *Studie I* is composed with only sine-wave tones; such is the case with *Studie II* also, but with the difference that spectra of sine-wave tones are emitted in a resonance chamber and then recorded again. This distortion of the individual sine-wave tones resulted in noise-like acoustical phenomena, of more or less dense composition, possessing much greater power and intensity. *Gesang der Jünglinge* goes a stage further: electrical impulses are used to produce acoustical phenomena. An impulse generator provides sequences of impulses of a particular frequency —or impulse-duration—and these sequences of impulses are filtered in order to produce timbres of yet another entirely new category. This all served to prove that by using impulses one could establish an extremely variable array of timbres. *Kontakte* was composed exclusively with the use of impulses; it is a piece displaying what is for electronic music a particularly extensive scale of timbres.

Equal participation of all parameters

Once more we return to the idea which, in terms of musical theory, forms the point of departure for electronic music: the composer can compose even the sounds for a piece (by putting them together in the ways we have described) and therefore the selection of timbre families is in fact just as important for a piece as is the choice of proportions for organizing time and for the interrelationships of pitches and dynamics. With this, equal participation of all the properties of sound is achieved for the first time. Rhythm, metre, melody, harmony, dynamics and timbre (composed sound) can all be organized in terms of general serial formation, hence using a single proportional series.

This takes us straight from technical considerations to the musical and aesthetic aspects, and here we may refer directly to words Stockhausen himself has used in conversation:

'The same proportions that I use to organize time I can now also use for the intervals needed to compose certain spectra; the same proportions which regulate the maximum intensities of different sounds, I can also use for the intensities of the individual partials in a spectrum and of the individual noise bands in a sound complex of coloured noise; and the same proportions which serve to control the durations and intervals of entry of sounds and noises having the most varied gradations, I can also use to organize the inner evolution within a sound, only now of course all on a very reduced time scale. The sequence in which partial oscillations in a spectrum enter will determine the way in which different sounds will vary in their "attack" phenomena, and the sequence in which they end will determine the variation in their "desinence" phenomena; moreover within a single sound partials or formants can appear and disappear again within a short time so that the sound will develop a very complex internal structure; this is usually called a "volatile" structure in contrast to the "rigid" structure of, say, *Studie I* and *Studie II*, where all the partials begin simultaneously, end simultaneously, and have the same intensity throughout the sound. In acoustics, sounds of this latter type are called "stationary" sounds, as opposed to "non-stationary" sounds. One can produce extremely differentiated sounds in a synthetic way; one can control them, and accurately observe all the differences between various sounds. Wherever there are distinctions between different sounds, this is the result of composition; sounds no longer have to exist side by side as they do in instrumental composition, but can be composed in interrelationships of every degree.'

Anyone who has kept abreast of the work that has emerged from the Cologne studio since 1951—and it was in 1951 that the subject was first demonstrated in experiments by Werner Meyer-Eppler at the Darmstadt Summer School for New Music—will be able to confirm how much has been achieved in the course of some twenty years from the aesthetic point of view, in the refinement of sounds, and in mastery over the sound material. And from the point of view of technique, Stockhausen has summed it up thus:

'If I want to make sounds very similar, I introduce similar proportions for time, for intensity and for intervallic distribution within the sounds themselves. Or if I want to compose great contrasts, I choose proportions a long way apart from each other. I can compose a series of degrees of relatedness between sounds—in other words, mediate between the most various forms of acoustical phenomenon—by specifying degrees of relatedness to connect one sound with another. I can cause a transformation from one sound into another to happen in an orderly way right in front of the listener's ears, for continuous transformation—the timbre continuum—has become a simple matter with electronics.'

Thus it is quite in order for us to speak of real progress in technical mastery and in the aesthetic results. Hitherto European studios had worked exclusively with apparatus that was originally built for other purposes, purposes of technical measurement. At any rate generators and filtering equipment already existed. In contrast to this, America is today the scene of researches and technical realizations in such fields as automatic sound synthesis, computer technology and synthesizer techniques. However, Stockhausen is convinced that to set up the whole paraphernalia merely in order to reproduce the instrumental sounds we already know is a questionable venture. On this point Stockhausen lays particular emphasis on his demand that electronic music should really *be* electronic music; its character is not to be found in imitating what already exists, but in lending itself to the discovery of completely new processes and facilitating their technical realization, so that with them can be achieved a synthesis of utterly new and unknown timbres such as can correspond to the requirements of a musical composition. In Stockhausen's view computer technology is still at a purely scientific experimental stage; its primary objective is to solve the problem of transforming all possible sound data into an impulse technique so that electronic apparatuses can be used to transform electrical impulses into sound in the most rational and economical way possible.

Stockhausen's progress towards electronic music started with his analysis of sound, whose aim had been to enable him to achieve for himself a synthetic 'composition' of sound. Viewed in the perspective of musical style, electronic music is entirely in keeping with the term New Music as it was understood during the 1950s, for the movement towards electronic music was rooted in the quest for a total serial organization of sound. This could not be achieved with instrumental timbres, since these can offer no scale of timbres quite as clearly defined as is, for instance, a scale of pitches on the piano.

Electronic composition in practice

It is because of the way electronic composition is orientated towards new discoveries that—just as in previous times composers discovered in their composition new shapes, new rhythmical turns and new harmonic–melodic formulations—now they are finding new sounds and constellations of sounds too. With Stockhausen composition is preceded by experiments. And he has significantly stated that 'For the most part I have an approximate idea of the entire course of a work without knowing in detail which sounds will be involved in this or that section.'

Let us now see how all these factors come together. The technical possibilities make their own contribution inasfar as they are at the composer's disposal and will lead him in a certain direction. The experiments preceding composition are geared to certain previously thought-out processes of production and to the proportions governing the composition of the sounds—and this will all be derived from ideas about the rhythmic agenda a composition will follow. For instance a work can have a rhythmic agenda whose defining boundaries are the pointillist and the statistical. On the one side the single sound, and perhaps even its components, can be clearly heard; on the other side many different sounds may be compressed together in simultaneous or successive conglomerations within so short a time that they can no longer be perceived as individual sounds at all. As we have already described at some length, such processes yield totally new acoustical compounds. This therefore means that the composer, if he wants to produce any sort of acoustical compound by electronic means, must bring with him a very definite compositional conception with all its relationships worked out. The real work of composition begins with the selection, in the preliminary period of experimentation, of the sound family or families—in other words, groups of interrelated sounds—for a given piece. With all his compositions using electronically produced acoustical phenomena Stockhausen's procedure has been to work on the composition at home in the mornings and to tackle the practical studio work in the afternoons, evenings or nights. There has thus been a continual reciprocal effect between musical thinking and sensory experience, and to this Stockhausen attaches especial value, for—as he says—much of what one has devised has then to be corrected, and conversely practical experience brings with it completely new ideas for the composition. This sort of combined activity, with its interchange between idea and realization within the framework of a daily curriculum, has not been a regular feature in music since the baroque age, and Josef Haydn, during his period at Esterházy, was probably the last composer whose works were still produced concurrently with their practical testing out, and benefited accordingly.

The unity of realization and composition

For Stockhausen the unity of realization and composition, a unity no longer to be split up 'because the one has almost become the other', is very typical of electronic composing. He has little confidence in those composers who would 'think something out with insufficient knowledge and practical experience of work in an electronic studio', and would then not trouble to attend to the task of constantly controlling every stage of the realization. Stockhausen takes this still further and is quite unambiguous in attacking two widespread misconceptions. It is far from the truth to imagine, as people usually do, that electronic equipment might one day be common property whose techniques could be learnt and passed on as if it were some instrument to be learnt in a traditional way, or else could be preserved in an archive and obtainable at will from some sort of filing cabinet. And the second misconception to be disposed of is that it is principally a question of quantitatively extending the range of sounds already available, merely to bring 'unheard sounds' to the ears of the listener in the sense of an 'unlimited' extension of the domain of sensual delicacies.

The superficial aspect of sounds soon wears off and is quickly exhausted; this goes for the effect of unprecedented electronic sounds just as much as for instrumental sound effects, quite regardless of the way such sounds are introduced—whether as a shock tactic or in an 'insinuating' manner. For the composer the discovery of a sound is no yardstick unless he is necessarily led to it by an inner logic. The sound world typical for a work must obey the law that the composer himself has invented and discovered. The simultaneous process of discovery and invention for any given work imparts a personal imprint to the material and creates the distinctive character which enables one to identify different compositions.

This unity of realization and composition referred to here demands of the composer a basic technical knowledge even if he has a technician at hand to help him. The composer must know what he wants so as to be able to tell the technician what to do. However, it is a mark of considerable inventive talent on the part of the composer when he can think out such processes of combining and composing sounds as can actually be tried out in practice. Technically the further development of 'montage' could well make matters a great deal easier, for composers have long had to resort to such primitive operations as the use of scissors and sticking-tape. With the present collaboration between composer and technician, one thing that composers have long been attempting now appears redundant: the notation of electronic music. Stockhausen has told how he made precise working drawings of his electronic compositions, even the most complicated of them. To a great extent these took the form of an attempt to describe precisely what had been done. Thus: I use such and such an apparatus, introduce such and such a frequency, and so on. Such documents are progress reports for the present and for the future, preponderantly destined for the attention of composers. Thus the score is something more than a mere aid to realization; it is a textbook for composers.

One discovers much in listening only when one knows what to listen for. A great part of musical knowledge and musical theory is possible only through the study of scores rather than merely listening to music. The question as to the relative importance of a composer's thinking in electronic music is one that Stockhausen leaves open, while stressing the fact that the tapes produced have only a limited durability. We must beware the widespread fallacy which holds that the high quality of our technical accessories (tape and gramophone record) enables sound to be preserved 'through all eternity'. In the course of time, tapes, like films, constantly deteriorate and their technical quality ceases to be acceptable. Consequently a work that exists only on tape or on disc has a much shorter life than does a composition that is reproduced from a score by an instrumental ensemble. Naturally an electronic composition can later be reconstituted once more on the basis of indications in a score—when, where and by what means is not of so much interest to Stockhausen; for as a composer he lives in the present.

But there is another area that seems to him all the more important: collaboration with the technician. In the present form of the composer's work in realizing electronic music Stockhausen sees only a transitional stage. The ultimate solution seems to him to lie in the education of technical assistants who would not be composers themselves but would be able to assist the composer in his work by following his instructions, and to contribute their own ideas on the processes and methods to be used in the production of new sounds. Today no such specialists yet exist. Many and various things would have to be at their disposal: an education in acoustical engineering and in music, as well as a special feeling for contemporary music and for solving the problems it presents, so that they could collaborate fully and independently with the composer. If the question arises of setting up a new electronic studio somewhere, then today it should no longer be thought of simply as a matter of installing a quantity of equipment; but the establishing of a studio will have to be conceived in the spirit of those who will work in it—in other words, one must first employ the right people. Stockhausen sees the direction in which things in general are developing as a movement towards specialization. His ideas on the subject can be summed up as follows: Just as today there are special ensembles such as the Cappella Coloniensis—an orchestra of specialists from different European countries who have taken up the task of giving the most authentic possible performances of old, and in particular baroque and pre-classical music—so we shall see orchestras of specialists devoted to performing classical or romantic concert music. In contrast to this, electronic music will be used for radio and television productions and for the production of film music; such music, for all its varieties of stylistic dependence on the past, will still be specifically contemporary music and to that extent will justify the new means used for the production of sound. Stockhausen has no illusions that this means will not suffer repeated abuse; but that is not a speciality of electronic music, for it happens with instrumental music as well; in electronic music, too, there will always be composers who draw up their material in a completely non-functional way simply for the sake of effect. 'But this should not disturb one in the slightest and above all should not deter one from presenting either music that is really worth discussing or new inventions and ideas of a musical kind, and then allowing them an existence on a broader basis through automatic production by radio and television corporations.'

The prospects for the future, then: leading acoustical engineers will collaborate with composers who will be responsible for sketching out projects. Electronic music will be true to itself—a necessary and independent adjunct to instrumental music; both will coexist in new ways without rivalry and in complement to each other. Finally the creation of such music as is played directly in the presence of an audience has itself received a completely new impetus in recent years. The development of electronic music meant nothing if not that work hitherto performed by men has more and more been transferred to machines, so as to leave man time and energy for tasks that only he can perform, thereby concentrating human endeavour more and more on creative work, on invention, discovery and planning. The future will need practising musicians as does the present; perhaps not so much those who can play an instrument as musicians who give evidence of their musicality in controlling what comes out of a machine, in rectifying it and in bringing it to the level of a musical result which will satisfy their conceptions and demands.

Kontakte

Stockhausen's *Kontakte* exists in two versions: one is purely electronic (*Kontakte* for electronic sounds), and the other is called

Kontakte for electronic sounds, piano and percussion. (The word 'sounds' is used here in the sense of a general concept, not in its special acoustical sense.) In producing the sounds of *Kontakte* Stockhausen latched onto some very fundamental relationships. The basic material consists of electrical impulses provided by an impulse generator with variable impulse rate (impulse frequency) and variable impulse duration. The impulse generator used operates between 16 impulses per second and 1 impulse in 16 seconds, and with impulse durations between $\frac{1}{10000}$ of a second and 1 second. These impulses are fed through a feed-back filter (an electrical filter with variable bandspread) so as to produce filtered sounds. Stockhausen spent much time conducting experiments with the aim of producing a given timbre in such a way that the result is a rhythmicised impulse sequence. From the practical point of view, Stockhausen took single impulses that he had recorded on tape and stuck them together one after another at given intervals of time. If he wanted to make a periodic sound, he made such an impulse sequence into a tape-loop—in other words arranged for the same impulse sequence to constantly repeat itself. It was now a single period in a periodic sound. If for example one proceeds from a rhythmicised impulse sequence a second long and accelerates it a thousandfold, one hears a note at 1000 Hertz, in other words the single period then lasts $\frac{1}{1000}$ of a second, and the rhythmicised impulse sequence within this period will then determine the timbre. This means that extremely varied rhythms of impulse sequences, when they are later accelerated, will yield extremely varied timbres. In this way timbre can be precisely controlled, since timbre differences can be determined by rhythmical organization (a purely temporal form of organization). And so timbre is the result of a linear temporal organization that is constituted of impulses.

Conversely, if one wishes to pass over from a periodic phase-sequence (hence a sound whose pitch is clearly recognizable) to a noise, then one simply has to stick together impulse sequences which vary in a given distribution around a central value of phase duration. For instance: 1st phase = 1 second; 2nd phase = 1 plus $\frac{1}{10}$ seconds; 3rd phase = 1 minus $\frac{1}{10}$ seconds; 4th phase = 1 plus $\frac{1}{2}$ seconds; 5th phase = 1 minus $\frac{1}{4}$ seconds—then the difference between the extreme phase durations in these five phases amounts to $\frac{3}{4}$ seconds. By simply sticking together phases of such impulse sequences distributed within given limits around the central value of 1 second one will no longer have a note—a sound with a precisely identifiable pitch and having a constant phase length—but a noise; and the band width of the noise will be determined by the interval between the smallest and the largest phase lengths and by the density of the phases deviating from the central value. Thus the transition between a 'note', having a given pitch, and a 'noise' can be determined by means of rhythmic composition.

The consequences of these experiences are of uncommon importance: namely that one conceives of sound as not simply something that is put together from different components simultaneously superimposed, but as the result of a linear sequence of impulses in time, and that it is the temporal intervals between impulses alone that regulate the distinctiveness of timbres and above all the transformation of timbre.

If one now further provides the impulse sequences with the most varied intensities (by recording impulses of different intensity and sticking them together) one comes to a further aspect that is decisive for the production of timbres. Stockhausen produced the greater part of *Kontakte* with this kind of impulse technique and thereby for the first time created a compositional relationship between what he calls microtime, which regulates the inner processes within a sound and the constitution of timbres in general, and the macrotemporal procedures that we then hear as so-called rhythmic-metrical relationships between these individual sounds. Thus whether one is looking at the larger or the smaller temporal relationships is simply a question of perspective—of whether one is in the realm of timbre composition or in the realm of melodic-harmonic and rhythmic–metrical composition. For the composer everything becomes a single parameter, a single dimension of

determinacy. The consequence of this is that the organizing principles that regulate a work can actually be used multilaterally for all
its aspects.

Telemusik and Hymnen

From *Kontakte* (1959/60) to *Telemusik* (1966) and *Hymnen* (1966/
67) is a leap of scarcely imaginable magnitude. This does not however mean to say that there has been a development by virtue of
which Stockhausen, with his later group of works (*Telemusik* and
Hymnen) has left the older works behind him, as perhaps the first
two symphonies of Beethoven are largely overshadowed by the
Eroica. This sort of stylistic development, that we can retrospectively survey and demonstrate in numerous composers, particularly of the 19th century, cannot be detected at all at this date in
Stockhausen's music. What *can* be observed are the various territories which he has so far opened up one after another, and everything points to the conclusion that his creative powers still bear and
hold in readiness many possibilities for the future.

With *Telemusik* and *Hymnen* begins a new chapter in the story of
Stockhausen's work with electronic sounds. The first impulses
leading him to a new path of invention may have come to Stockhausen from Varèse's *Poème Electronique*, dating from 1958.

Poème Electronique was created as a counterpart to the architecture of Le Corbusier for the Philips Pavilion at the Brussels
World Fair in 1958. Le Corbusier designed the pavilion in the ex-
terior form of a triangular tent, with an interior, in his own words,
in the form of a cow's stomach. The outcome was a series of hyper-
bolic and parabolic curves, and it was from these that Varèse's
music, which he called 'organized sound', emanated unceasingly
through countless loudspeakers. At the same time one could see
projected images that Le Corbusier had himself selected—paint-
ings, photographs, written characters and montages—in respect of
which the two artists had attempted no matching of any sort between image and sound. The sound material that Varèse recorded
on tape and transformed with electronic equipment is extra-

ordinarily diverse. The listener rapidly recognizes organ chords, percussion sounds and human voices, machine- and clock-noises, and bells, of which the composer came across a great variety in Holland and Belgium. Varèse made no comment on what he wished to express in his *Poème*. Perhaps a remark he made about the human voice heard at the end of his composition can be taken as indicative: 'I wanted it to express tragedy—and inquisition.'

In one of his thirteen lectures that we referred to above, Stockhausen had this to say about Varèse's work: 'Varèse is alone in his generation in having composed a work of electronic music and furthermore in having heralded in this *Poème* a modern formulation of compositional relationships whose true significance can only today be recognized: namely the sequential presentation and superimposition—even though sometimes abrupt and unmediated—of events of a heterogeneous nature (for instance, extremely realistic events, events resembling musical hoardings, and freely invented events).' This is a fairly straightforward identification of the compositional elements in Varèse's work. But the creative imagination hastens on to the next essential step, which here has to be taken in full consciousness of where it leads. Stockhausen continued: 'Anyone living today—Varèse was at the time living in New York —is confronted daily with the hurtling together of all races, all religions, all philosophies, all ways of life . . . of all nations. In works by the musician Varèse this bubbling of the cauldron is aesthetically portrayed . . . New York, that prime blueprint for a world society, is without question an indispensable experience for the contemporary artist. Ideas one might have about possible integration, about a coherent unification, or about possible syntheses of the influences issuing from all parts of the globe, all these must be tested against living experience if they are to lay claim to any truth.'

In these last words there already appears the idea of integration on a worldwide scale, an idea upon which in turn both *Telemusik* and *Hymnen* are founded. In no circumstances must this universality be confused with uniformity.

Before going into these two electronic works in detail, there is perhaps room for a personal recollection. The first performance of *Mixtur* took place on the evening of 9 November 1965 in the series of concerts 'das neue werk' given by North German Radio. The news of Varèse's death in New York on 6 November had just arrived. Before the first performance Stockhausen had the opportunity of giving an account of the genesis of his new work, and he prefaced these details with a tribute to Varèse. His words on that occasion, spoken freely and without preparation, deserve to have been published, for I must confess that I have never heard or read any declaration made by a younger composer about an older colleague that was more grateful, more appreciative and more sympathetic towards such creative greatness, human warmth and artistic significance as passed on with Varèse. Varèse had been born in 1885, Stockhausen in 1928, so the difference in age amounts to more than forty years.

With Varèse and Stravinsky the above-mentioned musical conception was still a matter of collages, in other words of a superposition and juxtaposition of stylistically heterogeneous events; as such they heralded the forms of contemporary society by 'forecomposing' them. In Stockhausen's work one can no longer speak of collages; one must speak rather of intermodulation. This means that apparently incompatible phenomena can be reciprocally modulated with each other in a way far transcending mere coexistence with and against each other; this procedure heralds the unity of a world which will maintain differences intact and at the same time will enable a total effect of 'higher unity' to be produced. Thus his works become modern projects for future forms of society and of life; all our contemporary crises of ideological, racialist and religious conflicts suggest that we stand urgently in need of such visionary projects. While the world approaches catastrophic rock-bottom, already there are some who, guided by their intuition, are looking far beyond the low ebb of human disintegration and committing their whole conscious lives to the creation of a universal and unreserved harmoniousness.

Since a gramophone recording of *Telemusik* has been made

available by DGG, Stockhausen's introductory essay, citing as it does various sound-sources, ought to have been published too, for it seems indispensable for a first—and even for a deeper—understanding of the work. Here Stockhausen listed some of the sound events which he integrated into his *Telemusik*; these are all 'found objects' and are mentioned elsewhere in this book (in the chapter 'Notes on the works'): music of the Japanese Imperial Court, from the isle of Bali, the southern Sahara, from a Spanish village festival, from Hungary, the Shipibos of the Amazon, the Omizutori ceremony in Nara, from the worship-bound China of the Kojasan temple, from a Japanese Nō play, and so forth.

Stockhausen's previous electronic compositions, with the exception of *Gesang der Jünglinge* whose initial basic material was a boy's voice, were realized exclusively with electronically produced sound material. With *Telemusik* and *Hymnen* a new process is introduced: the material now also includes recordings of found musical pieces (of anonymous origin in *Telemusik*) which are transplanted in their own characteristic acoustical clothing and then transformed and modulated in varying degrees.

In recent times the word transplantation has attained a worldwide familiarity in connection with heart surgery; for more than fifteen years I have already been trying to systematically introduce the concept and practice of transplantation into musical thinking. This will involve the creative transplantation and adequate adaptation of an alien material, and in addition to these two activities, procedures of transference, conversion and fusion.

Such fusion can be found both in *Telemusik* and in *Hymnen*, where the sounds of the original material are conjoined to overlapping ideas. What Stockhausen has in mind is a universal humanism, a single idea to span the world and to unite all peoples, the idea of what is common to us, namely our humanity, our human existence on this earth. In this consciousness of our fate, and of our existence as human Being, Stockhausen conducts an integration of musical examples whose situation is that of individual peoples, nations, cultures and sects, having arisen in their midst and remaining indissolubly bound to them. Individual examples to which Stockhausen has applied his process of fusion are listed above. What he used as initial material was not the score as such but its sound, its phenomenal form, which was available to him in recordings on tape or disc. And the same is equally true in *Hymnen*. Here he used the anthems of numerous peoples, that is, of communities of people organized on a national basis. They are printed in the collection *National Anthems of the World*, edited by Martin Shaw, whose second, expanded edition was published in 1963 by the Blandford Press in London. However, the initial material for the composition of *Hymnen* consisted of the sound of performances, whether for chorus or orchestra or both together. In his introduction to *Telemusik* Stockhausen himself tells of the veritable whirlpool of an experience that his encounter with Japan was for him. Two great emotions permeate his words. The first is the positively stunning emotional impact of meeting people of the Far East, and the other is gratitude for this experience. Together they unleashed in Stockhausen a vision, 'a vision of sounds, of new technical processes, of formal relationships, images of notation, of human relationships, etc.—everything at once in a network that was too entangled to be presented as a single process: This was something that was going to occupy me for a long time.' And of the musical encounters, of the residue of authentic folk art he had experienced, of the quotations that he integrated in *Telemusik* Stockhausen says: 'They all insisted on participating in *Telemusik*, often simultaneously and crowding in on each other . . . they had to feel "at home", not "integrated" by some administrative act, but genuinely united in a free spiritual encounter.'

The principle of transplantation and integration of pre-selected, alien material in music is an old one, and to find its first beginnings one has to look to where two cultures have collided—perhaps in Ancient China with the encounter between the traditional music of the court and an autochthonous or foreign musical folk culture. Here a considerable number of musical processes were fulfilling themselves. To this same category belong the fusing processes between Gregorian chant and national characteristics of church music in polyphonic music, the encounters of baroque music, of the Viennese classics and of the Romantics with the folksong of Central Europe and of the more westerly Eastern European countries, and also the meeting of folk art with art music in the 20th century, of which we may cite the music of Béla Bartók as a representative example. What is characteristic of these processes in every case, however, is the fact that the composer has always transformed only elements of the model—such elements, that is, as melodic substance, harmony and rhythm, and occasionally, though no more than peripherally, the intonation of sounds too, hence the pitch differentiations to be found in Bartók.

What Stockhausen has accomplished is much more comprehensive. He directly affirms the sound world of the exotic, transforming it and relating it with electronic possibilities in a completely new conception. He gives us visions in sound of distant, foreign lands which, for the moment, are yet no longer 'distant' or 'foreign', since the compositional perspective unites them in a completely new kind of vision—a vision of a single universal musical community of all peoples.

One example will suffice to illustrate this. In *Telemusik* moments appear in which, for instance, the melody of a Shipibo mother singing to her baby is modulated with the rhythm—and only the rhythm—of a *sevilliano*, and the product of this is in turn modulated with the harmonic and timbric structure of electronic sounds composed by Stockhausen himself, the result being modulated with the dynamic curve (intensity profile) of a priestly song recorded in the Todaiji temple in Nara during a Buddhist ceremony. The original five-channel composition superimposes these multiple intermodulations of events in up to five layers, which are then unified by using several ring-modulators—for the most part in the high registers—to form new symbioses. In such intermodulations each component retains some of its unalterable character traits, its 'personality', and at the same time undergoes a transformation in a higher unification with characteristic traits of other 'alien' phenomena. This one example should already suffice to make it clear that in terms of quality such conceptions far transcend the notion of collage.

Stockhausen was able to make his first excursion abroad when he went to Paris at the beginning of 1952. In the biographical chapter of this book it is related that here Stockhausen for the first time made the personal acquaintance of students of every nation. One has to remember that Stockhausen had grown up in the perspective of national and even provincial short-sightedness which had been concomitant with nationalist politics, and that his mature consciousness had developed at a time when these politics were being demolished piecemeal under the annihilating blows of the Allied Forces. Stockhausen's student years coincided with the first steps towards politically rebuilding the essentials of the state known as the German Bundesrepublik, a confederation which has come to command a leading role in economics, but whose political thinking has to this day always remained narrow and extremely provincial. Coming from such a confined atmosphere, Stockhausen found in Paris a breadth of outlook which must have fascinated him. And the many journeys he has made since then, taking him around the whole world, have given increasing depth to this experience.

It may be of interest to record that while still a student Stockhausen wrote a short story 'Humayun', whose characters and situations were drawn exclusively from Indian history, and to this day the reciprocal interpenetration of East and West, Orient and Occident, Asia and Europe, has occupied his life and work with constantly increasing intensity. Most recently, for instance, the writings of the Indian Sri Aurobindo have come to mean a great deal to him as a corroboration and elucidation of his own conscious thoughts, and he has told me of a conversation lasting several hours that he had with the nonagenarian Dr. Datsei Suzuki at the house of that world-famous philosopher of Kamakura Zen Buddhism in 1966 shortly before his death.

One of the long-term results of all this is the composition *Hymnen*. As the work begins with an 'international gibberish of

Karlheinz Stockhausen, 1964

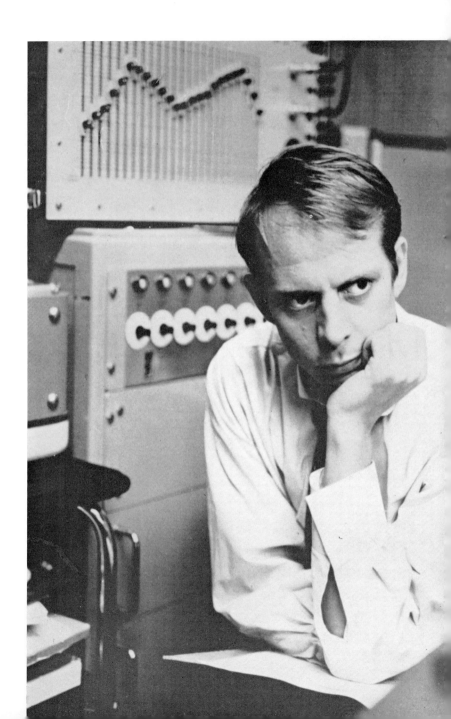

Karlheinz Stockhausen, 1970

Peter Eötvös, Harald Boje, Aloys Kontarsky,
Karlheinz Stockhausen and Christoph Caskel who performed
Stockhausen's music at St. John's Smith Square during the
English Bach Festival, 1971

short-wave transmissions' and closes with a vision of a 'Utopian realm of *Hymunion* in *Harmondie unter Pluramon*', there must unquestionably be a programme hidden here that embraces as great a vision of a pragmatic Utopia as could be conceived today, as we move into the last third of the 20th century. The words Hymunion, Harmondie, Pluramon are chosen entirely for their hidden verbal meanings (hymns–union, *harmonia mundi*—harmony of the world, pluralism–monism), so as to tell us that the work reveals the conception one very forward-looking contemporary has of the world and of life—a contemporary living in the present and squarely facing today's demands on humanity and the problems humanity has to solve in the future. The French music critic Claude Rostand wrote of *Hymnen*: 'The whole work is of fascinating complexity and is full of hallucinatory impressions; in it Stockhausen has probably reached the summit of his production, in a work that is as much that of a technician seeking a new language as that of an individual human searching for a new sense of life.' This is a concise way of putting what I too experienced and felt at the first performance in Cologne.

On the construction of those parts that were completed by the date of the first performance Stockhausen has said the essential, and this is given in the chapter 'Notes on the works'. The first performance was preceded by a press conference in which Stockhausen made known further particulars, of which some details will complete the picture.

In all Stockhausen had collected 137 anthems, certain of them being present in different versions. About forty anthems (nations) had been worked into the composition at this point (first performance: 30 November 1967). As we have stressed above, only sound recordings of the original hymns were used, some of which had to be either made on the spot or requested from the countries concerned. In the original anthems Stockhausen sees a highly 'collective material', which he conjoined with electronic sounds. The anthems, seen from their perspective of national associations or of the scale of values of their musical character, are not themselves to be considered as relevant details, but Stockhausen attributes absolute value to what he has made of them. Thus there remain no direct political references to speak of, as if the anthems were, in a sense, 'actually being performed', when, say, during the second region four centres appear in the music: the anthem of the German Federal Republic, a group of African hymns intermingled and alternating with the beginning of the Russian anthem, with a second German anthem from the past then breaking through, unmediated, after which there arises an extended verbal reflection. From the preselected material grow compositions of timbre—far beyond any possibilities of day-to-day political associations; the given material is drawn into that which is newly composed. Thus, belying the suspicion of mere collage which has often been voiced in connection with this work, its value attains that of an artistic creation having a great number of stylistic modulations in which the realistic coexists beside both the associative and such sections as are to be heard as broad stretches of purely musical structuring.

For a commentary on the work's details, one will naturally have to await the availability of a version on disc.* Stockhausen speaks of the initial material as 'found objects' and he sees this procedure as a further development along the lines of the harmonization of a Bach chorale in Alban Berg's Violin Concerto, a procedure equivalent to the reproduction of an object in the context of a picture. Stockhausen says that for ten years he had worked at the logical construction of an autonomous world without associations or objects, and also without recollections or reminiscences. This manner that he had formerly represented might be called 'abstract', 'ego-orientated' or 'turned inwards', and leaves room only for the ferment of the individual imagination as it flows freely—the composer's and each individual listener's 'world of inner fantasy'. On the other side stands the concrete world of the external, the world of objects, pictures and quotations, of everyday sounds and noises. The dualism between these two worlds is now to be elevated into a higher unity, the external is to be joined to the internal. In this

* Not yet available when this was written. (Translator's note.)

sense Pluramon means a bridging of the gap between monism and pluralism. To Pluramon, the fourth and to date last region in the composition *Hymnen* is devoted.

Hymnen seems to me to be the summation of all that Stockhausen has composed up till now, but again not in the sense that with it he has left earlier compositions behind him; as was said above, we are not in the presence of an evolutionary type of thinking that leads forward from one work to the next. But summation here means the result of the masterly resuming of all previously available means in a specific work, the anthems themselves forming the starting point for an electronic composition. The work is also a summation in the sense of the power of imagination which is at his disposal here in inexhaustible supply and almost incredible profusion. The properties of sounds are a formal factor which is also particularly determinant for the sound of the fourth region. Here Stockhausen achieves a high degree of solemnity, an absolutely hymn-like quality. More and more expansive sounding calls and answers are heard until—at the very last—an antiphony is struck up between the sound of musical events that are motionless in space and a natural sound of breathing in and out. It is a confluence, a return to the peace of nature, a harmony of dying sound after the sometimes fearful disharmony of people and of elements through which we have more than once been dragged, a calm of the All as is presented in a similar way at the end of James Joyce's novel *Finnegans Wake*. Naturally these observations should be taken as personal comments on a first impression; their nature is entirely subjective, but the world of electronics is an aesthetical stimulus to such subjectivity, and makes it wholly legitimate. Every listener, musicians included, should have the courage of this subjectivity and the courage too to confess their subjectivity in words.

In this connection it is worth saying a few words about Stockhausen's most recent work, although it is not of an electronic nature; it has to be mentioned in this context because once again it bears all the traces of a synthesis between the Eastern and the Western worlds. It is called *Stimmung* ('for sex-tête') and is a composition for a sextet of vocal soloists. The six soloists (two sopranos, mezzo-soprano, tenor, baritone and bass) are seated in a Yoga posture on cushions laid out in a circle on a low platform in the middle of the audience who sit grouped around the platform. In the middle of the platform stand six microphones to pick up the voices of the six soloists and relay them over loudspeakers in the auditorium. The work has several alternating sections which hang together in a logical way. One section consists of the calling out of a large number of magical names, names of gods, from all the parts of the world —from the ancient cultures of Europe, Asia and America as well as from present-day primitive peoples and developed cultures. If this already provides an impetus for meditation, this impression is confirmed by the incantatory repetition of single syllables in which there inheres something of magical adjuration. Repeatedly, too, vowels are sung on the same note, and the transformation is mediated by a highly suggestive range of tone-colouring. Singing alternates with speaking, and in both a meditative psalmody predominates; the singing is either in solos or based on a constantly recurring chord which sounds positively tonal. Often a soloist gives his 'part' (*Stimme*) to a partner, who takes up the incantation. The whole piece takes place in a dynamic range between *pianissimo* and *mezzo forte*; it is a piece of chamber music. It eschews everything that is hectic, everything that is ecstatic in the sense of being loud, rapturous or outside-of-itself. It is entirely an ostensible act of devotion, an exercise in the gentle and the meditative. While for long stretches it achieves a state of spiritual intensity with the sensual medium of the human voice, this kind of meditation is several times interrupted by textual recitations which appeal in an unambiguous way to the erotico-sensual. In these spoken texts one is directly reminded of the erotic freedom of the ancients, or of the association between *sexus* and *spiritus* that is peculiar to the Tantric art of Eastern Asia.

Aesthetic aspects

Earlier in this chapter we were concerned principally with technical aspects of electronic music. We must now consider all the aesthetic aspects that are allied to these. In this respect reference must be made to one thing in particular: in selecting and composing timbres for a piece the composer of electronic music should pay attention to the need to avoid as far as possible the use of sounds which are already known, or have already been used in other electronic compositions, so that he can create a personal world of sounds for each single work, wherein the associations attendant on already familiar acoustical phenomena and musical works are excluded as much as is possible.

From the point of view of the listener's reaction, this will prevent no-one from listening associatively. We know that such associations are extremely personal and can bring alive memories of events in life, images of colours and movements, parallels from traditional music and much more besides. In the end everyone must wait and see how he gets on with new experiences; for it is possible for everyone listening to use his powers of invention or of discovery if he tries to recreate or follow what is offered by the composer in a work. One cannot blame electronic music for the entirely polymorphous nature of the associations that may occur in listening to it. Yet it is still important to largely exclude associations of certain natural sounds, of instrumental music, of vernacular speech, and of all the known repertory of acoustical signals. All this of course does not alter the fact that instrumental music and electronic music have so far fertilized each other, and had an inspiring effect on each other, even sometimes combining their resources, as in the example of *Kontakte*.

Basically, instrumental music can be distinguished from electronic music by the fact that in the latter we have a completely determinate music whereas the former is a music of maximum variability which can change from one performer to the next, and can take on quite different forms in the hands of different interpreters. But Stockhausen has also thought of the idea of making electronic music variable for permanent performances. With this in view he has made certain proposals. For replaying electronic music, machines should be built so that a given electronic material, with given rules of combination behind its production, can be constantly varied from one replay to the next. There are in electronic music very variable possibilities that can be automatically regulated so that determinate initial structures having determinately defined rules of combination can be linked together in constantly changing constellations from one replay to another. With a four-channel composition single channels can be closed according to the context, while others are perhaps opened again, and combined with each other. Thus a work having different possibilities to select from could reach the listener in continually new forms. One might also conceive of several tape recorders running simultaneously and—by stopping the tape recorders at different intervals—the times at which each layer was heard would be made variable. Naturally the material must then be composed in such a way that it can be variably combined. Or one might work with very long tape loops, each of them timed differently, thereby making it possible for the context to change over very long periods of time.

The influence of electronic music on instrumental music has in the first place been an effect of its sounds, which have transformed the use of instruments. This has primarily been a matter of composing sound-mixtures that are typical for a work and are unrepeatable because of the way in which the rhythmic aggregations are composed so as to produce single sounds or single notes. Attention has also been directed to the composition of single sounds and constellations of sounds. Here the effect is not that of a single instrument playing a note on its own but a whole admixture of different instruments producing a single sound. In this way unmistakable 'new' timbres can be constituted for any composition. Here a vast amount of variety is available—in fact one can create whole sound families that will remain typical for a single composition. They will then be unique and integrated elements of this one work.

What still remains for us to discuss is the possibility of a form of composition which could well represent a further development, perhaps even an altogether new development (and of which, as Stockhausen has remarked, he has not yet garnered any experience of his own). I am referring to composing by computer. Our methods of sound production and sound processing are still basically an extension of our conception of conventional instrumental music, even though with new principles. So far it has always been the case that the composer 'puts together' his music according to a musical conception that he has before the outset or that forms during his work. In work with complicated composing machines it would seem that the composer generally knows nothing of the music that will be produced. In other words he would define (now in reverse) not what he wants, but what he does not want. For—as Stockhausen has said—ever since Schoenberg's time we have really become used to the fact that the musician will have an increasingly precise idea of what he does not want, but will tend much less to have any preconception of what he does want. In this connection we may interpose a story that is told of Debussy. When he was asked how he really went about composing his music he replied: 'I conjure up all the music that there is, and then I leave out whatever fails to please me.' And there is a grain of truth in this. The composer might be faced with a certain choice of sound elements, then define certain principles of combination, and finally try out all the possibilities on a computer which has been programmed with all the required preconditions. We can imagine what would actually happen. If the composer used principles of combination that were based on earlier, already known ones, then most of what emerged would be already known and in existence. However it would be different if he tested out principles of combination of which he himself did not know in detail what results they would lead to. Here he could arrive at new results, new discoveries, and even (in an experimental sort of way) new compositions. Such a computer would offer a great number of models for the composer to choose from. The results of his choice would again be combined with each other by the composer to form larger structures, complexes and sections.

In his Cologne Radio lectures, Stockhausen had something to
say which is of particular importance as a pointer to an aesthetic for
electronic music. He was speaking about *Continuo*, the electronic
composition produced by Bruno Maderna in 1957: 'In Maderna's
Continuo one becomes aware of the great range of differences of
intensity between the merest breath of a sound and massive con-
glomerates of extreme loudness; it has only become possible to do
this with such fine nuances in electronic music and it gives the
dynamics an importance such as this aspect has never before had in
music. On account of this too there arises from time to time the
impression of enormously vast spaces—extremely slow movements
within the tempo of magnified time, so to speak—and one loses
one's sense of direction with regard to durations and time proportions, finding oneself in a world of feeling that one can at most
believe oneself to have experienced only in dreams.' When I had
the opportunity to hear the work—it was in a programme of electronic music one evening in the 'Musik der Zeit' series of concerts
on West German Radio—I quite spontaneously noted at the time
that it reminded me of the prelude to Wagner's *Lohengrin*; not, of
course, in any thematic way, nor tonally or rhythmically, but rather
it has in common with Wagner's orchestral work a soft beginning
in the ethereal-sounding upper registers, a gradual dynamic increase accompanied by a sinking into deeper regions, until an
extreme climax is reached, after which this electronic work again
takes wing very softly into what seem infinities of altitude. In the
above quotation Stockhausen was seeking to demonstrate in
Maderna's work what he himself had composed in the way of extremely broad spaces and slow times in his *Carré* and *Kontakte*. My
own observation is no less subjective than Stockhausen's, which he
associated with his impression of Maderna's *Continuo*, but here it
seems to me that we have a first clue of how we may establish ways
of judging artistic procedures which can no longer be described by
our conventional vocabulary.

Stockhausen has given another sort of clue in his attempt to describe the electronic composition *Divertimento* by Castiglioni. He

said: 'In this work there are scarcely any melodic or harmonic formulations since the sounds are continually changing, constantly
revolving, being displaced and concealing their pitches in more or
less rapid slidings. Thus movement as such becomes more important than that which is moved. Since there are no shapes imprinting
themselves on the mind, one must use images such as "nets of
sound", "grids", "webs", or "splinters" in order to characterize
such procedures . . . completely new principles of musical time.'

Here new concepts are introduced which can perhaps become
foundations for aesthetical categories.

To the listener encountering electronic music for the first time
Stockhausen has given the following advice: 'Electronic music is in
the literal sense impossible to view, and on this account is suited to
radio listening where there is nothing to view in any case. For myself I can say that I listen to such music best and my imagination is
most free when I am alone, just listening, preferably with closed
eyes in order to shut out the things around me too. Then the inner
eye opens to visions in time and space which overstep what the
laws of the physical world around us permit; spatial perspective
and the logic of cause and effect in temporal events are both suspended. Electronic music has liberated the inner world, for one
knows that there is nothing to be seen outside oneself and that there
can be no sense in asking with what and by what means the sounds
and acoustical forms are produced . . . The inner world is as real
and as true as the outer and I think that music should serve the
experiencing of this inner world more than ever before, for here
everyone experiences himself most strongly as an individual and
learns as well to see and hear the outer world afresh.'

Naturally such a surrender to listening does not just mean one
should feel encouraged to enjoy the free, arbitrary subjective associations of a dream with no frontiers. Above all Stockhausen means
a participation of the self in the movement, the dynamics and the
peculiar spatiality of this music. This is the path to human experience of oneself and through this to an experience of the outer world
as it can be revealed by an encounter with the inner world.

These quotations are taken from the series of lectures entitled 'Do you know a music that can only be heard over loudspeakers ?'. And in the course of these same talks I also picked out the following statement that Stockhausen made in connection with an electronic composition by the Argentinian Mario Davidovsky: 'I feel that after hearing this piece I am no longer the same person as before.' It seems to me that here lies the core of what is decisive in Stockhausen's relationship to music—and what he also thinks decisive for the listener. The statement expresses Stockhausen's idea of a criterion for what can be made possible by music.

Spatial location in music

Antecedents

The conception of space is an immanent corollary of the phenomenon of music, though in fact this relationship is already a feature of sounds and noises before they ever become part of music. In all acoustical events there is present a definite indication of location—even though this cannot easily be conveyed by words. Language has found no distinction by which to characterize it, and has indeed never attempted to, since life offers no practical necessity that would justify such an attempt. 'High' and 'low', 'bright' and 'dark'—these are psychological properties of acoustical perception which describe—and that in only a very imprecise way—impressions relating to locations whose reality is that of aural psychology rather than of physical space.

When someone sings or plays an instrument for himself alone, then the spatial phenomenon can only exist for him in a very restricted way. The sounds he produces with his instrument or with his voice may be high or low, but they are not perceptibly localized within the instrument from which they proceed. However, the case is quite different when there is a clear-cut separation between the performers and the listeners, or if the performers are divided into groups, whether within an instrumental ensemble or a vocal one. Everyone sitting in an orchestra becomes familiar with the fact that the instrument of his colleague makes a sound which reaches him from another place. The listeners too can clearly perceive the different positions; technical reproduction of this phenomenon has today led to stereophonic recording and playback.

The fact that the performing group in a concert-hall will be seated on a platform, or—in a church—in the choir loft, is as familiar to us as is the individual positioning of the various sections within the group. We find it natural to sit within a prescribed area confronting the performers as listeners and spectators. Very few people realize that in its present form, the 'concert' represents a relatively recent form of performing practice. It was preceded by a completely different angle on the relationship between music and space.

In the Cathedral of St. Mark's in Venice, modelled on the Church of the Holy Apostles in Constantinople, there were two organs in facing choir lofts. Adrian Willaert (ca. 1490–1562), when he elaborated the practice of instrumental and vocal polyphony, was apparently stimulated by the possibilities of acoustical presentation afforded by the two organs and the vocal and instrumental choirs allotted to each. This technique, already current, then became characteristic of the Venetian school which, though founded by the Fleming Willaert, was shortly to be represented exclusively by Italians.

The technique is notable for its systematic and absolute (rather than merely relative) spatial division of the performing body, which takes up separate positions at different stations. After Willaert's eight-part *Vespers* (printed in 1550) the Venetians soon developed a markedly imaginative treatment of sound in their use of separately stationed choirs (*cori spezzati*). This treatment of the choirs and choral effects with its exchanges and combinations was elaborated to the point where the deployment of acoustical space became an art in itself. The individual performing groups were positioned separately. Choral sections in compositions were often set off against each other in 'dialogue form'. Echo effects became prominent. At the end of the 16th century splendid and colourful ways of enhancing sound even included the combination of vocal and instrumental timbres in five 'choirs'. Considerable surface effects were generated by featuring a preponderantly chordal style. There was a marked retreat of polyphony in favour of homophonic effects. Chromaticism made an increasing appearance in music. A melodic language full of imagery and affect was developed, sometimes taking in realistic tone-painting.

The use of multiple choirs, such a conspicuous principle of music-making in the early baroque and at the start of the high baroque, was taken further still, probably reaching its climax with the *Festal Mass* by the Roman Orazio Benevoli, which was written for the dedication of Salzburg Cathedral in 1628 and called for 53 parts (16 vocal and 34 instrumental, besides two organs and *basso continuo*). This *Festal Mass* of course represents only one side of the technique's possibilities: that of surface splendour and of great pomp. The other side, the dramatic and mystical, is exemplified by Heinrich Schütz in a work like 'Saul, was verfolgst du mich' (*Symphoniae sacrae, III*, 1650) for three choruses, orchestra and organ. The voices crowd in on Saul from all sides as if in a vision, rising from the darkest depths, powerfully unfolding, and finally mysteriously dying down.

The practice flourished less after the middle of the 17th century, but the *St. Matthew Passion* of Johann Sebastian Bach contains a late echo of it. Subsequently examples become much rarer, being restricted to such occasional instances as Mozart's *Notturno* (K. 286), written for four groups each of two violins, viola, cello, double bass and two horns. Certainly Mozart's only aesthetic justification for this layout is in his echo effects. For these the music is always cut in half so that the impression of an echo is realistic, though in the minuet the effects of this innocent playfulness are made an organic part of the composition. In his Seventh Symphony ('The terrestrial and the divine in the life of man') Louis Spohr used a double orchestra (1842). The sound demanded in Berlioz's *Requiem* (1837), with its five orchestras and eight pairs of timpani in the 'Tuba mirum', is well known, and the acoustical spatial disposition of the Grail scene in Wagner's *Parsifal* (1882) merits attention. Titurel's voice issues from the 'depths of the grave', the Knights of the Grail sit at stage level, the voices of the attendants come from the partial elevation of the cupola, and the voices of the youths from the topmost height of the cupola.

The idea of sound-filled space, of a music which surrounds the listeners on all sides, also occurred to Arnold Schoenberg. Thus in the great orchestral interlude in his *Jakobsleiter* he had the idea of using four distant orchestras which would join the main orchestra in addition to female choruses with one high and one extremely high solo soprano. In September 1917, when he was called up for military service, he broke off work at this point. It was never completed, but the technical problems posed by using the distant orchestras were to occupy his attention twice more; once was in 1944, when he proposed that separate microphones should be used to transmit the sound of the distant orchestras through loudspeakers to be positioned at different places in the hall. This was the solution adopted for the first performance in Vienna in 1961, where a tape was played back through a four-channel system. In its poetical conception the end of *Jakobsleiter* recalls the scene of the Grail in *Parsifal* just as the latter in turn recalls the ending of Goethe's *Faust*, Part II.

A few more examples from the early 20th century must be included here in order to confirm how strongly the idea of distributing music in space possessed the minds of various composers for short periods quite independently of each other.

In his ballet *L'Homme et son désir*, composed in 1918 after a text by Claudel, Darius Milhaud set up the music on four levels, corresponding to the action. In his conversations with Rostand, Milhaud says of it: 'I accordingly set up a special group of musicians for each side of the stage and one for each playing level; hence the differently constituted ensembles: vocal quartet, oboe–trumpet–harp–double bass; two percussion groups, piccolo–flute–clarinet–bass clarinet; and finally a string quartet. All these units often play in different metres and remain in some way independent of each other.'

Dating from the year 1914, and composed in the train of a nationalistic upsurge of feeling for the German nation, Max Reger's *Eine vaterländische Ouvertüre*, Op.140, was dedicated by the composer to 'The German Army'. In bar 234 a distant orchestra enters (3–4 trumpets in C, 3–4 tenor trombones) with the chorale 'Nun danket alle Gott'. In the principal orchestra are heard, supported by the organ, the national anthem 'Deutschland, Deutschland über alles' and the two militaristic folk-songs 'Es braust ein Ruf wie Donnerhall' and 'Ich hab mich ergeben'.

As early as 1908 the American Charles Ives had introduced spatial distribution of the orchestra in his short orchestral work *The Unanswered Question, a Cosmic Landscape*, and Ives again had recourse to the separation of sound-sources in his Fourth Symphony, written between 1910 and 1916. The isolation of sounds has already long been a requisite of theatre music, the *locus classicus* being the trumpet call in Beethoven's *Fidelio* and in the *Leonore* Overtures. The signal call here denotes an impending arrival, whereas in Mahler's Second Symphony it denotes resurrection and foregathering, and in Schoenberg's *Jakobsleiter* the combination of the various bodies of sound symbolizes the release of the soul and the spirit from the corporeal. There is no question of such extra-musical associations in Stockhausen; the three ensembles of *Gruppen*, with their very differently constituted forces, are subject to the formal principle of groups and are hence an organic feature of the music.

Traditional music corresponds to the philosophical climate of the time at which it was created, and in this perspective the world was conditioned by a *single* sort of time: things happened in *one* time alone. After 1900 it was the natural sciences that brought about a turning point in our attitude to time. The classical physical concept of time was relativised. The concept of organic time was introduced, and Viktor von Weizäcker's formulation 'Time is a function of life' became central.

Modern compositional practice is founded on the relativity of the concept of time. Stockhausen has always stressed the concept of multitemporality—plurality of time. Musically this is founded on the phenomenon according to which each sound has its own time. Proceeding from this fact, one has to think in terms of strata of time.

It is to this multitemporality that multispatiality corresponds; in *Gruppen*, as we have seen, the spatial division into three orchestras is geared to thinking in temporal groups and to the necessity of a practical realization using traditional ensembles. The characteristic times proper to the sounds are spatially separated so that polyphony of time coincides with polyphony of space.

In *Gruppen* and in *Carré* respectively, three and four ensembles are installed in separate places. Stockhausen has logically pursued the idea of a new conception of space and time; he has worked it out in such a way that a composition is no longer performed in a single area, but the different time strata can be heard simultaneously in different spatial areas. The most recent result is *Musik für ein Haus*, first performed at Darmstadt in 1968.

New halls for new music

In the most immediate past the first composer to attempt to include the direction and movement of sounds in composition and to open up this new dimension of musical experience has been Stockhausen, in his electronic work *Gesang der Jünglinge*. The work is composed for five groups of loudspeakers, to be spatially distributed around the listener. To fully appreciate the work one has to hear from which side the sounds and sound groups emanate into the area, from how many loudspeakers at a time, whether in clockwise or anticlockwise rotation, and to what extent they are fixed, to what extent mobile.

The old indivisible relationship between music and space here receives a new impetus, movement of the sound, for the sounds continuously 'wander' from one to another of the loudspeakers placed around the audience. Suitable listening areas for this kind of 'music in space' do not yet exist. Stockhausen thinks that the ideal would be a spherical area furnished with loudspeakers at various points. In the middle of this spherical area a suspended platform of some transparent and acoustically conductive material would hold the listeners so that they could then hear the music composed for such an area coming from above and from below them, in fact from all directions.

The idea of this globular listening area recalls the spherical theatre of Andy Weininger. This is not a theatre affording the experience of spatial perspective with focal points and vanishing points; rather the area itself and the relationships within it are meant to be structured and experienced as form, colour and light. The spherical theatre is a spherically shaped frame in which the audience would be grouped together rather as in an amphitheatre on the inner surface of the lower half of the sphere; the

Karlheinz Stockhausen

position of the acting areas would not be on a circular level stage (as in the Greek theatre) nor in a perspective-orientated display-box (as in the baroque theatre), but would be in the cylindrical area between the upper and lower poles of the steel sphere, broken up with spiral stairways, suspended gangways hither and thither, and so forth. Thus was born the idea of the non-perspective stage.

With the composition of *Gruppen* for three orchestras and *Carré* for four orchestras and choruses the practical question of how space must be utilized appeared in a new form. Here are Stockhausen's practical proposals. The most important properties that he envisages for such areas are as follows:

1. A spherical, circular or quadratic area such as will facilitate orchestral positioning at any desired place around the audience and/or in the middle of the audience.
2. No permanent platform; instead, a large number of small movable daises.
3. Parts of the floor at variable elevations.
4. Seating arrangements to be alterable at will; no fixed seating.
5. Fixtures for loudspeakers and microphones around the walls and in the ceiling.
6. Alcoves and/or balconies at different levels for small instrumental groups.
7. Doors not interfering with any circular disposition of orchestral groups around the walls (as many doors as possible, distributed evenly round a circular area).
8. Electrically controlled echo that can be matched to suit any given conditions of performance.
9. A studio outside the hall for relaying over loudspeakers and for recording.
10. Separate lighting for the hall and for portable music-stand lamps.

These ten points of Stockhausen's enumerated here are to be seen as amounting to a proposal of which they are the unconditional requirements. The whole idea is to be understood as a

precursor of Stockhausen's conception of a 'music building' hous-
ing several halls. Music's new multiple sort of time finds its most
appropriate and logical complementation in such a multiple sort
of space.

Space in Stockhausen's works

The first performance of *Gruppen* for three orchestras took place
in 1958 in the Rheinsaal des Messegeländes, Cologne. One's first
surprise came upon entering the hall: the quadrilateral area was
arranged diagonally so that the central orchestra took up the whole
of one side of the hall at the front, the second took up the whole of
the left-hand side and the third the whole of the right-hand side.
The listeners found themselves in the middle of the three orchestras.

Stockhausen had worked on the composition itself for three
years, with some interruptions. The programme note he wrote
for the first performance is reproduced on pages 37–8. The
orchestral layout of *Gruppen* is a consequence of its spatial disposition. Thus longer or shorter groups of sounds, noises and
combined sounds and noises are to be presented in different tempi
at the same time. In order to achieve this, to play it correctly and to
render it audible, a large orchestra of 109 players was divided up into
three smaller orchestras. Each smaller orchestra was under its own
conductor—at the first performance in Cologne these were Bruno
Maderna, Pierre Boulez and Stockhausen himself—and was installed in the hall with adequate room between each. The three
orchestras are of roughly equal sizes and in each the following
instrumental families are represented: woodwind, brass, plucked
and bowed strings; each of these four families is further subdivided into a 'sound' group, playing exactly determined pitches,
and a 'noise' group, playing only approximately determined pitches.
For the transition from sound to controlled noise within each instrumental family there is a selection of many percussion instruments of
metal, wood and membrane. With instruments such as the piano,
the celesta, tubular bells and cowbells, sound and noise can be
combined in a single instrument.

What, then, of the aesthetic impression? Here I propose only a subjective report, a spontaneous impression arising from two performances in Cologne in 1958 and a further performance in Donaueschingen during the Autumn of the same year. The formal outline of the whole comes over surprisingly clearly, thanks to the spatial disposition of the orchestras; this is also partly due to the colorations, and in the third place to the dynamics. In its total effect this piece, lasting roughly 24 minutes, is extremely impressive by reason of Stockhausen's supreme mastery over his materials and the strength of his imagination. In its constantly changing colour complexes, and in the vast range and diversity of its emotions, paralleling the richness of the instrumental colours, the work immediately recalls middle-period Schoenberg and the athematic, atonal period of German Expressionism in which he worked.*

Stockhausen has written in connection with *Gruppen*: 'It is always a question of functionally directed sound, rather than of sound effects.' In fact this association of sound with function, incorporating the sound into the whole, is here completely convincing. The ear can take its bearings at first hearing from the organization of the timbre groups: the beginning is almost impressionistically tender, like chamber music, then in the following section all three orchestras play *forte*; in the third section there is first a delicate piece of string writing in the first orchestra, then all three play together and alternately, preponderantly *piano*, in a kind of development section. Then the combination of the three orchestras leads to great climaxes: long percussion solos, concertante trumpet solos, powerful brass sections, alternating and interpenetrating, with constant tense pauses between the sections; a piano solo comes in, then there is a passage for the percussion of all three orchestras with the brass entering later: this is the ultimate climax. What follows has the character of an epilogue, sounds taking their departure. The whole of the music features a neo-expressionism that has the typical superabundance, the discontinuity and the

* For a view closer to Stockhausen's own, see p. 193. (Translator's note.)

extreme contrasts of this style, and is permeated by enormous pressures of expansion.

We will venture nothing of an analytical kind on the subject of *Carré* either; at the time of writing the printed score is not yet available. Again I report my first impressions. For the first performance the festival hall of the Hamburg exhibition site 'Planten on Blomen' had to be made ready. In *Carré* the four performing ensembles (each comprising a chorus and an orchestra) are situated on platforms against the walls with the public seated diagonally across the 'square' (*carré*) they form. Thus for half an hour four choruses and four orchestras disposed in quadrangular fashion make music—spatially speaking—against each other, with each other and amongst each other. Here is what the constitution of the whole orchestra looks like: 2 flutes, alto flute, 2 oboes, cor anglais, 3 clarinets, bass clarinet, 3 saxophones, 3 bassoons; 3 trumpets, trumpet in D, bass trumpet, 4 trombones, bass tuba, 6 horns; piano, vibraphone, cimbalon, harp (with harpsichord); 8 percussionists: 8 tom-toms, 4 bongos, 12 cowbells, 4 cymbals, 4 hi-hat cymbals, 4 gongs, 4 tam-tams, 4 sets of Indian jingles, 2 bass drums, 4 snare drums (very high-pitched); 4 choruses (8-8-8-8); 4 groups of strings, without double bass (8-8-8-8).

Bearing in mind that this ensemble is split up into four sectional groups, the result is that each of these will have an almost chamber-music-like constitution. To continue, however, in a totally subjective vein: here it is scarcely any longer a matter of music in the traditional sense. The chorus eschews all text, singing instead vowels and consonants with extremely varied colorations, and clapping their hands, clicking their tongues and snapping their fingers. There is barely anything approaching a theme or a motive in the orchestra; rather one is compelled to speak of groups—of groupings of perhaps two notes, of *glissandi*, with solo instruments often at the extremes of their range, of ecstatic outbursts from dense instrumental groups and of resounding long-held chordal complexes. It is a never-flagging hypertrophy of ideas and impressions which mill round the listener from all four sides; new entries are always appearing, never repeating themselves, and embracing every mood, from a cry to laughter, from ecstasy to mourning, from the playful to the dramatic, from the prankish to the tragic. At first one feels taken aback, but then one cannot for an instant hold back one's astonishment and admiration. One's aesthetic involvement with the work is unceasing, and after all these impressions and experiences one has to reconsider one's answer to the question of 'What is music?'; for *Carré's* methods are musical ones and the impression it leaves is of a work of art.

And it is as a work of art that this work will be heard and judged. In a note in the programme for the Hamburg first performance Stockhausen concedes that it is sometimes best to close one's eyes so as to be able to hear better, and his cordial wish is that this (his) music might afford a little inner calm, breadth and concentration, for it is better to find oneself than to lose oneself in something external. It was during hour-long flights that Stockhausen made every day for a number of weeks in America that *Carré* came to him, was experienced and gradually allowed to form. In the realization of the score Cornelius Cardew worked out some of the composition plans independently. One must take one's time if one is to absorb this music into oneself; it does not carry one along with it, but leaves one in peace; Stockhausen has no story to tell here, for though each moment is indeed related to other moments, it could yet still exist for itself alone. Thus one could confidently miss a moment if one did not wish to or was not able to go on listening.

A glance at the four scores that were prepared for the first performance deepens one's initial impressions. We read in the directions for performance: 'The figures in seconds for the durations of the groups are average values, which have been laid down after several readings of the score. Thus, as instructions for any performance, they are to be seen as only approximative. A group is indicated by a number enclosed in a square: eg. $\boxed{4}$. The sequence of units giving the beat for each group is shown in capital letters. The beats within these units are indicated by arabic numerals: thus, A 123, B 123 etc. Each 1 corresponds to the downbeat at the beginning of a bar. The duration of each beat should be proportional to the spatial distribution of the music on the page, relative to the duration of the whole group. The durations of the fermatas are: V = short; Λ = medium; ⌒ = long; ⌐.⌐ = very long.'

The greatest care is accorded to the treatment of the human voice too. Stockhausen distinguishes between the execution of a) exactly prescribed pitches (normal notation),

b) approximate pitches (notated thus:)

and c) free pitches ( ), in which the melodic steps are only approximate. For the diction special symbols are introduced giving extremely precise differentiations as laid down in the *Principles of the International Phonetic Association* (Department of Phonetics, University College, London WC1).

The sociological aspect, the questions about the possibility of practical performance, of performing areas and of the role of the public—all this is discussed elsewhere. We have already spoken of the idea of the spherical performing area for presenting electronic music; Stockhausen is particularly keen to point out that this idea is only one proposal among many. The spherical form seems to him favourable on account of the fact that one would be able to hear from all directions; the sphere should have scarcely any resonance of its own, for this would already be given by the loudspeakers provided. The erection of a listening platform in the middle of the area would mean that one could hear as much direct sound as possible, for one would be at an equal distance from all the sound sources around one. Stockhausen thinks equally highly of other solutions. In this context he recalls an idea that was put forward by Henri Pousseur: performing areas would be encased within each other, and connected by passages and corridors, so that the sound could come from different areas, providing both indirect and direct sound; music with instruments could here readily be integrated into electronic music. The essential lies in the proposal that new musical space prescribes no

directional orientation of the sort to be found in the traditional
concert hall with its fixed platform, permanent seating fixtures
and so on.

Stockhausen's idea of a 'music in space' and its conception in
some detail have rapidly claimed a sizable following, including
amongst others Pierre Boulez, whose *Poésie pour pouvoir*, after a
poem by Henri Michaux, uses a speaking voice, distorted on tape,
other *musique concrète* sounds and three orchestras. This work was
first performed at Donaueschingen in 1958.

Let us return to the starting point of our observations, namely
our remarks about the relationship between music and space. For
the first time in the history of music the Venetians of the 16th
century and their followers introduced physical space as a component of the art of musical composition. At this time, however, the
practice is accounted for neither by a musical aesthetic in our
modern sense nor in any written description of it: we can therefore
only construe the Venetian school's motivating ideas from the
compositions themselves. These ideas seem to be of a completely
different nature from those which occasioned Stockhausen to
allow notes to sound from different directions in space and with
different forms of movement in space. Let us again quote Stockhausen himself:

'The first compositions of electronic music and of "pointillist
music" in general were extremely homogeneous in their sonority
and in their form. All the musical elements participated on an
equal footing in the shaping process and all the properties of the
notes were constantly renewed from one note to the next. Now
when all the tonal properties are constantly changing at the same
rate, and when no one property remains constant for a relatively
long time, so that another property comes to predominate (for
instance, longish note sequences in a high register, then in a low
register; or several notes remaining equally slow, then fast; or a
note group played on the strings, then another on the wind; or
first many loud notes, then many soft ones); when, rather, pitch,
duration, timbre and intensity alter note for note ("point for point")

then the music finally becomes static: it changes extremely fast so
that one is always traversing the whole gamut of experience in the
shortest time, and thus one gets into a state of suspension: the
music "stands still".

'If one once again wished to articulate longer periods of time,
there was only one possibility: to allow one tonal property to
predominate over all the others for a while. But under the pro-
visons existing at the time that would have constituted a fundamental denial of the spirit which had given birth to the idea of
an equal participation of all the tonal properties. So a solution was
found by spatially distributing periods of time of differing lengths
and of homogeneous note-structure, giving them to different
loudspeaker groups or instrumental groups. Thus it first became
possible to articulate longer pointillist structures by giving them
mobility in space, moving them from one place to another. This
even provided a solution to the problem of how to make simultaneous superimpositions of such pointillist structural strata
comprehensible through a spatial distribution of the sound; the
preceding dissolution of all "polyphonic" principles and of the
"part" in general as a formal concept in music left as the only
available possibility a permanent reduction to the single layer (as
in Asiatic music). The scattering of "points" upset the "simul-
taneity", since superimposed points yield at best point sequences of
greater or lesser density, and only lines, in other words continuous
strings of points, would make it feasible to present different simultaneous processes. But if one now splits up a point structure into
two groups sounding simultaneously, the one from the right and the
other from the left, then it is perfectly possible to experience two
layers of one and the same sound structure.'

In the note he wrote to accompany the DGG recording of
Gruppen Stockhausen said that the spatial separation of the groups
was in the first place the result of the superposition of several
layers of time displaying different tempi, a situation which could
not have been met by a single orchestra for technical reasons
of performance. This was the decisive factor in his completely

new conception of spatially distributed forms of instrumental music. 'The total process embodied in this music was partly determined by spatial dispositions of the sound, by the direction of the sound and by the movement of the sound (alternating, isolated, fusing, rotational movement, and so on), just as it had been in the electronic music *Gesang der Jünglinge* for five loudspeaker groups, dating from 1956. The work is consciously composed as a whole (there are no "movements" in the traditional sense) and is a synthesis of "orchestral music", "chamber music" and "solo music".'

Gesang der Jünglinge was composed in the years 1955 and 1956, and exactly ten years later (1966 and 1967) came *Hymnen*. This represents a complete synthesis of all the experience acquired in a decade, which is incorporated in a programme that must be described as often markedly dramatic, in every way justifying the need for spatial distribution of sound. The work offers possibilities not only of superimposing individual musical ideas, but also of temporal continuity and of spatial presentation such as earlier music was capable of only occasionally and even then only by suggestion. To give some idea of this let us examine the single case, out of an infinite variety of examples, of what happens at one point to the national anthem of the German Republic. The melody of the song —in the original recording for chorus and orchestra—is reduced to motivic and periodic splinters, a counterpoint is then added, and the sound of the voices is split up into its constituent parts; finally instrumental sound is isolated from vocal sound. In the final chord cries of 'bravo' and ships' sirens are heard. We now realize that— from constantly changing positions in space—we have been witness to a launching, and we know too that at the same time we have been witness to a typical process whose events held us absorbed in direct participation.

It finally remains to answer the question of why music that is written for spatial performance should be transmitted on the radio. It is better, in Stockhausen's view, to see a photograph of a plastic object than not to see the object at all. Perhaps one will then get the urge to see the object in its original form. And the same argument applies to this kind of radio broadcast.

Musik für ein Haus

It must have been for about ten years that Stockhausen had been harbouring the idea of writing a piece that he wanted to call *Kammermusik* ('Chamber Music'). The basic idea was to construct on the stage or platform a series of chambers (in the manner of a multiple set), installing musicians in these and isolating or combining each sound event issuing from the various chambers, while giving the musicians the opportunity to change chambers so as to produce constantly changing distributions of the one chamber ensemble. The idea of this 'Chamber Music' was never realized, but it has meanwhile been subsumed in *Musik für ein Haus*.

Musik für ein Haus ('Music for a House'), owing its existence to the work of the participants in Karlheinz Stockhausen's composition studio, had its first performance on 1 September 1968 in the Georg-Moller-Haus at Darmstadt. Stockhausen himself had taken charge of the process planning, and the compositional realization was in the hands of Junsang Bahk, Gregory Biss, Boudewijn Buckinx, Rolf Gehlhaar, Mesias Maiguashca, John McGuire, Costin Miereanu, Fred van der Kooy, Thomas Wells, Jaroslav J. Wolf and Jorge Peixinho. The interpreters were Eberhard Blum (flute), Heinz Holliger (oboe), Josef Horák (bass clarinet), János Mészáros (bassoon), Georges Barboteu (horn), Pierre Thibaud (trumpet), Vinko Globokar (trombone), Harald Bojé (electronium), Aloys Kontarsky (keyboard instruments), Saschko Gawriloff (violin), Othello Liesmann (cello) and Georg Nothdorf (double bass). The composition was presented continuously from 1800 hrs. to about 2200 hrs. The acoustical happenings were located in four rooms situated on two floors. Directions for improvisation were given to the individual instrumentalists; their various improvisations were now picked up by microphones in each room, fed to a mixing desk, partly distorted by electronic means, then played back again on the loudspeakers of the other rooms, so that amongst the musicians themselves there was constantly an experience of reciprocal stimulation. The public had the opportunity to move around freely in all the rooms. Listening was intuitive, freed from the pursuit of interrelations. A fifth chamber provided the opportunity of listening simultaneously to the musical processes occurring in all four rooms.

New music and society

Aural bias

By 'biased' and 'unbiased'* we refer to two different ways of behaving towards the rational and the emotional. Our relationships with the objects of our reason or of our feelings may be direct; then we shall be unbiased. However we shall be biased whenever anything intervenes between our capacity for reaction and its object, weakening, inhibiting or totally negating our openness.

In German, the words meaning 'prejudiced' (*voreingenommen*) and 'unprejudiced' (*unvoreingenommen*) offer an even sharper characterization of this mental and spiritual behaviour. They designate the intention or tendency to adopt a kind of behaviour—thus a relationship—reinforced by a particular manner, indeed a rigour, in doing so. One may 'have a predilection' (*vorher eingenommen sein*) for something or not. And one is prejudiced because there are good reasons against not being.

The man who listens to music too is subject to this kind of behaviour, indeed is reliant on it. Bias comes to us already in the first years of our life; through the music of our environment we grow up inseparably in the world of our tonal system and in the expressive world our music inhabits—in the first place, nursery songs, folk songs and popular songs.

The musical understanding of many people, in other words their capacity to follow music as an experience, never leaves the realm of the simple song. For the lowliest consumer of music as for the most cultivated professional musician the environment of our central European music creates a bias against everything that does not belong to the realm of our tonal system and our modes of expression (all non-European music, for a start). The extraordinarily refined music of the Arabs, the highly significant music of the Chinese and the orchestral music of Java, all this is for us a book with seven seals. We can probably attempt to describe the impression it makes on us. But already such an attempt will be biased

* *Befangenheit* ('bias') also, and even primarily, means 'embarrassment, constraint'. (Translator's note.)

by our accustomed way of experiencing music. The symbolism of exotic music will escape us.

Very few people give a second thought to this fundamental bias. We always speak of music as meaning our Western music, and in particular Central and Western European music of the last two hundred years.

It is at the price of this limitation that we acquire a relationship with our own music in which we feel at our ease. For every increase in our attachment we pay out further costs without gaining any clarity on the subject. The musical scholar, the incipient music student and the initiated novice are all educated in the mental imagery of our music. They are introduced to customs of composition and of formal classification and to the history of music; they set foot in a hierarchy where artistic and aesthetic principles hold sway, even though they may not always be formulated in clear paragraphs. The freedom with which the artist moves in this region is relative, not least so because freedom and restrictions are not simply governed by rules, and the possible meanings of the mostly unwritten laws are very different. For instance, we are familiar with the names of some composers in the hierarchy who are recognized at the time as indisputably great. The symphony passes for the most demanding form, and the string quartet for the most intimate ensemble in Western music. Thus musical education is a familiarization with this hierarchical order, whose nature is extremely seldom critically doubted by music teachers. Consequently many fundamental opinions are handed down and perpetuated from one generation to another.

It is no longer primarily music that we hear, but always music associated with the names of composers and the type or genre to which a piece of music belongs. This begins when we learn an instrument: every piece that we play is docketed by a title and the name of a composer; already we are playing under a suggestion. The effect continues throughout our whole life. Every concert advertisement 'lures' us by the programme just as much as by the names of the performers. If a symphony by Beethoven is announced, we always hear it in the concert in a prejudiced way, influenced by the experiences that have already accumulated for us around the name of Beethoven, and aware of the knowledge that everyone associates with this composer in particular. Already the word symphony is for everyone a complex of ideas and experiences reinforcing the individual's listening to a single work.

Thus it is clear that only with difficulty, if at all, can we separate the experience of music from what we 'know' of music. The concept of the symphony or sonata genre creates a prejudice. Through the Viennese classics and the Romantics, and through Beethoven more than any other composer, these forms, by now a matter of history, have become yardsticks of value, models and examples against which subsequent music is measured. Such historically standardized values have often enough veiled our view of the present. A great many of the judgments in musical history which later times were able to correct in an unbiased way can be explained simply in terms of aural bias. Every plus must be paid for by a corresponding minus.

To hear in an unbiased way—a wish, a precept. It means that we must from time to time wipe off the dust from opinions we have grown attached to, even old and well-founded judgments, and pass them under critical review; it means that we must submit our own musical experiences to revision and constantly expose ourselves anew to the living, spontaneous impression of listening if we are not to stand still letting our ears become still more thickly coated with prejudice and bias than their natural covering already makes them.

Autogenous disposition

The history of music has seen many judgments corrected by posterity. They are evidence of a continuing, unceasing change of attitude. This is a fact about the human spirit and is as little to be ignored as that an individual can escape from his habits and take up an isolated stand. It is a basic law of intellectual life, as there are laws of nature to which human life and the possibilities of human knowledge are subject. In his autobiography, Stravinsky has put this realization in the following terms: 'It is in the nature of things —and the uninterrupted progress of development, not just in art, but equally in all branches of human activity depends on it—that epochs which have just passed into history fade away from us whilst others, further back in history, become closer to us.'

This capacity for perspective on the one hand and on the other the adjustment associated with it may be combined in the concept of autogenous disposition. The word disposition refers to a type of mental and spiritual behaviour, of which we are here describing one particular manifestation in listening to and evaluating music. This behaviour varies from person to person even though in their essentials the factors which determine it are originally the same: individual factors, factors of environment and education. The first of these, individual factors, are to be equated with the concept of musicality, by which is meant the individual capacity for assimilation, the 'ear for music'. The factors of environment already begin to take effect at an early stage in the home. Education, encouragement, music-making and visits to concerts and the theatre belong in this category. The educational factors are again of a more individual nature. The disposition for listening to music can be individually varied by studies in musical history or in general cultural history. One can, for instance, acquire a particular capacity for assimilating the music of earlier periods through special preoccupation with these periods.

This grouping of the factors which determine autogenous disposition in listening to music permits a more exact insight into their essence. Although we put musicality first, since it is the 'organ', the instrument without which music can awaken no resonance, this in fact looks after itself. It is the inborn precondition in contrast to the additional propensities which are acquired later. However, common to all three groups of factors is the specific form in which they take effect. We call them 'autogenous', spontaneously effective, in other words in many cases their effectiveness is not consciously experienced. Autogenous disposition creates not only the form in which one experiences listening to music, but also that reaction to listening to music which consists in both emotional response and discrimination. With this we have again touched on the outlet for our thought processes: judgment and evaluation.

We have distinguished between inborn and acquired characteristics determining the mental and spiritual behaviour of autogenous disposition. The pedagogue and the cultural politician will have to direct their attention chiefly to the second kind, the circumstances of environment and education. For it probably lies to a large extent within their powers to create, to educate and to form autogenous disposition in listening to music. In the West, where musical life remains as always decisively anchored in the institutions of the concert hall and the opera house, choral societies large and small, chamber music ensembles and amateur groups, it will be difficult to make a strict separation between a first experience of music and an educational experience. From this point of view, what is to be educated in a listener to music is even more than merely the ear—the 'receiving set'—and musical apperception—the mental faculty of assimilating what is heard to the value of the work of art. What has to be created is the broad intellectual framework, the autogenous disposition to evaluate and to weigh up a work of art while still enjoying it, and to appraise the whole of its artistic significance, assigning it a place both in its own particular stylistic milieu and in the broader perspective of cultural history so that, from this standpoint, it can be grasped and understood afresh, in full, individually and moreover equitably.

On these changing relationships between work of art and observer (or listener) Goethe made the following rather self-critical remarks in his *Maxims and Reflections*: 'It used to occur and indeed still happens to me that a work of fine art displeases me at first sight, because I have not grown towards it; however, let me once suspect it of any merit, and I will seek to gain access to it, finding then no lack of the most gratifying discoveries; I become aware of new properties in things and of new faculties in myself.'

Out of the 'fifties

The first German performance of the piano piece *Mode de valeurs et d'intensités*, played by the composer, Olivier Messiaen, was heard on 26 May 1952 in the series of concerts organized by Hessische Rundfunk, Frankfurt am Main, in their International New Music Festival. At the time I noted: 'Here music has reached a limit of the ear's capacity for relating sounds to each other—a limit such as never before existed. A purely linear music, it demands the colours of the orchestra; pure abstraction. No longer is any synthesis of connective listening possible. We shall have to change our ideas. Learn to hear afresh.'

Two months later, the first of Stockhausen's premières took place in Darmstadt, that of *Kreuzspiel*. I summarized my impressions as follows: 'It was not by chance that it was in the audience that the radicals provoked the sharpest exchanges. The climax of a confrontation that had become a veritable concert of whistles followed the twenty-one-year-old* Karlheinz Stockhausen's *Kreuzspiel*. He completely renounces melody and rhythm in the conventional sense, restricting himself to a pointillist sketch of a musical idea which denies itself any really artistic utterance.'

In Autumn of the same year we heard in Donaueschingen the second work by Stockhausen: 'Karlheinz Stockhausen, already known from Kranichstein, a pupil of Frank Martin and of Messiaen, born in 1928, was represented with the first performance of a two-movement *Spiel* for orchestra. He contributes something quite new, a music of purely static character, without the sort of development familiar in Western music. It remains in the sphere of the illustrative, the idea, a pure contemplation unfolding in musical space. It requires of the listener a completely new conception of the phenomenon of music, and of the orchestra a way of playing different from the customary one. When, after the brief ten minutes that *Spiel* takes, applause was mixed with whistles, one yet had the feeling that neither the audience nor the orchestra had proved

---

* At the date of the performance Stockhausen was of course twenty-three. (Translator's note.)

familiar enough with the exigencies of the composer for his music, the completely new demands on performers and listeners. In 1920 new music broke away on its own path with élan, today it tries to woo and to convince by means of the idea.'

The autogenous disposition of my generation constantly saw the events after 1945 as a parallel to those after the First World War. We had to learn differently. Today we know that new music cannot be compared with the turning taken around 1920.

One incident which deserves to be recorded in the annals of contemporary music took place at the first performance of Stockhausen's second cycle of piano pieces (*Klavierstücke V–VIII*)* at the Marienhöhe seminar, Darmstadt, in 1955: 'A scene, recently experienced, is sufficiently memorable to be entered in the annals of Kranichstein. Marcelle Mercenier, the pianist from Brussels [she is the dedicatee of *Klavierstücke I–IV*], was giving the first performance of the second cycle of *Klavierstücke* by Karlheinz Stockhausen. The composer was turning the pages for her. This is not the place to argue about why the audience's initial attentiveness to the complete novelty of this musical language soon changed to laughter. It is not the first time that the composer—who is now in his mid twenties—has met with such a reaction to the paths he has chosen. None of his works has escaped meeting with incomprehension; always the same effect of shock on the public; but nothing deters Stockhausen from pursuing his ideas further. During the performance a guest arrived who had long been known to seasoned habitués of Kranichstein: a cricket, having found a pleasant spot under the platform, began to chirrup. For many it was a familiar occurrence, but for others it was one more excuse to conceal their inability to understand in laughter.

'In Vienna Schoenberg and the music of his pupils had met with pitched battles in the concert hall. In Kranichstein it was quite a different story. Who would have been likely to get over-excited about Stockhausen? Only incomprehension of this music and lack

---

* On this occasion *Klavierstücke IX–X* were not played—see page 22. (Translator's note.)

of the self-assurance and energy to want and to defend anything else can account for this indifference.

'It became too much for the composer. Perhaps mainly disappointed that no-one even wanted to pay attention to a first-rate performance by the pianist, he snapped the score shut and left the hall with his manuscript in his hand. An embarrassing situation. The reaction was one of constraint and renewed laughter. Then the Italian composer Luigi Nono stood up. He is four years older than his German colleague, is a friend of his, and shares his belief that only lack of compromise and personal integrity can be the answer to the attitude of the public. He fetched Stockhausen back, mounted the platform with him and turned to the public. A few words, spoken by Nono in his straightforward way, sufficed to restore calm and to shame the audience: "You ought to listen to the end and air your views afterwards." '

Five years after the first of Stockhausen's first performances I drew up a balance sheet. The actual occasion was the first performance of Stockhausen's *Klavierstück XI* (interpretations I and II) at Darmstadt: 'Right from the first, Kranichstein has been a platform for the young generation. This idea—whose continued pursuance has made it unique the world over—has to this day not lost its vitality. The young generation has a right to experiment, and our critical distance from them is not thereby narrowed. As director of the Kranichstein Summer School, Dr. Steinecke has always presented the concerts with works of the young generation as studio performances, not allotting them to the concert hall but reserving a place for them on the Marienhöhe where the courses take place. These concerts are performances in professional circles and it was never intended to draw the public at large into the argument.

'In the last seven years at Kranichstein we have been witness to an exciting breakthrough by the young generation. Three names in modern music have come to the fore: Boulez, Nono and Stockhausen—three names from the three central countries of European music. As being especially characteristic of their artistic personalities let me cite Nono's *Il canto sospeso*, Boulez's *Le marteau sans maître*, and Stockhausen's *Zeitmasze* for wind instruments and *Klavierstück XI*—in Kranichstein in 1957 some of these works could only be heard on tapes, while Stockhausen's *Klavierstück XI* was having its first performance here. That these three composers have from the start followed a very lonely path is proof at this stage only of the startling effect of their first pieces. That this was a self-prescribed path, prescribed as a result of an intellectually keen understanding of the situation, is testified by the intellectual concentration of this music, its structure and the way it materializes in sound. Today we know more: that this path has led ever more distinctly from the realization of an idea to an individual and broadly comprehensible communication, the expression of the human, without sacrificing any of the rigour of its musical logic. And with this the label of isolation too begins—in the eyes of the public—to fade.

'This is not the place for any analysis, and neither shall we attempt to find any expression for the emotional character of this music as it speaks to us today: this would merely brand the music with a shibboleth! The main thing: it is music. We can live in the knowledge of having in the last few years lived through a chapter in the history of music. That out of the ruins of the war and post-war years life has sprouted forth—real, new, artistic life—this fact allows us to face the future with every confidence.'

Then came the first performance of *Gruppen* for three orchestras in Cologne. The notes I took of my first impressions at the time are reproduced in the chapter 'Spatial location in music'.

In 1960 Hamburg saw the first performance of *Carré*, dedicated to Herbert Hübner, the director of 'Das Neue Werk', Hamburg, who commissioned it. In addition to the impressions given in the chapter 'Spatial location in music', I noted the following: 'And again it was proved beyond doubt that Stockhausen far surpasses any other composer in West Germany today in invention, in ideas and in the organization of totally new possibilities. He conducted the forces with magisterial command, and he was supported—in quadratic (*carré*) formation, of course—by three further conductors:

Michael Gielen, Mauricio Kagel and Andrzej Markowski. The chorus and orchestra of North German Radio stuck devotedly to their task. This first performance must have been the event of the season.'

Here—with these quotations from published reviews and private notes—something thoroughly personal and subjective has been said, something about spontaneous impressions and artistic quality; the quotations are deliberately appended as giving an account of a confrontation with Stockhausen's work as a composer—a confrontation lasting some years. They should show that these impressions have chopped and changed.

The chapter 'New forms in music' substantiates in detail how Stockhausen's music, beginning with the pointillism of *Kreuzspiel* in 1951, grew out beyond this form without however wholly giving up this aspect. From one work to the next a constantly increasing variety of creative possibilities has found its way into Stockhausen's music, and a state of some rigidity in pointillist music has more and more given way to a new flow. To put it more graphically: Stockhausen's music has constantly become more like 'music'. What this music has to offer the listener could easily be outlined by emotional definitions. Although in his music Stockhausen completely renounces the dramatic as it is established in forms featuring contrast, there are in most of his pieces moments when one holds one's breath, so strong is the dynamic, volcanic, almost uncanny force. As Stockhausen says, this effect is in no way intended at such points and he himself does not know of them at the moment of writing them down, but such effects come from certain configurations that may sometimes be long, sometimes short. This takes place in a sphere which has to do neither with the clear-headed perception of musical ideas nor with quality. Thus Stockhausen is deeply convinced that his music is an untragic and undramatic music (dramatic in the sense of an expounded construction with climaxes and conflicts). His music is a form that is markedly open, has an equal distribution of potential, and is extensible at will, rather than being in the long run determined by a *'fatum'*. That there is no longer this 'fatality' in his music is inherent in its new formal principles, its mediation. 'There really are only principal matters or else nothing at all', says Stockhausen.

The path to the listener

A few words here on the participation of the listener. There are compositions that the listener knows so precisely that at every point he is already orientated to what follows. Now it is not correct, however, to claim this as a result of the 'inner logic of the work' in which everything is supposedly logical by virtue of compelling us to think in this way. To illustrate this with a comparison: If we read through a very complicated mathematical formulation and one that is simpler, then the logic of each will be equally rigorous, but we shall require more time for the more complicated one; one idea may be very much richer than another, but this alters nothing of the idea's logic. Applied to composition this means that there will be qualitative differences. There are musical ideas and possibilities for development which are by their very nature polyvalent. If there exists such polyvalence in the composition then it is no longer possible to say that one can follow the work unequivocally and exclusively at one hearing—even if one really knows it. For polyvalence is unresolvable; in other words, one can hear in different directions according to the way one is listening. The listener is the interpreter.

And here we return to the works of Stockhausen. In comparison with the composer of former times they are small in number, and this is also true in comparison with some of today's composers or with such as write a lot of 'utility music' which is aimed at immediate comprehension; theatre music too largely belongs in this category. Stockhausen writes slowly; this is not because of any lack of facility, however, but rather because much is concentrated into each of his pieces and he does not rest until he has achieved a maximum density of relationships. This can also be seen from the problems he poses himself and from the time he takes to resolve them. Moreover, the degree of complexity will be related to the possibilities of reproduction. The effect is a reciprocal one between composition on the one hand and performance on the other, covering the whole range of tape, gramophone recording and concert. His creative powers seek to concentrate themselves on the multiplicity of the given means of presentation available instead of being squandered over a multiplicity of works. Naturally it is also Stockhausen's wish that 'as many as possible' should participate in his work, but to him this does not mean the same thing as making something to suit everybody at any price. 'I must formulate my ideas, my musical conceptions, as I always have done, and then I just have to wait and see how the music goes down. And if the number of those interested is very small, then in the long run it is my personal fate to have something to say to only a small group of people. However I do not see this as any reason not to do what I have to do.' There are examples enough in history; one need only think of the singers of the Schola Cantorum, where only specialists of many years' training in this art-song could perform. People could listen, but they had not the slightest chance of singing the works themselves or of aurally checking the music. Such a stage is always reached in times of marked inventiveness or during such revolutions in musical language as disturb even its technical details. At such times the number of those who can participate directly is always notably small. Besides, the question remains open as to how many people, in percentage terms, actually listen to the radio programmes in which specialist music is performed. Again and again Stockhausen has spoken of the spontaneous response he meets with in those who participate intensively in new music, making tapes so as to be able to listen again repeatedly. Much is also due to the creation of a public. But what is this in comparison with the audience for any quiz programme or the publicity machine for light music? The number of those interested in new music is still relatively large in comparison with many specialist areas of, say, the humanities.

In the consequences that may be drawn from the ideas surrounding 'unending form' there is a fundamentally new path to the listener. Stockhausen has enlarged on this: 'A new practice of performing and listening in which each individual helps himself freely to musical works would counteract, if not altogether eliminate, the general passivity of the listener—in my opinion the chief culprit behind the schism between musical invention and participation in what is invented. Everyone would have free access to the works according to his capacities, his knowledge, his assiduity, his industry, his patience; and this access would not remain confined to the so-called élite of concert-goers and listeners to musical broadcasts who seek to subsist passively under the conditions of present methods of performance and distribution—despite the relatively few concerts containing contemporary music (in which a new work can rarely be heard more than once); and despite the very few broadcast concerts containing new works (which have to give way unprotestingly to popular relays of political debates or to boxing matches). One consequence of passivity is an increasing lack of freedom to confront new inventions and discoveries and to participate in them in the literal sense; it ends in lack of participation, indifference and finally in ignorance, an obdurate insistence on the known; it stifles the urge to follow the constantly increasing tempo of changes in the arts. The innovations in the practice of performance and listening described above would give each listener the opportunity—which would certainly be quite appropriate to the works—of taking his time, in fact of taking as much time as he needed for the personal perception of a creative work; "for things that happen must have someone to happen to, someone must stop them", Beckett writes in his book *The Unnamable*, and at another point: "For he who has once had to listen will listen always, whether he knows he will never hear anything again, or whether he does not . . . silence once broken will never again be whole." '

The specialization of musical life

The concert is a sociological problem of a special kind. It has only existed for a mere two hundred years and had its fullest impact during the nineteenth century. As it exists today it appears to be an offshoot of a certain development. The concert halls are only full when the same traditional works are always on display like museum pieces. The percentage of concert-goers is infinitesimally small compared with radio listeners; concert giving is linked with certain locations and these again in certain towns. It remains an open question whether this practice can be reborn and transformed or whether it is the manifestation of a last remnant of a given form of society. Equally it remains an open question whether the new performance practices we have been describing, particularly in the chapter 'Spatial location in music', contain in themselves any possibility for complementing or even renovating concert life. The fact is that the concert is becoming fossilized into a museum-like institution and that in contrast music is gaining more and more ground in radio broadcasts and television transmissions. On the other hand in individual works new music has become so specialized that the ideal conditions for listening are solitude, repeated hearings, in a room at home, perhaps in the smallest circle of intimate friends. Music has become so condensed that it demands room for itself. This it has through radio broadcasts, gramophone records and tape recordings. Thus all the social links of the concert hall are disappearing. This apparent disintegration is also to the good, namely in specialization, since the various institutions such as the theatre, the concert hall, radio, television, and record companies, are individually giving thought to the matter of reorganizing themselves from the bottom up. Stockhausen has never wanted to wipe out and annihilate the past, tradition. Quite apart from the emotional aspect, it will always serve to instruct. 'In order to know what we ourselves are doing we must also constantly gain some perspective from what has been done in the past, in other words, we must constantly get to know it and test it out.'

For precisely this reason Stockhausen supports the establishment of musical museums: collected repositories of works—comparable with collected editions—in different interpretations and first-class recordings; in sound archives which offer the opportunity to prepare recordings for study in listening studios and to make them available for broadcasting too. Naturally it must be insisted that these recordings are essentially to be made by highly qualified specialists. These facilities would enable us to use the past for what it is—a reservoir of experiences, of creative achievements—and as a spur to new activity. The overestimation of the historical past cripples more than it encourages. It would be impossible to risk the step forward without also being prepared to sacrifice something from the past.

Thus musical life will become more and more specialized—there can be no question about that. The question is much rather whether this will be accompanied by further automation. Are we seeing a development which will lead to the sort of specialization in the so-called cultural orchestras that has long since overtaken jazz orchestras? Musical life, musical organization and musical practice as we know them are founded on the fact that the appointed player serves with the orchestra until he has reached the age at which he is entitled to a pension. Thus the point of view from which it is organized is that of the security of the individual's existence, not the point of view of his special accomplishment. Today it already transpires that many a performance of a new work founders because the orchestra of some town refuses to do it. Only specialization will ensure a higher quality in the future; perhaps it will come about so that in one town an excellent wind ensemble is built up, in another town a string ensemble, with both groups travelling about and in certain cases coming together as a single orchestra. It is utterly wasteful for twenty or more rehearsals to be given to a work only for all the achievement to vanish with a single performance, instead of making a performance more secure by playing it repeatedly in other towns, enabling the musicians to play themselves into the work, and achieving a correspondingly good response.

All these proposals—and Stockhausen has no illusions on this score—cannot be realized overnight, and not even in a few years. Only very, very slowly will they impress themselves on public awareness. 'But that in no way prevents such ideas having to be expressed some time, for otherwise they would never come to fruition at all. It takes a very long time.' It has been said often enough in the course of the last fifteen years that something must have been amiss if in Germany concert halls were being rebuilt as if merely to restore classical–romantic concert practice, only with less stucco— but on that account for the most part with worse acoustics too.

Why ? For want of ideas or for lack of courage. The architectural appearance of concert halls is still determined by two confronting areas : the platform and the rows of seats. But already there are also conceptions which go much further, and Stockhausen is especially grateful to a number of architects for conversations and exchanges of ideas, just as he in turn has provided stimuli that are already having an influence on architects, painters and poets, choreographers and technicians.

Musical theatre

The new performing practice has thrown into the open problems which in the broader sense are associated with musical theatre and can be put to fertile use in it. The contrast between the new instrumental music and loudspeaker music extends to the visual aspect: in the former there is a completely new kind of action, in the latter complete immobility. In order to relieve this immobility Stockhausen has considered linking musical composition with visual composition. In the project for semispherical and spherical performing areas it is also arranged that optical forms can just as well move about, swooping low and allowing coloured 'sound images' to unfold. The artist's task would now be to make of this a composition, a form, which would be, in effect, new and in which experience in the cinema and in television could play a part. Until now Stockhausen has never used opera or ballet in his work, since neither of them interest him; for him the problems to be solved have been of a purely musical nature. If at first he completely excluded those areas, this was quite deliberate on his part.

In the theatre the social conditions of performing practice are particularly restrictive. Yet the new forms of music allow us to consider the inclusion of the performers' actions in the formal plans

too. Indeed, why not ? For it is a concrete consequence of composition that musicians move about while playing; thus this movement
will be endowed with an independent meaning too, it will become
emancipated. The basic tendency is to integrate into the composition every phenomenal aspect of music, everything that can be
observed by the senses. In this way one necessarily comes to the
idea of 'musical theatre'. By this Stockhausen understands both
something more and something other than what is included by the
concept as it is known in history. For him it means 'a composition
of movement which arises through the production of music and
during the production of music. This does not mean that a musician could not move if he had nothing to play. On the contrary, he
very well might move, even if not producing notes, so long as this
moment was included in the total composition.'

The first signs appear in *Kontakte*: at given times the pianist
stands up, moves to a tam-tam installed elsewhere in the area at
some distance from him, strikes it and returns again to the piano.
Then there is another passage during which percussionist and
pianist—they play at the extreme right and the extreme left respectively—go to the middle of the hall, and meet there (one of them
having arrived somewhat before the other); one of them plays the
gong, the other the tam-tam; then first the one to have arrived last
goes away again, followed by the one to have come first. At the
beginning of 1962 Stockhausen was commissioned by the National
Arts Theatre of Baden-Baden and the Civic Museum of Wiesbaden
to write some music of about 20–30 minutes' duration in connection with Oskar Schlemmer's *Triadische Ballett* and his costumes
for it, which would represent variations and moments for this piece.
The three towns of Baden-Baden, Recklinghausen and Wiesbaden
planned for 1963 an exhibition which had the working title 'Art and
the Stage'. Those responsible for the commissions had been at the
first performance in Cologne of Stockhausen's *Momente* and had
been particularly attracted by the inclusion of unusually lively
audience reactions in the composition and in the interpretation.
After some hesitation Stockhausen accepted the commission. He

composed new 'moments' and extended them as a score for solo soprano, instrumentalists and dancers, so that the composition of movement (for lighting technicians, soprano, instrumentalists and a selection of Schlemmer's figurines, each one of which was permitted only certain determined movements, speeds, intensities and durations of movement based on the construction of the 'costume') is worked out according to purely musical formal principles. Thus Stockhausen took over from Schlemmer's *Ballett* only the figurines, as 'historical costumes', for which he composed things to be played, as if they were 'historical musical instruments'. The composition of movement, too, was built up on the same basic idea, in conjunction with song, instrumental music and dancers in costume (and/or actors), and it points the way towards a new form of musical theatre. Here too—just as in performances of new spatially distributed music—the spatial proportions of the theatre are entirely obsolete. Stockhausen refers to the conceptions of new theatrical spaces which Schlemmer had already published almost forty years ago and which were simply ignored in the whole programme of post-war reconstruction of theatres and concert halls.

In October and November 1961 Stockhausen had the opportunity to perform his composition *Originale*—Musical Theatre, at the Theater am Dom in Cologne:

On entering the auditorium one finds oneself facing the open 'stage'. An open space of about 4 × 5 metres, like a platform, and on the rear wall a curtained window; from the ceiling hang an aquarium with goldfish, a cage with budgerigars, several metal mirrors, and—right at the back—a cage with two white doves. On the right near the platform the pianist David Tudor is sitting at a grand piano, and on the left stands Christoph Caskel at the percussion (both in evening dress), with a film camera and two tape recorders in front of him. At the rear of the platform stage there are chairs on which the actors from time to time take their seat. A cameraman and a lighting technician are busy with projectors, tripods and cameras, setting up props; the stage manager settles in front of the right near the platform on a raised structure like a bar stool, which is reached by a ladder; he issues orders. Stockhausen is sitting in the front row.

The playing begins without any noticeable start. Are they actually playing or just preparing? Music has started (Stockhausen's *Kontakte* for electronic sounds, piano and percussion), and the stage manager continues to give his orders. One has the impression that a tape recording or a film take is about to be made—an impression which is strengthened when after a few minutes the music breaks off. It has been recorded on tape; the tape is rewound and then played back. We hear the same music, now with the recorded voices of the stage manager, the cameraman, the sound technician and the lighting engineer. During the playback a Korean clambers up a ladder and turns over a large hour-glass filled with salt, which begins to run; he utters a brief piercing cry. A child is sitting upstage on the platform, playing with building blocks without paying the slightest heed to all that is going on around it. A lady in a coat moves from the front row of spectators onto the platform and takes articles of clothing from two boxes. She lays aside her coat—all this without the slightest contact with the public—and tries on clothes. A Japanese violinist in evening dress comes forward and then steps back again, having played a few notes.

The music has stopped altogether. Tudor and Caskel are dressing up (ceremonial robes and fencing outfit). Called upon by the stage manager, one of the actors comes forward and speaks a classical monologue. The lady and the child have disappeared from the scene. Then an actress enters and recites, apparently quite independently of her colleague. This two-part counterpoint of improvisatory speaking voices is finally augmented to five parts by the arrival of three further actors. It is everyone for himself, each playing a type, in a world which he lives and acts out. Suddenly four of the actors freeze in living tableaux and the other seems to apostrophize the audience in a harangue. Once more, this moment dissolves into rapid movements and whispered speech, then changes to cheerfulness when the door of the auditorium is flung open admitting a locally well-known woman newsvendor who offers the public the evening edition and calls out the headlines. Stockhausen stands up and conducts the actors, as he does the instrumentalists, the lighting engineers and the sound technicians.

Then comes the 'scherzo' of the evening, the entry of the Korean composer Nam June Paik—a bizarre, grotesque scene.

The tension is released: all the participants are again on the stage and are eating oranges and bananas, feeding a pet monkey, fishes and birds, and watering indoor plants. (Tudor is in oriental female costume with a mask.) Quite suddenly everything is still and quiet. Absolute calm, only the cooing of the doves. Each of the participants stares fixedly for about two minutes into the eyes of a spectator. (The public's solo, with astonishingly different reactions from one evening to the next.) Then everything is again set in motion and speech, and the music begins once more. The remnants of the fruit are swept up and the painter Mary Bauermeister prepares her scene.

Music from *Kontakte* is heard. The painter kneels in front of the easel and squirts colours onto the canvas, colours that can only reveal themselves in their iridescent beauty in the artificial light of an ultra-violet lamp. The lights go up, the picture vanishes and the easel is carried out.

The stage manager climbs off the ladder and recites from Stanislavsky. Again the actors enter, rigid as marionettes. They fall down on the stage with their heads towards the audience and read out alternate words from the newspaper. They fall silent: the poet Hans G Helms has stood up and is reciting from his work *Fa:'m Ahniesgwow*. As background music melodies are heard on musical boxes. Now the actors read from the obituary notices in the newspapers, and with darkness drawing in again they fall asleep. Mary Bauermeister has lit some sparklers.

In the silence electronic music is again heard. Suddenly a film begins. Images of machine parts flash across the screen, mixed in with close-ups of the actors. The painter blows soap bubbles over their prostrate figures. A last section of *Kontakte* then begins, and the lights go up.

Stage manager Caspari mounts the platform, cuts up a cushion and strews feathers over the sleepers.

Music. The actors rise quickly, all the participants join them, each holding a camera, and they take flashlight photographs of the audience. Bit by bit the stage empties. *Kontakte* comes to an end and Caskel (now in a red porter's jersey, top hat and ruff) reads from his calendar while playing.

Originale is a musical composition. The macrorhythm of scene continuity and the ordering of moments are musical. The individual scenes are composed musically, regardless of whether or not there is any 'music' in them. The verbal counterpoint is musical, as are the 'monodic' word melodies and the polyphony of speaking voices.

The proceedings are senseless as long as one is associating sense with causality and logic. But they stand in relationships with an overall artistic reality. Their interrelations lie between reality and non-reality, between relatedness and contrast, in quite different dimensions, together forming a new unity.

The organization of the course of events is of a dynamic and rhythmic order. It leaves a lot of scope for the actors' individual interpretations and takes into account the spectators who invariably participate with vocal interruptions. Thus each performance is a 'first performance'; the 'composition' is a show that is started afresh every evening.

The tendency seems to be towards a new form that will efface the cruder contrasts between concert hall and opera house. The articulation, the differentiation, the variation of density—all these correspond to the serialization and the interweaving of the various musical branches.

Complexity

It is a far cry today from the will to invent dramatic or lyrical constructions, far from the epic, the obtrusive, far from the narrative and documentary, from the educational, the instructive, the illusionist, the 'entertaining'; far from commercial intercourse even in the works that make use of the platform area so full of conventional and historical associations. Instead we have spiritualization, concentration, compression into the formula. These are now the horizons to which art, the artistic, the music of Stockhausen aspires. Again and again problems of this kind have been focused in individual periods of previous ages. For Webern, for instance, it was a chief problem to bring into a synthesis everything that was vertical and everything that was horizontal. A fundamental idea in music, grasped by Webern in traditional concepts of music. Beyond its purely musical aspect this means that everything is at the same time in stasis and in flux, everything is intermixed and unmixed, everything is simultaneous and successive. And in Webern's historical situation it meant an attempt to synthesize sonata and fugue; not the schemata themselves, but their intellectual principles. 'Every small creation is a moment within the great totality of creation' (Stockhausen).

Such intellectual phenomena are brought to life in the complex form of the work of art. This does not refer to the 'forces' used—the 'conscription' of three orchestras or of four orchestras and four choruses. Any concert-goer can easily confirm that the ensemble of instrumental and vocal forces in *Gruppen* or *Carré* is not only relatively small but is small indeed compared with the works for 'large forces'. A performance of the *St. Matthew Passion* or the *Missa Solemnis* in a moderately large town provides work for more people than both of these works by Stockhausen put together. The size of the forces is a decision which has to be made from one instance to the next, from one work to another. There are conceptions which demand full orchestral forces, and there are conceptions which require only one man. For this reason it is completely irrelevant to try to find in *Gruppen*'s wealth of timbres a parallel or a return to late romantic or expressionistic orchestral music of the years before 1914. The complexity is of an intellectual order. We have already spoken above of the listener's ability to follow music.* The propensity towards complexity is in part determined and influenced by the experience of musical reproduction. To the extent that we

* See pages 172 ff. (Translator's note.)

hear the works often and repeatedly, we constantly discover new connections and relationships. And when the formulation of musical ideas becomes constantly denser, constantly richer in tiny details, and constantly more complex in its relationships, it does require repeated listening. Today it already happens that judgment is pronounced on the status of a work on the basis of a single hearing. It is up to the listener to open up its complexities and to uncover its multiplicity of relationships. Naturally there are enough works of traditional music of which we can never learn everything, but most of these are constantly repeated in concert halls and on the radio and the listener's interest will tend to shift, once he knows the works, to the secondary, the subsidiary. It is for this reason that the interpreter has been able to assume the dominant position that he occupies today. Concert-goers and possessors of gramophone recordings nowadays occupy themselves less with the work than with how someone has performed, hence with the form of realization, a matter which belongs on the periphery and leads further and further away from musical ideas and towards the superficial and the unintellectual.

The question of complexity is again a question of the connections between art and life. The identity, the indissoluble unity of art with life must be accepted; and it must be realized how essential it is to bring artistic concerns into harmony with practical life. All material problems, and all economic problems, too depend on the resolution of intellectual problems, and not *vice versa*. The undervaluation of intellectual work is the greatest danger that threatens us if we give up those traditions which always take their support from an intelligentsia, submitting instead to the wishes and needs of population groups whose level of awareness is for the most part somewhat lower.

We have already spoken of the undramatic and the untragic in Stockhausen's music, to the effect that it is basically founded on technical considerations. What has been achieved is the overthrow of the dualism between static and dynamic forms. In historical terms the static side corresponds to sequential forms such as suites, variations and song forms—these are open, non-directional; the dynamic side corresponds to the developmental forms, fugue and sonata form, which are closed and directional. The multilayered thought that is so characteristic of the West is now no longer a stratification of 'parts', of the harmonic, the vertical, but a stratification of characteristics, of processes. Our thinking becomes more and more complex: one time we hear one extra layer, another time it will be a different one, just as we do in a Bach fugue, but taken a stage further; it is illusory to believe that in such complex music one could hear all the 'parts'—there can be no question of that. It is a question rather of a formal polyvalence which shimmers like the sun on the sea. The many dimensions of a Beethoven quartet or a Bach fugue cannot be replaced or 'overthrown' today by a wilful, deliberate neo-primitivism. The new forms are the forms of new thinking; new thinking is more complex and more polyvalent than ever. 'The present problem humanity has to solve is a universal problem of the intellect: to outgrow primitive controversies and to clarify our thinking through what others have thought. A mediation between extremes. A recognition of complexity. A polyphony of thought.' The conquest of space and the increasing intermixing of peoples must be paralleled by an inner process of 'mediation', 'and I am certain that if we do not mediate the dualism within ourselves, if we do not accept the complexity, and instead toy with simple solutions, then we are incapable of mastering the present with the force of intellect; and this is just what *will* bring about the great drama. It is not a matter of assimilating ourselves, but of expanding ourselves and taking in that which hitherto seemed foreign and even hostile to our conventions and our way of life.' This is as relevant for the intimate as it is for the universal problems of humanity.

The multidimensional, multilayered characteristic that is at the core of Stockhausen's thinking, is here borne by an idealistic faith. Stockhausen considers us to be at the beginning of this task. For him, the objection that we simply could not solve it does not exist at all. Finally, too, it is a concern of the generation to which Stockhausen belongs to see different phenomena connectedly from a higher point of view and to live accordingly, not denying or excluding foreign forms, so as to be as multifaceted as is at all possible. The earth is becoming more and more of a unified *Lebensraum*. Technology serves to conjoin and to combine. Serialization attempts—without levelling down—a universal mediation whilst still recognizing extremes of complexity.

Universal thinking and traditional thinking

Universal thinking should not exclude traditional thinking. We cannot do without it. But we must see what rapid steps universalization is taking. This is not least due to modern possibilities of communication. Today people the world over are concerned with Stockhausen's music.

The second half of the twentieth century is laying bare sociological problems such as have never before been manifest in the history of music. Their core is in the concept of specification. It is becoming ever clearer that the division of music into genres barely offers any further possibility of bridging the frontiers. There have been times in which music found its meaning and objective in the service of worship, and at other times art drew on elements of folk music as a binding force in the phenomenal form of contrasts. Today such bridges in individual areas of style have been completely pulled down. So one has to be satisfied with the fact that the Viennese classics with their unified vision belong in the course of events as a unique historical phenomenon, an unrepeatable melting-pot for the fusion of the highest art forms with the simplest folk elements. Serial music has a highly specialized technique of composition which, for instance, will reject 'tonal' elements from its sphere. Outside this sphere they may still have validity. This does not prevent musical listeners from penetrating into these different spheres and being able to follow each one individually.

The pages of this book should have made it increasingly clear that with his music Stockhausen consciously wishes to break through the isolation. He wants to bridge over opposites; his music is not the monologue of a solitary, content with his lot, who would both envisage and proclaim the individualistic as his objective. Stockhausen guards against the misguided imputation of esotericism which he must often meet with, but demands recognition of his intellectual and creative achievements. It is misleading to constantly measure the present against the few exemplars remaining from the past. Stockhausen has quoted Whitehead on this: 'Nothing unnerves a man more from his duties in the present than that kind of admiration which compares the greatest achievements of the past with the average failures of the present.' One should bear in mind that the number of people has increased to the nth degree, but creative powers have by no means grown proportionately. No collectivity and no automaton can ever replace creative power.

Looking at things in all these aspects, let us once again say something about their relationship to the past.

Stockhausen has remarked: 'What it comes down to is the musical idea, and that idea must become clear.' The 'original' sound of traditional music cannot in any event be reconstructed, and in the work of, say, the Cappella Coloniensis, Stockhausen sees an interesting hobby, an attempt to give us an idea of tradition. 'But,' he continues, 'none of the essentially musical ideas of this time would be lost if we played this music with modern instruments.' Only in the realm of electronic music does he consider colour and its reproduction as of critical importance; previously no-one at all had thought in absolute terms of timbre. Stockhausen pursues his logic so far as to say that for him the ideas of Beethoven in a string quartet are not even 'lost' if it is realized not on strings but with four other timbres—for instance, electronically. We do not know Beethoven's conceptions, 'but what I do know are my ideas about Beethoven. I think through Beethoven's music when I hear it and what he may have thought I cannot know.'

It is not Stockhausen's intention to denigrate the value of works of the past when he maintains that, particularly in the baroque era, in classical and romantic times, there were much greater possibilities of working from the standpoint of a certain routine, known as *métier*: a facile hand, and an academic training in forms of melodic, harmonic and rhythmic articulation. One recognizes the genius of the great composer less by his 'craft' than by the precision and novelty of his utterance, and by the surprising concision and the individual imprint of its continuity. The older technique of composition can be described as 'working with familiar objects': a theme is invented or adopted, and expounded, worked out, combined, placed in new contexts: shapes are shown in a new light. In the new music of which we are speaking here, the reverse is true: in a composition new shapes are constantly created, new constellations and figures with a relatedness established by a force that takes both fundamental and simultaneous effect upon the shapes. The old motivic–thematic composition has given way to a composition that grasps as a formal criterion that which is essentially binding— what makes up the essence of a theme—which may be flowing, smooth, perforated, broken up, or abrupt, and which, whenever it appears, elicits a new manner of playing. The elements of the language of the Viennese classics were a material that was already preformulated.

Today we find ourselves in a wholly different situation. It is a question of the spiritualization of the totality of artistic production. The problems which are raised in composition are not solely confined to music. Ideas about organization extend further when Stockhausen sets about giving plastic reality to a philosophical idea, a scientific idea, an observation or a discovery in the form of a work of art. Not all ideas can be given form with results of a musical kind. The musician proves his mettle in his capacity for thinking things out in musical categories, finding formulae that will clarify intellectual connections in relationships of musical organization. Here we may think of the example of *Zyklus*, which mediates between the static and the dynamic and as a synthesis of open and closed form. Such ideas, which are universal, stimulate Stockhausen to composition. This leads to works of the greatest complexity. The more universal the ideas, the more stimulating—if seen broadly— does the work become for the reflective listener. A formula that is applicable to life emerges from the work. Thus Stockhausen is constantly in search of a new form. No form can be repeated. The different forms described in detail in the chapter 'New forms in music' are no mere schemata, but modes of formulating and types of formulation.

At this stage Stockhausen retrospectively evaluates the traditional forms as being of exclusively historical interest. Sonata form, as a formal development, is representative of a closed epoch. It was the culmination of the forms perfected in the classical period, forms born of dualistic thinking. 'Anyone still using this formal concept today is enlisting a corpse. He is trying to recapture a time and an intellectual situation that have expired.'

To recapitulate: Serial form means equal participation of all the elements and mediation between extreme opposites. And these are the ideas of our century, not to be denied: open-ended conception; the dissolution of the hierarchy of the ruling and the subordinate. In serial thinking the mere contrasting of different characteristics is superseded by the relatedness of all to all. The stratification of the characteristics of an aesthetic image is typical of modern thinking. In the course of a chosen form every characteristic can come into contact with every other. A fundamental idea in working with series is mediation, hence also the mediation between characteristics. Stockhausen sees works in several movements as representing an obsolete form. If one is thinking in a logical manner there is always only one work: a single work in which the perspectives of feeling and with them too the perspectives of compositional technique and methodology constantly and unpredictably change. The essential is that things should be related, not just presented or juxtaposed.

Invention and discovery

In observing these relationships one distinction Stockhausen met with has proved to be very fruitful, namely that between invention and discovery. He explains:

'Invention stresses finding one's way; one thinks for so long about a problem until one has found out the best form from many

conceivable solutions (and so one says that the invented form is the
solution for which one has been searching). On the other hand one
may also conduct experiments and researches and come upon a
form, find it, in this way. If I call the first an invention, then I can
describe the second as a finding; but in place of the word "finding"
I choose the word "discovery" so as to indicate that here one un-
covers something that was previously hidden.

'Invention and discovery are concepts associated with time: the
invented was not previously present; the discovered was previously
present but unknown.

'Invention proceeds from the conception of a formal problem
from which is deduced the intended selection of elements and the
formulation of principles of combination—so-called rules; the resulting form is thought out, planned and systematically established.
Thus invention can be represented as a deductive method of composition: the composer envisages a form which is to fulfil quite
definite conditions that he has laid down (and from which he then
deduces all the particulars).

'Discovery, on the other hand, proceeds from an indefinite
formal expectation, in which one will playfully combine elements
and gropingly deliver oneself over to chance: everything possible is
tried in the effort to find everything; the corresponding form is
established unexpectedly and empirically. Formal discovery can
therefore be described as an inductive method of composition: the
composer conquers and explores a form which is unknown to him
and which he has happened upon by chance. Most discoveries are
made in attempts to invent something quite definite that has previously been theoretically formulated in a working project; in seemingly accidental happenings (and not least in "mistakes" in the
working out of one's ideas) completely new forms are discovered.

'Invention and discovery have a common goal: the will to give
form to material. This will is expressed in the composition: the
composer presents, in other words, he writes down and/or realizes
in sound, forms both invented and discovered.

'I would not describe invention as conscious and discovery as unconscious composition, as often happens; rather I proceed from the fact that both arrive at conscious presentation and perception through the stages of the unconscious mind. Thus discovery can be quite as conscious as invention; the difference lies in the fact that the goal of conscious work in invention is more the work to be presented, and in discovery it is more its workings.

'Invention and discovery are modes of creation: they bear forth new forms. Even if with different composers, or with a single composer at different times, the one or the other seems to predominate, they still complement each other, and in particularly fortunate cases both are combined in equal measure. No matter how high the degree of consciousness there may be in composing, the perception of a form once presented must be conscious and systematic. Formal creation is only complete when it is precisely perceived.

'What happens in creative labour—the invention and discovery of forms—is repeated in the listener's perception. In listening to a given piece of music the *invention* of form means thinking out a form (or forms), conceiving forms, "giving form" to the music heard. Indeed such formal invention is stimulated and opened up by the music; but in this case it cannot be a matter of a single form which would be the same for all listeners; for formal invention assuredly creates new forms. I would call this "creative listening" (rather than "re-creative"), since the listener, in perceiving what is heard, will invent his own new forms while relating what he hears to the whole of his mental landscape and producing conceptual forms by the strength of his imagination (thus not passively allowing music to happen to him and merely seeking to follow it, to become acquainted with what in his opinion is already present and "only has to be transmitted"). In this case, "precise perception" refers to the act of mentally bringing together in a single form all the ideas that come to one in listening, without omitting a single one: it means the most intense concentration possible. In listening to a given piece of music the *discovery* of form means coming upon a form (or forms) of which one had no suspicion as a listener, and which had lain outside one's own conceptual field. This demands an open and alert attentiveness for the unexpected, and the capacity for accepting things of an alien nature which one has not invented oneself (or "thought into the music", as one might say). As soon as one excludes from the outset that "which does not suit one", that which seems to one "strange", "unattractive" or "repellent", then one is a poor discoverer. In listening, the discovery of forms—in contrast to the invention of forms—demands prolonged encounters and intensive study. Here it is equally true—keeping in sight the genuine perception of form—that formal creation is only complete when it is perceived both consciously and as precisely as possible. In this case, "precise perception" means the exploration of all the details of a work and seeing them in relation to works that are already familiar.'

Historical foundations

It is right and proper that to serve our understanding of the present should be seen as the ultimate and highest goal of historical research, illuminating the present through the past and exposing possible points of reference. How can we use our historical knowledge to explain the situation of new music, its stylistic and aesthetic manifestations since 1950, the work of Stockhausen ? Does our study of history offer us a hand-hold; does it hold any sign of a bridge for our understanding ?

In the last ten years it has been affirmed on a number of occasions that around 1950 there began a new epoch in the history of music; one might say that this claim has already become something of a commonplace. Yet so far no extensive foundation and fundamental groundwork has been laid, no basis for this utterance, which itself is more of a hunch than a perception. To be regarded as such, a 'new epoch' must necessarily be distinguishable from previous times by something decisively 'new', but for this phenomenon to be recognized there must first be clarity about what can be taken as characteristic of 'previous times'.

In a comprehensive work that appeared under the title *The Age of Thematic Processes in the History of Music* I was concerned to demonstrate the general thesis that is central to the understanding of music of the period between about 1700 and about 1950. My investigations show that the common denominators are the musical shape called the 'theme' and the process of thematic development. This factor unites even forms of language that are as far removed from each other in their harmonic guise as those of the major-minor period, the age of free atonality (between 1909 and 1923) and that of twelve-note music (after 1924, and partly surviving today). What is essentially new since 1949 is the renunciation of the traditional concept of the theme.

From its Latin root, the word 'process' takes its suggestion of a movement which progresses in a planned fashion towards a goal, thereby producing changes; it is a movement associated with direction, wreaking transformations at each step. The prefix *pro* in the verb *procedere* encompasses the idea of having one's sights set on something, directedness, intention and the will to alteration and transformation, always in respect of the new, the next step. In *procedere*, and likewise in process phenomena, there is a dynamism, the will to development, with a steady end in view, with one's sights set on a new form, a new world rising above the old.

The material in which these process phenomena are reflected in music is the theme. In the period of thematic processes the essence of the theme must be grasped by understanding the process and conversely the phenomenon of the process by understanding the theme. The theme is the material that is capable of forming and of being formed—forming in the way that the great classicist Goethe commanded: 'Artist, give form.' Until very recent times it has not been fully recognized that the concept of the theme can be defined only be reference to process phenomena and then only if these are constantly in view. A definition might be essayed as follows: Each theme is an entelechy that must by definition hold in its individual sections the potential for its own development. The forces that the process-like phenomena release and in this way propel to the fore are primarily of an intellectual kind, rather than of an emotional character.

The concept of progression must be seen as a concomitant of the concept of the thematic process. And this enables us to see the difference that exists between a simple phenomenon and a process. The phenomenon does not tend towards anything, it is not determinate, but is a mere passage of events, of time; whereas among the determinant factors in the classical process will be a target, a teleological impetus, a determination, a final step and a final objective. Thus a final destination and a conclusive character are always proper to the great works of the period of thematic processes. They find their most remarkable expression in certain works for the stage, as in Mozart's *Magic Flute*, Beethoven's *Fidelio*, Weber's *Freischütz* and the works of Richard Wagner; they are correspondingly to be found in the symphony, in, say, Beethoven's Third, Fifth and Ninth Symphonies, Schumann's Fourth Symphony, the First Symphony of Brahms, Mahler's *Resurrection* Symphony, and Tchaikovsky's last three symphonies, to cite only the best known examples.

Works of this kind are witness to an evolutionary image of the world, defined by a specific beginning and reaching a predestined, foreseeable end. This view is the Western, historical view, bearing the imprint of Christian revelation and theology. The 'world' is defined on the one hand by the beginning, the creation, and on the other hand by the end, 'the end of time'. Between the two points marking the beginning and the end lies the process of creation.

The essence of the thematic processes of the period between 1700 and 1950 must first be recognized before one can judge how strongly and decisively Stockhausen's conception of processes, which we have already extensively discussed, stands out against them. In Stockhausen, processes are not determinate; they do not progress to a final goal that would coincide with the finish, the end, of one of his conceptions; moreover they are not associated with themes.

For the period of compositional invention associated with the theme came to an end in about 1950. In place of the theme there now appear new musical shapes, whose properties, inasfar as we can yet say anything conclusive about them today, have been the consistent concern of the present book. Thus it represents an attempt to systematically sketch out for the first time the new features of music since 1950.

Let us now take an example of a special historical question: Is there a connection between *Zyklus* for solo percussionist and the historical past? To establish connections here requires us to broaden our canvas still further.

The concept of the rhythmic series first made itself felt during the twentieth century in minds that were preoccupied with history, particularly when they encountered rhythmic series in late medieval music in the context of the isorhythmic motet; it again made itself felt when rhythmic rows transmigrated into more recent music, as in that of Alban Berg (*Lulu*) and above all in the piano study *Mode de valeurs et d'intensités* by Olivier Messiaen (1949); and finally it made itself felt when the Indian *raga* became more familiar in the West.

To clarify the concept I would distinguish between a thematic–rhythmic mode and the emancipated rhythmic mode. The concept of the mode is here used in exactly the sense in which it is understood for pitch modes too (Gregorian modes, Indian modes, modes in folk music, etc.). The final historical outcome of the concept of the mode was that of the series. It was a condition of this that melodic modes, rhythmic modes and subsequently timbre modes were all emancipated from strictly motivic–thematic associations. This process of emancipation can be traced through history, and only today, after the development since 1950 of a non-thematic music following the emancipation of the serial parameters, are we clearly aware of it.

One sort of thematic rhythm, for instance, is the dotted rhythm that characterizes the introductory *grave* section of the French overture. Since dotted rhythms often return as a type it is justifiable to speak of them as constituting a rhythmic mode. The *locus classicus* of the thematic rhythm is the dominating rhythm of Beethoven's Fifth Symphony; differences of pitch often appear only of secondary importance during the course of this work, while the primary importance belongs to the characteristic rhythmic shape in which we recognize the properties of a rhythmic–thematic model. The significance of such rhythmic modes in thematic writing and the part they might play in constructing whole movements had already been recognized before Beethoven by Haydn and Mozart, and details of their technique show how superb was their mastery in this field.

The first example of purely percussive composition, in other words of music without fixed pitch relationships performed entirely on percussion instruments of indeterminate pitch, is to be found in the transitions from the second to the third and from the third to the fourth scenes of *Das Rheingold* by Richard Wagner. The 'notes' here approximate to the note F and should be heard in four different registers. The rhythmic motive, the so-called 'smith motive', is simply a 'note'-repetition. It is already familiar to the ear from the second scene of the opera as an individual melodic-rhythmic motive with associated pitches. What then happens in the two interludes is a reduction to rhythm. The rhythmic sequence is a thematic-rhythmic shape. An earlier example of similar rhythmic emancipation is the famous opening motive of the first movement of Beethoven's Fifth Symphony. At the beginning it appears as a major third then as a minor third. The intervallic step frequently changes, generally in accordance with the harmonic context. At certain places the motive appears simply as a note-repetition, but its connection with a melodic differentiation of notes stays in the mind. The motive is a thematic-rhythmic mode.

The other route leading towards the rhythmic series is that of abstracting it from any melodic association in the first place. Here too there is an example in the music of *The Ring of the Nibelungs*. At the beginning of the second scene of *Das Rheingold* is heard a Valhalla (or Wotan) motive, and the motive is conjoined with a kind of signal which is pure note-repetition. This rhythmic sequence appears throughout the whole of the *Ring*, heralding the emancipation of the rhythmic series.

The percussion writing in Wagner's *Das Rheingold* is only a 'conditioned' abstraction, since the rhythm that the anvils play as the so-called 'smith motive' has already imprinted itself on the ear in the second scene in conjunction with pitches and text. The first to take the final step in the emancipation of the rhythmic was Darius Milhaud. The relevant passages are to be found in Milhaud's opus 25, the score of *Les Choéphores*—the central section of the *Oresteia* of Aeschylus—written in 1915. Milhaud's percussion passages comprise a group of strictly developed rhythmic themes in polyphonically conceived writing. The single rhythms are individual themes, their character being produced not least by the instrument they are played on, its relative flexibility, the brightness or darkness of its timbre. The writing is structured entirely in traditional metres; the movement is in bars of $\frac{4}{4}$ or $\frac{6}{8}$ time which, once set in motion, are never altered by any changes of time-signature.

Quite independently of Milhaud, the Italian futurist Luigi Russolo in 1913 took the step of abandoning the traditional theme and the thematic principle by composing sequences of noise-like sounds for instruments he himself had constructed for the purpose (*intonarumori*, or 'makers of noises'). Here what it actually amounted to was the overthrow of all thematic shape. In Russolo the music is still always metrically notated (the score, of which only the first two pages have been preserved, prescribes $\frac{3}{4}$ bars to begin with), but at the same time the listener cannot become aware of the metre, because in this music there are no longer strong and weak beats, and the characteristics of the traditional rhythmic motive—memorability, obtrusiveness, vitality—appear to be completely lacking; great numbers of individual sounds are run together in the manner of *glissandi*.

Milhaud (1915) and Russolo (1913) had taken the first steps along two paths which were later to be further explored.

The path on which Milhaud had struck out was primarily continued by Edgard Varèse, who also proceeded to cut out the human voice from his work. The work of historic importance here is called *Ionisation* and was composed between 1929 and 1931. It requires thirteen performers who play a total of 37 percussion instruments; in addition to these, two sirens and, in the last seventeen bars, bells, glockenspiel and piano are also included; thus only towards the end are instruments of fixed pitch used. Varèse's *Ionisation* is the precedent for every percussion work that has since followed. Looking at this score, one quickly recognizes that Varèse concentrates on rhythm as a vehicle of expression. The rhythms that are heard are almost throughout abstractions in that they have seceded from the dominion of the melodic, having no pitch outline. But they are still melodic motives reduced to rhythm, and are developed individually according to traditional principles. The thematic process, as it has governed music since the late baroque era, is here simply confined to the rhythmic. Correspondingly, as a composition, *Ionisation* can also be understood formally in traditional terms as a kind of sonata movement.

Stockhausen composed his *Zyklus* for one percussionist in 1959. He wrote a text about the composition which is published in *Aufsätze* (Cologne 1964, Volume 2: *Texts on my own works, on the art of others, and documents*) under the title '*Zyklus* for one percussionist— explanation of the score'. This is indeed merely an explanation of the score, and in no sense is an introduction to the music in historical or aesthetic terms. In an extremely systematic way, Stockhausen voluntarily confined himself to what a single player can do, and continued in the direction travelled by Varèse by taking as his point of departure melodic shapes from which the pitch is subtracted and allotting the rhythmic language (melody) to the percussion. The result is that by applying entirely new formal principles he has created a variety of rhythmic gestures and expressive possibilities that can never fail to astonish.

The total emancipation of the melodic through a single-minded concentration on the rhythmic is unquestionably a mighty turning-point in the history of Western music. In the scope of its significance it is perhaps best grasped through a comparison, however questionable such parallels might be. If one thinks of painting, putting the realistic depiction of an object as an image by means of representation in the same category as that to which in traditional music the theme or motive associated with melodic elements would belong, then the emancipation of melody, of rhythm, of dynamics, and of timbre is a phenomenon which parallels the transition from representational to non-representational painting.

Had the ideas of the Futurists and their upshot in the construction of instruments and in Russolo's scores really been forgotten already when, in the middle of the century, the composition of noise-sounds became a significant stylistic accessory of New Music ? It is a question that at present we cannot yet answer. Which composer—in around 1950—was the first to use clusters in instrumental compositions and to shift material about in a *glissando*-like way ? Was he familiar with the corresponding concepts in sound and the piano compositions of Henry Cowell, or with the sound-world of the Theremin instrument which produced the sort of electronic music that could be heard shortly before 1950 ?

Evidently two different paths were taken towards the realm of noise. The first impetus was sparked off by the Futurists—before 1914. Those first twenty years also saw the corresponding compositions with tone clusters by Cowell, who in 1912 appeared for the first time in San Francisco to demonstrate new techniques of his own for playing the piano (tone clusters) in which the piano is also played with the forearm, elbows and fist; this resulted in aggregations built up of minor and major seconds. At the end of the 'twenties Leon Theremin toured Europe and America with the electronic instrument that bears his name.

The second impetus began in around 1950. To all appearances the electronic music that had come into being at the start of the 'fifties and the sounds of *musique concrète* soon led instrumental music along tracks similar to those it had taken about forty years previously.

The first example in instrumental music of the texturally composed cluster that is moved in a *glissando* is to be found in Stockhausen's *Gruppen*, an immediate development from his *Studie II*. Whether compositions such as the orchestral work *Metastasis* by the Greek composer Yannis Xenakis (first performed in Donaueschingen in 1955) stand in direct relation to the Stockhausen work remains an open question. What is more certain is that Ligeti wrote those works of his which rest entirely on the effect of cluster phenomena after studying the score of *Gruppen*, and that Penderecki composed his own similar works after the first performance in Hamburg of *Carré*, which exhibits a great variety of textual examples of cluster effects. The effect of the cluster is in fact noise-like. It consists of heaps of notes, bands of frequencies, making it impossible for the listener to analyze the individual components of the sound. In the true sense of the term, clusters are composed sounds.

This is exactly how they are to be achieved. The effect of the sound complex lies in each of its frequency bands, in its dynamic profile, in its internal colouration and in its duration. This is why the frequency width of such aggregates is exactly laid down in scores; the same goes for the density (semitones, microtones) within the band width, and equally for the opening and closing pitch registers. The musical phenomena strike the listener through their changes of co-ordinated contrasts, which can be heard to complement each other. Stockhausen has often spoken of the inherent time of sounds. Here there comes into effect a new time-space feeling such as is no longer comprehensible in terms of the conceptions and measurements of conventional metre. And the traditional theme has been left behind *en route*.

The great change of around 1950 can also be understood from the point of view of form. Every musical composition is the outcome of a reciprocal working of centripetal and centrifugal forces whereby, in a single work of art, in different epochs, and even in the personality of a single composer, the one or the other direction of force will alternately predominate and subside. Centrifugal forces create forms whose individual sections pull away from each other. The effect of the force is diffusive; the sections will be at variance, they will push out into further expanses, they will be explosive, they will have no common denominator, they will form contrasts, and these contrasts will not be balanced by any concern for counterpoise or by correspondences. On the other hand centripetal forces bind together; they will strive towards a mean, even if this is frequently no more than imaginary, they will unify, their effect will be one of balance. The musical forms that are constructed from centripetal forces are related to a central point. This alignment round a centre will exist in the form of bilateral symmetries only in very specially laid out examples.

There can be no question that the period of thematic processes primarily built up forms related to a central point, and in fact one of the greatest achievements of the period was precisely this. Centripetal forces produce balancing forms, whereas centrifugal forces produce moment forms. The formulation of the concept of moment form in connection with a very definite conception of form can certainly be attributed in the first place to Stockhausen. Any formal unit that can be recognized by a personal and unalterable characteristic he calls a 'moment'. A 'moment group' will refer to several consecutive moments that are related to one another by one or more characteristics without their personal identity being put in question. The logical consequence of this is the concept of open forms, or else forms that may be designated as endless—forms that have always already started and can always continue further. By definition such forms reject a single relationship to a central point. Stockhausen's *Momente* refers to the concept of moment form in its very title, and aptly so, for *Momente* is 'not a closed work with unequivocally fixed beginning, formal agenda and ending, but a polyvalent composition of independent events.' Another consequence of the effects of predominantly centrifugal forces can be seen when the interpreter by his own free selection—hence also by chance—can permutate individual sections of a composition.

In Stockhausen's works of the most recent years, however, one feels there is a tendency to bring centripetal and centrifugal forces into a synthesis by means of concentrating on a number of centres in a single form, to create multipolar processes. Before anything conclusive can be said about this we must wait a while and observe how the development of such forms proceeds.

A musician's philosophy

Stockhausen is one of those artistically creative personalities for whom composing is not the sole expression of their creative being, but for whom the spoken and the written word is also a helpful and indispensable form of self-expression. Stockhausen's words constantly affirm that for him artistic creation is a way of understanding himself in the world. And many of his lectures are marked by an urge to help the listener to understand not him, the composer, but his music, so as to find in it ways and means of achieving a transcendental awareness reaching beyond himself as a person and his human existence, an awareness which is not depersonalized but which attains the suprapersonal by way of the person.

It is possible that with some of the composers of previous times too this double activity of composing and writing—whether poetry or theoretical description—was not founded simply on a duality of talents but was an extremely fundamental inner necessity, a principle of self-knowledge, the better to understand oneself. Guillaume de Machaut was a poet-composer, Jean-Philippe Rameau a composer and theoretician, and in Wagner was to be found the most sovereign abundance of combined talents. Even though today we accord Wagner the highest respect only as a composer, yet this personality can at the same time be equally understood as a dramatist, in his verbal works of art, and as an essayist, in his writings on aesthetic theory; meanwhile one should not fall into the trap of measuring Wagner's music against the yardstick of his own aesthetic theories.

Many of Stockhausen's utterances are perceptions about himself and, as such, are indispensable to him; the urge to inform is something he shares with many musicians of earlier times, and equally with such of his own generation as Pierre Boulez. To try to reduce Stockhausen's labours solely to theoretical comments on his own composing is just as unreasonable as reproaching him on the ground that he should leave philosophizing to the philosophers. Composers who have ventured into the field of aesthetics and philosophy of art have frequently offered nothing but extremely stimulating aphorisms or peripheral comments of a subjective kind about the position of their own works. This kind of writing will quite simply block the musician's path towards the systematic and towards any self-contained edifice of philosophical doctrine, but this is not so when it is a matter of musical theory. Stockhausen's lectures and literary works are in many ways a source of irritation about which there are conflicting opinions. But this does not alter the fact that he has always tried to grasp problems of composition and of listening at their roots; wherever he has gone too far in his pressure to systematize and to unify essential matters of aesthetics, he has always corrected himself in his own works of art.

Whoever knows how to follow what Stockhausen has written will again and again discover one fundamental note, a motto, a deep-rooted basis: contemplation, meditation on the place of man in the world and in the cosmos. In the long run these are all religious bases. It will be from a later standpoint that some generation to come will one day reconstruct what intellectual influences Stockhausen has undergone, taken up and developed during his life, and what readings have been decisive for him. One such influence is already apparent today: in recent years Stockhausen has undergone something of an intellectual reorientation; his thinking and feeling have been deeply influenced by stimuli from Far Eastern and especially Indian religions. What seems to me particularly revealing in this respect is the text that Stockhausen published under the title 'Momente 1965' (it is reproduced in the present book in the chapter 'Notes on the works'). Here Stockhausen has said more about himself than in any previous publication, as far as subjective thoughts about himself are concerned. Having been acquainted with his creative work right from the start, it had already long seemed to me certain that one day Stockhausen would come across the worldly wisdom of the Indians and their way of life; for me this became an absolute and predictable certainty on encountering *Carré* for four orchestras and choruses, in which there appeared for the first time a way of articulating spaces and times in sound that had never before been heard in Western music. Here there is an obvious suggestion of an experience, an inner vision, of humanity as much as of art, which reaches out beyond the familiar and confined convention of Western categories of time and space. If in 1960 Stockhausen reported that he had 'found, experienced and gradually allowed *Carré* to take shape in hour-long flights that I had to make daily over America for six weeks', these exalted open spaces of experience are a first retreat from the temporality that consists in an earthbound connexivity of time. Here above the clouds, as Stockhausen says, he 'experienced the slowest transformation times and the broadest spaces.'

As a historian I am reminded of a parallel case from the 19th century: how could Richard Wagner, at the end of his opera *Tristan und Isolde*, have found and represented in his music the vibrations of the universe without an intuitive knowledge of what the Indian philosophers have to say about man and the cosmos and man's place in the cosmos ?

Two of Stockhausen's most recent literary publications may be drawn on to show still more clearly what is meant here. One is a comment on a question put by the *Journal Musical Français* on 15 May 1968, the other a letter of 15 June 1968 to the editor of the journal *Art International* (Lugano) in which Stockhausen comments on an essay 'The Waning of the Visual' by Harley Parker. The following extracts are quoted from these two writings, the first being from the 'open letter to youth':

'There was once a time when consciousness became so strong in certain animals that they finally became men. Now we are in a time when in certain men heightened consciousness is becoming so strong that they are approaching a higher form of life. Here on this earth. At the present time only a few will achieve this. But in every man the compulsion is more or less strong to overcome himself and acquire a heightened consciousness. Hence the crises that we are experiencing throughout the world and whose nadir is still imminent during this century. Everywhere in the world is felt the oppression, the panic, the feeling that something is impending that can only be compared to the first appearance of plant life amidst lifeless material, to the first appearance of an animal in the world of plants, and to the first appearance of man among the realm of the animals: a new step in the acquisition of consciousness. No matter how strong the desire in men for the next higher step of being, his terror and his resistance towards opening himself to this consciousness are just as violent. Single individuals, groups, parties and peoples believe that they have the supremacy and the right to suppress and literally feed on others. For we are unequal as far as intelligence and power are concerned, and we know that only individuals, out of their own inner resources, can achieve freedom and superconsciousness—just as only individual animals were able to attain the status of man.

'One can only become a higher man through conquering one's egocentricity and one's fear of losing one's way.

'Let us not try to erect new systems against the systems we want to do away with—because they are too narrow and tend to exclude, suppress and efface too much alien thinking. Our conception must be so broad that we see ourselves and the whole world from above, letting the old systems play themselves out, and neither continuing them nor adding any new ones that would have the exigencies of exclusivity.

'Systems are products of the reason that our forebears made the sole ruler of the body; in this way the soul became its own prisoner by giving all the supremacy to its former servant, reason. Let us realize that reason, if it is not constantly fed through the inspiration of the suprarational, is always recombining everything it has accumulated and that at any time it can assert anything it likes and the opposite both at once. One can use it for *everything*; it can represent every possible opinion, it can justify, support, refute, and so on, everything. And unless one learns to switch it on and off one simply raves on endlessly. It is just a useful instrument, no more, no less: a model computer. But WHO is using it? and for WHAT?

'It is the super-ego that should provide it with something to think about, and the super-ego gets its conception from the intuitive consciousness which it gets in turn from a higher consciousness

—that highest consciousness which conjoins every individual in a transcendental cosmic consciousness.

'Why am I saying things like this when I am in fact a musician and not a philosopher, nor anyone of that ilk? Because as far as possible we musicians should live entirely by intuition. Because I have learnt that everything new begins when one desires this consciousness and aspires to rise higher and higher. It is only secondarily that one is a musician, a specialist, a man with a profession. In the first place one is an individual spirit who must first identify with the universal spirit before he tries to impart to other spirits anything essential, anything that goes beyond the individual and is of some concern to every other spirit.'

Stockhausen then goes further into particulars and says that music should be 'above all the conversion into sound of a stream of cosmic electricity through heightened consciousness'. And he infers the following very definite demands for the musician:

'Those who wish to be musicians, following their higher voice, must begin with the simplest exercises of meditation, at first just for oneself: "Play a note with the certainty that you have as much time and space as you want", and so on. In the first place, however, they must acquire an awareness about what they are living for, what we are all living for: to achieve a higher life and to let the vibrations of the universe penetrate into our individual human existence. And musicians must prepare the future for the higher men still hidden within us: to set in vibration the whole body down to its smallest components in such a way that it becomes totally relaxed and receptive to the vibrations of the highest consciousness.'

These words are quoted from a call to youth. And the same letter ends in a special tone of exhortation:

'Great power is given to us musicians: our notes can kindle in other men the fires of longing to rise higher above themselves. Let us not abuse this power! It is not simply that the individual musician will vibrate in the height of heights; what matters is that the field of vibration around him will become so strong, so supercharged, that anyone entering this field will vibrate in sympathy.'

In his contribution to *Art International*, Stockhausen addresses himself directly to composers. Here he says:

'What then is to be done? In the first place make as many "works" as possible which will *at all times* remain open to the direct reception of the vibrations of the superconsciousness that are always "in the air". Hence, present as few objects as possible that congeal and freeze what has become consciously known and thus isolate it from the process of the *constant growth of consciousness*. This is of course not easy, since it is only with difficulty that we can part with our instrumental resources and our preference for "hard" material, and since the frozen art object is still generally regarded as the one worth striving for because it is that most fundamentally adapted to the acquisitive instinct.

'The artist must thus plan processes for the participation of practicians and mediums who can handle temporarily intractable instruments and fixed materials and can always connect them up to the stream of universal electricity. If in a process "finally" fixed objects are offered then they should be opened up, commented on, set in mid-stream, used as air-craft.*

'The hectic search for "total art works" is to be becalmed. It must become increasingly clear that one can set in vibration the whole of that consciousness which is our common deepest root through any region of vibration—acoustical, optical, tactile, and so on—provided one fulfils the higher proviso that every artistic enterprise should be linked up to the universal stream which must be allowed to flow through it so that the artist himself is no more than a mouthpiece, as purely tuned as possible, transferring the vibrations passing through him to the practising mediums, to the instruments, to the material and to everything that comes into the field of vibration.

'No matter how "unthinkable" these works may sound, they come neither from the subconscious nor from the rational, but from experiencing a progressively intuitive and superconscious activity.'

* Cf. 'winged vehicle' in the note on *Stimmung* (p. 67). (Translator's note.)

In order to be able to follow Stockhausen, a high degree of spiritual practice is here required of the reader, for basically speech is powerless to tell everything. Man thinks and is at the same time a thought, a manifestation of divine energy. In the face of absolute truth human language is useless. What remains open is the path of art and hence of music, for art is a path to the truth and to self-realization. This is as valid for the artist as it is for the spectator and the listener.

Stockhausen as innovator

If, as we have already said, the present is necessarily to be under-stood from the past, then the broader context to which Stock-hausen's work stands related in our time will be unfurled if we reconsider the point that I might here call the year dot—'dot' because this marks the beginning of a new epoch. The year dot is the ulti-mate end of the period of thematic processes. After numerous previous situations which were gradually pushing forward to this final point, the moment was reached when two styles came to their culmination. The one was that of the late Webern, no longer work-ing with themes but now only with the crystallization of musical ideas from intervallic centres. The other reached a peak in the piano study *Mode de valeurs et d'intensités* by Olivier Messiaen, where the logical pursuance of modes that have been strictly determined in advance embraces a totality of parameters—pitches, metre, dynam-ics and modes of attack. This piano composition is the first piece to have been written in the pointillist style. Its continuing influence on Stockhausen, Boulez and many others, especially among Messiaen's pupils, is well known.

If Webern and Messiaen had brought about the complete atom-ization of what had long been understood as the theme, the first—and already historic—achievement to Stockhausen's credit (and alongside his name we should cite some of the other young composers of the time too) is that of a new synoptical view. In place of the note–point in pointillist music there appeared the concept of the group. Stockhausen's two most important works in this connection are *Zeitmasze* for five woodwind players and *Gruppen* for three orchestras, two works written between 1955 and 1957.

In 1953 in Cologne, Stockhausen began his systematic technical work with electronic acoustical means and his artistic exploration of them. In 1953/54 came *Studie I* and *Studie II*, and *Gesang der Jünglinge* followed in 1956. Not only chronologically, but also from the composer's point of view, the shape of things was now already clear: 'We are no longer to think in terms of instrumental music *or* electronic music, but of instrumental music *and* electronic music. Each of these realms of sound has its own conditions and its own limitations.' Unlike many others, Stockhausen was always the very man not to have turned instrumental resources to the imitation of the electronic sound world.

As a by-product of electronic music, new spatial principles were found and transferred into the instrumental realm; thereby the theme of music and space acquired completely new possibilities founded on the principles of composition themselves and on specific ways of writing. The new ideas whose subsequent appearance in *Gruppen* for three orchestras and in *Carré* for four orchestras and choruses had all the logic of necessity are pursued in these two works in an aesthetically viable way; meanwhile countless imitators have taken them over.

An epoch-making breakthrough then followed: the reordering of the concept of time in music, in the first instance through electronics. The essential lay in the abandonment of the conventionally conceived conjugations of metre and rhythm in music. The revelation of the possibilities of electronics in composition necessarily brought with it the radical abolition of slavery to the bar-line and to the human heart-beat, and with it the discovery of whole new time-spaces for music; the basic unit for the musical experiencing of time, inculcated of old, was removed in favour of an oscillation and suspension produced by the inherent times of sounds. As early as 1954, in *Klavierstück VI*, the inherent times of sounds were included in composition as a new temporal function in place of chronometrical or numerical time. In *Carré* (1959/60) these musical possibilities were revealed in a completely new light. The spatial separation of the groups of performers was the outcome of super-imposing several layers of time, with different tempi, a manoeuvre which, from the point of view of performing technique, could not have been accomplished by using a single orchestra.

A consequential reorientation of the concept of musical form was entirely concomitant with these innovations in Stockhausen's music. Let us here try to grasp what is essential in the concept of centri-fugal formal tensions. In 1957 this 'openness' in a work's form led for the first time to the possibility of interchanging sections, in *Klavierstück XI*. With this Stockhausen first brought into play the concept of chance, of the aleatory, of a polyvalent technique of composition for large forms. In the handling of musical elements aleatory methods were of decisive importance in *Gesang der Jün-glinge* and also in *Gruppen*—although they are no longer recogniz-able in the final fixed version—as well as in *Zeitmasze*. It should be mentioned here that Stockhausen had already been stimulated to conduct experiments in aleatorism by Meyer-Eppler in 1953.* The actual creation of music became a function of the performer's actions and with this a completely new idea was offered to countless imitators in every part of the world. Meanwhile the aleatory, as Stockhausen understands it, is only a contributory factor in the entity which was to be defined in the concept of the typical process, or 'process model'. In his most recent compositions all the possibili-ties of this phenomenon are worked out. The work *Ensemble* (1967) is a special case, about which we have given a detailed account elsewhere in these pages.†

In several of his works Stockhausen has included the human voice. In Stockhausen the voice's presence is hardly any longer used to 'impart' something to the listener, in the way that we are accustomed to in our conventional vocal music, where the texts are

---

* This is described in the chapter 'The composer and his circle', on p. 237. (Translator's note.)

† See pp. 113–16. (Translator's note.)

almost without exception of a communicative nature. In Stockhausen it is much more a matter of bridging the old gap between
vocal music and instrumental music. Stockhausen's principal vocal–
instrumental works are *Carré* for four orchestras and choruses,
Momente for soprano solo, four choral groups and thirteen instrumentalists, *Mikrophonie II* and *Stimmung* for six singers. What the
singing voice imparts here—if we insist on this expression—are
parts of sentences without recognizable continuity, single words,
fragments of words and finally syllables and sounds in a scale of
phonetic differentiations which mediates between voiceless consonants and vowels. In addition it happens that the chorus is sometimes called on to make certain sounds beyond those made by the
instruments, such as, for instance, snapping of fingers, and so forth.
What is foremost here is the sound mixture that is sought and at the
same time the principle of the polyvalence of events. This new way
of handling language—here seen for the first time in a musical
context—could be seen as a parallel to the completely new kind
of linguistic organization practised by James Joyce in *Finnegans
Wake*.

In his origins Stockhausen is a German; his parents were of
peasant stock. But essentially he is a spirit who spans the whole
world. And in this he displays the characteristic universal breadth
which has come to all those who possessed greatness in their spiritual
life, no matter to what nation they belonged and no matter which
language came to them as their mother tongue. The first performance of an important work by Stockhausen was that of *Kreuzspiel* in
1952. And to this day (1968) Stockhausen has continued to unfold
the whole spectrum of a quite outstanding and significant talent
down to its farthest-flung creative details; he has attained a scope
of constantly increasing breadth; and now as then he is still—of
this there can be no doubt—in the full flood of his powers.

If since 1950 the contemporary music of West Germany has
again become a focus for the discussion of the world because of any
one representative of the younger generation, then it is because of
the creative achievements of Stockhausen. If at the end of the

eighteenth century it was in the person of Mozart that music rose above local and national style to take on the guise of a truly European music, then in our own times this same process is being completed by Stockhausen to its full extent in the shape of a music of the whole world.

The composer and his circle

The influence of the interpreter

Stockhausen's relationship with David Tudor and Christoph Caskel
has been one of close and friendly collaboration, particularly during
the years when he travelled through nearly all the countries of
Europe on concert tours with them.

While he was carrying out intensive studies in the field of electronic sound, it was partly thanks to encounters with the American
pianist David Tudor that Stockhausen achieved a new relationship
with instrumental music. He has never rehearsed any of his piano
pieces with Tudor; from the start, Tudor was not a 'performer',
but a partner. 'I shall see what can be done', Tudor often said when
Stockhausen would have suggested making alterations in the score.
For Tudor, scores are objects for the exercise of his intellectual and
technical imagination. He represents a completely different type of
interpreter from that which Stravinsky proposed as his ideal. He is
not an executant, but rather a creative accomplice.

An example will make this clear. In Stockhausen's *Klavierstück
VI*, Tudor, while studying the piece, tried out several solutions for
the pianistic attack, dynamics and tempo. At numerous places the
score requires an autonomous decision on the part of the player;
there are sections whose prescribed accentuation seems to be incompatible with the prescribed durations. Stockhausen favoured
altering the text so as to avoid all ambiguity. However, Tudor
realized that the ambiguity of the text offered the possibility of
different interpretations. The contradiction or ambivalence in the
text served to define a legitimate area of interpretation. Tudor's
decision was at the same time a decision in favour of the possibility
of different aspects.

This attitude gave support to Stockhausen's thoughts on new
instrumental composition. At first he had believed that there was
only one 'best' solution, namely the one that the composer had fixed
in the score. But in principle this view is only correct inasfar as it
concerns a narrowly confined stretch of historical time. With Tudor
Stockhausen could observe an interpretation of one and the same text
which, over long periods of time, repeatedly became the equivalent of

a re-creation. *Klavierstücke V–VIII* are dedicated to David Tudor.

It was at this time, in 1954/55, that Stockhausen began to write instrumental works in which degrees of variability and polyvalence of interpretation are differentiated and worked into the composition itself. In none of Stockhausen's works is any compositional principle repeated, and just as little repetition is envisaged in performance practice. First in *Zeitmasze*, then in *Klavierstück XI, Zyklus* and *Refrain*, a polyvalence of temporal, dynamic, timbre and to some extent pitch relationships is written into the music.

Experience with the completely new type of 'non-stationary' sounds produced by electronic means has shown particularly clearly what Stockhausen has called the 'inherent time of sounds'. Newly discovered sounds must first be experienced as having a life of their own and cannot be forced into any arbitrary rhythmical scheme. Each sound needs its own time in which to unfold, to be heard. This can be particularly well illustrated by the example of the instrumental music in *Carré*. At first Stockhausen had only a rough idea of how long, in terms of temporal measurements, a sound or group of sounds would need to develop. In the first draft, changes in time were notated as they revealed themselves in pitch *glissandi, crescendi* or changes of timbre. In the course of a reading with the sounds present in the aural imagination, each group was then timed several times over with a watch, and the average durations were inscribed into the score as approximate timings in seconds. In performance—under four conductors—special attention had to be paid to the sound at the moment of realization. Besides this there are passages using traditional rhythms for fast 'statistical' structures, in which the inherent times of sounds play no part. Many more possibilities for variable and polyvalent scores remain available for future use. As Stockhausen suggests, single structures, figures and moments might be erected without any definite intentions as to their context; only in the definitive combination of some 'version' would the reciprocal actions offered (or not) by the efficacy and extensiveness of the composer's thinking come into their own.

The percussionist Christoph Caskel, for whom Stockhausen

composed *Zyklus,* is another interpreter with whom he has been
associated over several years of work together. *Zyklus* was written in
1959 as a set piece for the international competition for the Kranichstein Prize for Percussionists, and is dedicated to Dr. Wolfgang
Steinecke, then director of the Darmstadt Summer School. It was
composed in close contact with Caskel, who demands extremely
precise and unambiguous notation and playing instructions, and
possesses an extraordinary sense of organization. 'What does this
mean, how do you intend that?'—such is his approach to notated
scores. In his practical way, he stimulates the composer to differentiate between the instruments at his disposal. This is important, as
some percussion instruments are primitive in the extreme. Unlike
the other instruments, they still leave ample room for improvement.
For *Zyklus* Stockhausen picked a number of instruments that are
not usually come across elsewhere—for example, slit drums and
cowbells. He uses three families of percussion: metal sounds, wood
sounds and skin sounds. Stockhausen proposes further possibilities
of development: gamuts of tuned membrane instruments (including higher registers), tuned metal blocks, tuned glass piping, differentiated choice of beaters, and so on. At present the percussionist is the most versatile of musicians, since he is not a specialist to
the extent that string or wind players are. How well Caskel has felt
his way into his task can be confirmed by anyone who has heard him
play *Zyklus* more than once. His playing constantly gains in nuances,
in imaginativeness and in its wealth of variation. Caskel's attitude
to polyvalent form is interesting. A polyvalently notated section
within a work gives him the opportunity to accommodate himself to
the contingencies of the instrumental and technical situation and
not just to seek a different version for each performance of the work.
It is his opinion that the polyvalence that has so far been written
into music, which represents only a slight gain for the listener, is
paid for too dearly by a loss in the quality of performance.

Anyone expecting Stockhausen to have identified the rhythmical
in *Zyklus* with vitalism, or anyone thinking in terms of jazz,
of primitive body rhythms, or of motoric rhythms, will be

disappointed. Primordially rhythm originates from vital forces, and even in the music of culturally more advanced peoples it has occasionally remained fixed at that stage. The possibility, peculiar to music, of transplanting elements gives the rhythmical aspect access into the regions of the expressive, the symbolic, the speculative and the rational. The sublimation of rhythm achieved by Stockhausen in *Zyklus* is founded also on the particular assortment of instruments used. The simpler the selection, the more 'primitive' and, equally, the more elementary the effect. But the more the timbres are susceptible to varied combination, the more differentiated, polymorphic and fluctuating will be the resulting impression. In *Zyklus* it is thoroughly irrational. The degree of sublimation and abstraction is primarily rooted in the layout of the composition (mediation between determinate and relatively indeterminate form through a series of nine structural types). Stockhausen further differentiates between three categories in each of the cited percussion families: those of determinate pitch, those of indeterminate pitch, and those producing noise. (Metal sounds: vibraphone—cowbells, gong, triangle—cymbals, tam-tam, jingles; wood sounds: marimbaphone— slit drums—guero; skin sounds: tom-tom (skin stroke)—side-drum —tom-tom (rim stroke), side drum-roll.)

The composer can only compose with what is offered him—in electronic music by the electronic apparatus, and in instrumental music by the instruments. To realize the ideas that haunt him he must think his way around the reality of his means. In *Zyklus* the choice of instruments for each situation in the composition is precisely laid down. The score indicates which instruments should sound and the manner in which they are to be played. Since then Stockhausen has gone on to be concerned with the idea of a variable designation of his instruments, indicating only the differences and relationships between the individual families. In doing this he need not demand specific instruments, but would have to give directions to obtain degrees between dark and bright (weak and strong), tonally pure and impure (with noise), simple and complex, of greater and lesser resonance, and so on. In this way compositions would be made open for all time. With the help of some or other instrumental group, one could then try to work out this or that differentiation of sound.

A further aspect is also essential: the use of the percussion in *Zyklus* erects a further barrier against the one-sided dominance of harmonic and melodic effects, drawing the attention rather towards rhythmic–metrical phenomena.

The composer's work with conductors also belongs in this section on interpreters and interpretation. Since the Romantics it has been considered paragonal in the art of the baton that the conductor should have the orchestra under his thumb. With several conductors working together on the performances of *Gruppen* and *Carré* new experiences were in store. At the first performance of *Gruppen* in Cologne, the conductors were Bruno Maderna, Pierre Boulez and Karlheinz Stockhausen (Hans Rosbaud taking Maderna's place in the subsequent performance at Donaueschingen), and for *Carré* in Hamburg the conductors were Michael Gielen, Mauricio Kagel, Andrzej Markowski and Karlheinz Stockhausen. Thus, with the exception of Rosbaud, all were conductors who are also prominent as composers. To quote Stockhausen: 'We create our common experiences; each tells me what he thinks about what is happening in his orchestra. I have asked my colleagues to communicate corrections immediately in rehearsal and to suggest alterations in the text if they think them necessary. And this equality of rights and of responsibilities in collaboration seems to me an entirely typical symptom of a new form of "interpretation", for in this particular work, *Carré*, we have to be prepared to react to each other, and must have complete respect for each other's conception, his dynamics, and his stick technique. I believe that this experience will always remain with me, and it should be possible to attempt even more often to work as a team on a single composition. It has a practical advantage as well: that of splitting up work in the rehearsals so that the orchestra and its individual musicians gain the benefit of particularized attention and less wastage of time; the result of this is an increase in quality.'

The principle Stockhausen used in *Zeitmasze*, whereby independent temporal structures reunite from time to time in a common tempo, was at first evolved only in chamber music. Translated into terms of larger ensembles and of the orchestra, this involves the necessity for coordinating the direction of independent complexes. In an orchestra there is as yet only a very limited possibility of musicians reacting to each other individually; only a few can sit close together and listen to each other. The coordination of larger instrumental groups has to be achieved by using several conductors.

Other friends and colleagues
Doris Andrae
Among his friends Stockhausen gives pride of place to his first wife Doris Andrae. It is to her that he is indebted for having made it possible for him to devote himself exclusively to his work from one year to the next, free from everyday worries. She accompanied him on many tours and made it possible for such friends as Pousseur, Ligeti, Cardew, Earle Brown, Heinz-Klaus Metzger, Tudor, Frederic Rzewski, Hugh Davies and Rolf Gehlhaar to stay at Stockhausen's house, often for longish periods; she created an atmosphere that was uncommonly congenial to his musical friends. To her Stockhausen dedicated *Kreuzspiel*, *Schlagquartett*, *Spiel* for orchestra and *Gesang der Jünglinge*.

Herbert Eimert
His association with Dr. Herbert Eimert has been uninterrupted since 1951. Stockhausen speaks with the greatest respect of this calm, cheerful man, who has always offered a ready understanding and willingness to help. In 1957 Stockhausen dedicated *Gruppen* for three orchestras to him. He remembers with gratitude the many nights spent with Eimert putting together or translating new articles into the small hours of the morning, or those evenings when such guests as Boulez, Pousseur, Cage, Tudor and many others would meet at Eimert's home.

Pierre Boulez

Stockhausen's association with Pierre Boulez has already been particularly close for a long time. Stockhausen first heard music by Boulez in 1951, and he first made personal contact with him in Paris the following year, a contact that has not been broken off since. Stockhausen has put it this way: 'No rivalry ever existed between us, and each of us has worked out his own way in life; there has always been collateral self-knowledge and mutual appreciation. I constantly admire in Boulez that which I have not and cannot have myself. Boulez is a composer for whom the quest for technical perfection is absolute, and this technique serves him as a basis for the formation of an unalterable personal style. His objective is the work of art, mine is rather its workings. Towards his goal, Boulez has not ceased to constantly lay hold on new methods which serve to individualize his work, and he has constructed a world which is his own world of language. Harnessed to this quest there is a constant endeavour to come to terms with tradition. In his work we find another successful résumé of the tradition of the West—and this at precisely the time when such a concept has become questionable. Boulez has a very definite idea that he must continue the French tradition, and he also has a clear idea of how he must continue it. He is decidedly intent on living on in his works; this is why he strives towards autonomy in his works, and why he constantly tends to build up "great works" from his store of experience and knowledge, whereas for me the conception of a work as a paragon seems devoid of interest inasfar as the further use of such a model is envisaged. Boulez has a synthesizing mind; he studies everything, absorbs everything into his system; and his urge towards synthesis can even successfully embrace the unification of phenomena so apparently opposed as those of the Viennese School and of French Impressionism. It is not surprising that he absorbs elements of Asiatic music; this too is well founded in the French musical tradition.'

It is as well here to recall a few data about Pierre Boulez. Born in 1925 in Montbrison (Loire), Boulez first studied mathematics and technology; after 1943 he studied composition with Olivier Messiaen and René Leibowitz. In 1946, on the recommendation of Arthur Honegger, Jean-Louis Barrault appointed him musical director of the Théâtre Marigny. From 1952 on he organized the Paris series of modern music concerts, the *Domaine musical*.*

Henri Pousseur

Stockhausen's friendship with Henri Pousseur dates from 1953. The Belgian composer was born in Malmédy in 1929; he studied in Liège and Brussels, worked in the Cologne and Milan electronic music studios, and has lived in Brussels since 1958, working for Belgian Radio. He is one of Stockhausen's most intimate friends. They have known each other from the time when discoveries in the new musical worlds they were exploring were really coming thick and fast. They readily and repeatedly told each other what they were working on at any time and what their new experiences were. In Pousseur Stockhausen admires two characteristics above all: the integrity of his personality and the acuity of his grasp of intellectual interrelationships. He arrives at artistic results by reflection rather than by aural intuition. His intelligence enables him to draw in ideas from areas previously unrelated: whether he is reading books on sociology, philosophy, politics, technology, mathematics or natural sciences, he can bring such ideas into harmony with musical ideas and develop them. The theoretician in him counterbalances the composer in a particularly auspicious complementarity.

Mauricio Kagel

Mauricio Kagel has lived in Cologne since 1957. He comes from a completely different environment in South America. Born in Buenos Aires in 1931, Kagel was a repetiteur and concertmaster with the Argentine chamber opera and at the Teatro Colon. At the same time he worked as a conductor for the radio, and was musical adviser at the University of Buenos Aires. As Stockhausen sees

* Gilbert Amy took over the direction of the *Domaine musical* in 1965. (Translator's note.)

him, Kagel is more speculative, more systematic, but also more inventive and exploratory than many Europeans, who are inclined more towards conventional musicianship and the perfection of their craft.

Whenever Kagel writes a new piece, he tries it out on all the instruments, a procedure which quite possibly no-one has ever attempted previously. He has an especial flair for sound effects. He delights in working up complex effects to sustain aural fascination. He claims that one of his principal concerns is with the 'psychologization of form'.

Kagel's ability to make musical use of stimuli from other fields is striking. He has a pronounced gift for thinking out in musical terms extramusical items, which might be ideas inspired by reading non-musical books. In this connection Stockhausen has made the following notable statement: 'It seems to me in general that one of the most essential talents of a musically creative person—perhaps musical talent itself even consists in it—is the ability to translate any idea whatever into music. One might see or read something, and thereupon get the idea of what kind of music one might make.' And on the same subject Stockhausen adds: 'Ideas do not always come from reflection on musical problems. I can equally well be stimulated by the work of an architect. I may have some experience, make some journey, see some landscape, and suddenly discover certain relationships which immediately give me a musical conception. The impression becomes transformed, transposed, and forms an independent musical idea.'

Cornelius Cardew

An example of fruitful collaboration between composers was that between Stockhausen and the young English composer Cornelius Cardew, who was born in London in 1936. Between 1953 and 1957 he studied composition and piano with Howard Ferguson in London, then lived in Cologne until 1960. For a year he worked closely with Stockhausen, particularly on *Carré*. Stockhausen had worked out the plans and had left a certain amount of latitude for discovering shapes or structures within given limits and provisions. Cardew undertook this work. A close comparison can be made between this situation and that of the architect's studio or with teaching in an artist's atelier.

Here is an example of the work done on *Carré*: for a particular structure it is specified that it should last 'very long', and also the instruments, the pitches, the intensity and the nature of transformation processes are specified. The chief change should take place, say, in the dynamics. For a chord of four specified pitches it is determined beforehand what forms should appear in the interpretation of the dynamic activity, and then—for instance—the form in which each note is brought out in turn from the chord is chosen. Thus Cardew was given the choice as to whether the first note or the second should be somewhat longer, in what order the notes should be played with a *crescendo*, and which instrument was to be selected from the given sound family.

Whilst Cardew worked in the afternoon after a preliminary discussion, Stockhausen could look through his realization in the evening and correct it. It would—in Stockhausen's opinion—be possible to take such collective work much further than in the case of *Carré*: it might amount to an equal collaboration, each participant reacting to the other and constantly offering fresh stimuli. Such a form of cooperative work has scarcely ever existed in music between composers. More frequently, though, it may be found between composer and librettist (one thinks of Bach, Mozart, Verdi and Strauss). But it should be remembered too that there must have been an active reciprocal influence between Dunstable and Dufay, and that one can point to such an influence between Haydn and Mozart and between Wagner and Liszt.

The idea of teamwork as a stimulus and exchange led Stockhausen further. Teamwork should not in fact mean a mere repartition of work in which an organizer, leading the team, assigns work to subordinate assistants who are the executive organs. Much rather the idea is that composers should mutually incite each other to greater things and benefit from 'feed-back' by working together at a problem and constantly showing each other new ways of looking at it. Thus what might be achieved is more than a mere reciprocal information, but a contact, a complex interreaction; and it would be achieved by working on a completely new level. Composition would become not the sum of two possibilities but the product of mutual correction, modification and stimulation. It would not consist of a continuing from the place where the other left off, but rather of new mutations of thought arising through the simultaneous presence of composers in cooperation. This leads to paths that one cannot discover alone. The thinking machines that are built today can take from man's shoulders such specific processes such as rapid combinatorial matching and the storage of experience in the memory. This makes it possible for man to concentrate on his really creative tasks, not only as an individual but also in group activities.

Gottfried Michael König

Gottfried Michael König was born in Brunswick in 1926, and since 1954 has been at the electronic studio of West German Radio. He is a composer and one of Stockhausen's technical assistants. Together, working in the studio every day (and at night too), they realized *Gesang der Jünglinge* (in about 6 months) and *Kontakte* (in about 10 months). Stockhausen reports that in König he came to value an uncommonly intelligent and cultured collaborator, whose judgment and criticism meant much to him, and whose modesty and sincerity won his respect.

Earle Brown

For several years there has been an exchange of ideas between Stockhausen and Earle Brown. He is an American, born in Lunenburg (Massachusetts) in 1926; a student at the Schillinger School of Music in Boston, he worked with Cage and Tudor in New York on the 'Project for music and magnetic tape'. He has been to Germany a number of times, and Stockhausen has visited him in New York. Conversations with him are particularly interesting to Stockhausen because Brown is a trained sound technician and has done much work for a record company. From this he has formed new ideas about recording procedures. Here is one of his ideas: A piece is recorded on tape, as has been the usual practice hitherto, but in different areas one after the other; the technician has his own score and mixes the 'composition' at the control desk. This idea led to further ideas and provided a stimulus towards new forms. A fascinating feature of the idea is that no-one except the technician would know what the final entity would be. It is already the case in television work that each individual cameraman works independently and the separate parts are selected and put together by an independent 'mixer'. Films of this kind, too, have already been made in America (see Whitney: *die reihe 7*).

Today's composer is not just active in composition; 'performing practice' has reappeared as an essential field making demands alongside those of composition. This is a new feature that is common to young composers and brings them together. It is not simply a question of writing music and communicating the experience of writing to others, but each has engaged in the propagation of music in his own way. Boulez has organized concerts in Paris, Pousseur plans programmes for Belgian Radio, and Stockhausen has arranged concerts and frequently has given talks about new music in late-night radio programmes. In the first place all this was latent in the situation after the war. One had to give performances of music oneself in order to have it listened to at all. Then again it is still inherent today as a result of the markedly experimental nature of the music. Composers began to organize small ensembles for themselves, to travel with them, to collect and exchange experiences. From the practical work of giving concerts came the opportunity to make recordings on tape and on disc. Hence the series of Boulez's *Domaine musical* concerts in Paris that the Vega company made available, and hence also the recordings that Brown made in the USA for Time Records.* To this was added the publication of

---

* These, together with further recordings made by Brown, now appear on the Mainstream label: see entries for *Zyklus* and *Refrain* in the 'Catalogue of Stockhausen's works', pp. 23, 24. (Translator's note.)

theoretical ideas in *die reihe* (Vienna), in the publications of the *Domaine musical* (Paris) and in Luciano Berio's *Incontri*.

Luigi Nono

A man somewhat apart in this context is Luigi Nono, a Venetian, born in 1924. He does not conduct, plays no instrument, seldom writes texts and organizes no concerts.* Nono and Stockhausen met in 1951 at the Darmstadt Summer School. There was an exchange of ideas between the two up till 1959; they taught together at Darmstadt and visited each other a number of times. Nono negotiated concerts for Stockhausen in Venice and Stockhausen introduced Nono's music in his lectures and late-night programmes, besides analysing parts of Nono's *Il canto sospeso* in his essay 'Speech and Music' (*die reihe 5*) together with Boulez's *Le marteau sans maître* and his own *Gesang der Jünglinge*. Stockhausen points out that at first—probably due principally to his latent ideological radicalism—Nono pursued a style whose conjunction of Webernian pithiness with Bergian emotiveness became markedly popular. After *Il canto sospeso* Nono restrained his manner of composition strictly within the limits of the technical and aesthetic criteria of a 'pointillist style'.

Luciano Berio

Through his work in the field of electronic music Stockhausen came into contact with Luciano Berio from 1954 onwards; Berio was the director of the Milan Radio studio for electronic music from 1955 to 1959. He arranged lectures and concerts for Stockhausen in Milan, published several of Stockhausen's articles in his periodical *Incontri* (Suivini Zerboni) and dedicated to Stockhausen his orchestral work *Allelujah I*. Berio is the 'musical craftsman' among the younger composers; his fluent pen has been responsible for a relatively large number of works in only a few years of composing (in-

---

* Nono has in fact undertaken a certain amount of conducting, as well as organizing concerts, some of them in connection with the Palermo Festival. (Translator's note.)

cluding pieces of 'elevated light music') and has always drawn a spontaneous response from a sizable public.

John Cage

In Stockhausen's work there are indirect points of contact with the American John Cage. Born in Los Angeles in 1912, Cage was a pupil of Henry Cowell and Arnold Schoenberg. He first set foot in Europe in 1954. Cage is at the extreme antipode of the European tradition; his work is a protest against our tradition such as is probably only conceivable on American soil. Cage demands of everyone a reappraisal of his own situation and his own world. He has no continuity of 'language', in contrast to the continuity of development usual in Europe. Stockhausen has known Cage's work ever since his first visit to Cologne, and they have met a number of times since. He stresses that with Cage there is a complete unity between a personal and an artistic world. A considerable number of discoveries, both large and small (for instance in notation) originate from Cage. He is a typical experimental composer; the musical result is the consequence of an experimental urge. He has an attitude of complete indifference to his own pieces and their fate, and cares nothing for any traditional concept of standards. He lives in a commune and is constantly in contact with people who play his music. Stockhausen summarizes his description of Cage as follows: 'How can one give any idea of all this ? First of all there is a concentration on new sounds, and on extremely determinate procedures, then there is a sudden *volte face*, a new line is taken, with indeterminate compositional procedures. A composer who draws attention to himself more by his actions than by his productions. And everything is mixed up with a good measure of philosophical thinking. A phenomenon that seems so completely beyond the pale, Cage represents, in his anarchic protest against the European tradition, the final destination of its own evolution—in a musical no-man's-land.'

However, Stockhausen can dispel one of the many misunderstandings that arise in assessments of the supposed influence of

Cage on European music. Time and again one reads that the incorporation of controlled chance in the work of Stockhausen, and subsequently of Boulez and Pousseur, was induced by the work of Cage. Stockhausen reports that the development of the forms he calls 'statistical', 'variable' and 'polyvalent' was germinated as early as 1953 by his researches with Meyer-Eppler into phonetics and information theory, and had made its mark on his thinking independently of Cage.

György Ligeti

A short time before the beginning of the Hungarian uprising in 1956, György Ligeti wrote from Budapest. He had heard late-night programmes and was interested in Stockhausen's music. A few weeks after the revolution Ligeti appeared in Cologne in a state of complete exhaustion, and lived for quite a long time with Stockhausen. Immediately after his arrival Ligeti had lost consciousness. He was taken first to hospital and then to Stockhausen's house, where he slept for 24 hours and refused all food. On waking he broke into a four-hour-long conversation about new music and electronic music, then he went back to sleep for another day and another night. Stockhausen analysed some things from his own work with him and recommended him to write an analysis of Boulez's *Le marteau sans maître* for *die reihe*. Later, however, the plan was changed, and Ligeti analysed instead Boulez's *Structure 1a* for two pianos. This is how the article that was to appear in *die reihe 4* came into being. After Ligeti had recovered and established a home for himself in Cologne he began his first experiments in the electronic music studio. Later he realized his *Artikulation* in the studio. Since that time Stockhausen and Ligeti have worked together at the Darmstadt Summer School on several occasions.

Alfred Schlee

Immediately after the first performance of *Spiel* for orchestra in Donaueschingen in 1952, the director of Universal Editions in Vienna, Alfred Schlee, approached Stockhausen and offered to publish his works. However at the time Stockhausen withdrew his first three scores (*Kreuzspiel, Schlagquartett* and *Spiel* for orchestra) from the public gaze. So it was another year before he could send his first score, *Kontra-Punkte*, to the publisher to be printed. The friendship between Schlee and Stockhausen was often severely put to the test when Schlee had to prevail upon his printers to comply with Stockhausen's 'impossible' demands—measurements given to the exact millimetre. His development of new notation occasioned violent discussions. Stockhausen describes Alfred Schlee as a man who in a time of incredibly rapid developments in music has demonstrated an openness and understanding for all new musical discoveries. He dedicated *Solo* for melody instrument with tape recorder to him, and *Mikrophonie I* to Schlee's youngest son Alexander, who is Stockhausen's godson.

Otto Tomek

Stockhausen has been in correspondence with Dr. Otto Tomek, consultative adviser to Universal Edition, since the beginning of the publication of *die reihe* in 1955. From this correspondence and from many meetings in Darmstadt, Cologne and Vienna, there sprang up a friendship between the two men. *Kontakte* is dedicated to Otto Tomek. The two worked in direct collaboration with each other when Tomek settled in Cologne as an assistant at the music division of West German Radio and was responsible for the production of several Stockhausen performances.

Ernst Brücher

In 1959 Stockhausen dedicated *Refrain* for 3 players to Ernst Brücher, probably his closest friend. As head of the Cologne artbook publishers Dumont Schauberg, Brücher is in contact with writers from all over and thus can offer a great deal to stimulate creative minds. Brücher edited an anthology of important articles from *die reihe* in book form under the title *Commentaries on the new music*, and his firm was commissioned by Universal Editions to print the scores of *Zyklus* and *Refrain*. Already on his first European

tours David Tudor was giving a number of premières and first
European performances of new piano music (particularly that of
young American composers) before a large gathering at the home of
Ernst and Majella Brücher, and in 1957 Stockhausen played electronic music there. He has said that in the most difficult moments
of his personal life Brücher alone stood by him.

Aloys Kontarsky

In 1962 the pianist Aloys Kontarsky gave the first performance of
Klavierstück IX, and with his brother Alfons Kontarsky he has
played the electronic organ in many performances of *Momente*.
His personal friendship with Stockhausen has grown up through
working together more and more. *Klavierstücke IX* and *X* are
dedicated to him, and since the days of *Mikrophonie I* (1964) in
which Kontarsky played the tam-tam, they have constantly
toured together. With Christoph Caskel and Stockhausen, Kontarsky has given many performances of *Kontakte* and *Refrain*; this
trio's interpretation of *Kontakte* and *Refrain* has been put on record
by Vox, with Stockhausen playing the celesta. Since his memorable
performance of all the *Klavierstücke* in a concert at the Darmstadt
Summer School in 1966, Kontarsky has given solo recitals of Stockhausen's complete piano works in many countries, and his performances have meanwhile been recorded on a CBS disc.

Harald Bojé, Alfred Alings, Johannes Fritsch, Rolf Gehlhaar

Like Kontarsky, the pianist Harald Bojé, the percussionist Alfred
Alings, the composer and violist Johannes Fritsch (who has often
taken part in Stockhausen's composition seminar at the Cologne
new music courses and at the Darmstadt Summer School) and the
German–American Rolf Gehlhaar (whom Stockhausen took to
Cologne as his permanent assistant after he had been one of the
twelve participants in the composition seminar at the University
of California in Davis during 1967) are all members of the ensemble
which performs *Mikrophonie I*; *Prozession* is dedicated to them,

and they have given several performances of *Kurzwellen* and *Hymnen*. Already they have given a completely new meaning to collective interpretation in our times.

Stockhausen has repeatedly spoken about the happy company of people this ensemble has turned out to be, a company in which—to quote Stockhausen—'in all the years of journeying together, of hotel-room existence, of carting apparatus around and concert-giving, not a single unfriendly word has been spoken and a splendid atmosphere of good humour has lent good speed to all our work.'

Michael Gielen

Since the first performance of *Carré* Stockhausen has spoken of the conductor Michael Gielen on frequent occasions and he recommends him whenever an opportunity to do so arises. Gielen and Stockhausen have conducted together a number of times in *Gruppen* for three orchestras, and Stockhausen arranged for him to direct the conducting course at the Cologne new music courses; Gielen conducted the first performance of *Mixtur* in Hamburg as well as further performances of the work, and his several performances of the orchestral work *Punkte* (premièred by Boulez at Donaueschingen in 1964, and later twice revised by Stockhausen) helped to secure a great success for the work.

Ladislav Kupkovič

Since the first performance of the chamber version of *Mixtur* (in Frankfurt, 1967) the Slovak composer and conductor Ladislav Kupkovič has belonged to Stockhausen's circle of friends. Kupkovič brought the Hudba Dneska ensemble to Germany from Bratislava and conducted two excellent versions of the work in the same concert; his performance has also been chosen for release as a gramophone record. Since then, Kupkovič and Stockhausen have met several times in Cologne and in Czechoslovakia, and Kupkovič has performed a number of Stockhausen's works in his own country.

Vinko Globokar

In the course of several encounters Stockhausen got to know the Yugoslav composer and well-known trombonist Vinko Globokar and came to value his friendship. Globokar took the initiative of working out a version of *Solo* and performing it (as did the Swiss oboist Holliger, who gave the European première of *Solo* in Basle). Stockhausen was so impressed by his integrity and artistic abilities that he recommended him as trombone teacher at the Cologne National College of Music and entrusted to him a course in teaching and interpretation at the Cologne new music courses.

Hugh Davies

Between 1965 and 1967 Stockhausen's assistant in Cologne was the Englishman Hugh Davies, who constantly accompanied him on tours, playing in the *Mikrophonie I* ensemble and in *Mixtur* (sine-wave generator); he took charge of correcting the proofs of the works published at this time (*Klavierstücke V–X*, *Mixtur* and *Plus/Minus*), produced the orchestral parts for *Momente*, worked on the printers' copies of *Mikrophonie I* and *Mikrophonie II*, engrossed himself for several months in the working sketches of *Gesang der Jünglinge* with a view to preparing a publishable score (which unfortunately did not come to fruition) and translated several of Stockhausen's texts into English. Since his return to England he has endeavoured to perform new instrumental-electronic music on the lines of Stockhausen's ensemble, and has founded a small electronic music studio in London.

David Johnson, Mesias Maiguashca

Two participants in the composition seminar of the Cologne new music courses were for some time technical assistants at the West German Radio electronic music studio in Cologne under Stockhausen's direction. The American David Johnson worked with Stockhausen on the realization of *Hymnen* from 1966 till the end of 1967, and at the end of his work in the studio he was commissioned to realize a composition of his own at the studio, which was first played at the Darmstadt Summer School in 1968; called *Telefun*, Stockhausen says of it that Johnson has here made a gigantic step forward.

Mesias Maiguashca from Ecuador was appointed Johnson's successor as permanent technical assistant at the studio; he impressed the ensemble as one of the best composers at the Darmstadt composition course in 1967 with his *Haus*.

Mary Bauermeister

In 1960 the painter Mary Bauermeister began to arrange for works by the younger composers to be played in her studio in Cologne. Among these there were many premières and first European performances. Composers and interpreters such as Cage, Tudor, Christian Wolff, Cornelius Cardew, Kurt Schwertsik, Kenji Kobayashi, Mauricio Kagel, Sylvano Bussotti, Nam June Paik, the critic Heinz-Klaus Metzger and the writer Hans G Helms acquainted an interested Cologne public and many foreign visitors (during the single week of the ISCM Festival in June 1960, for example, six concerts took place in the studio) with the latest developments, above all those of the young American school (George Brecht, La Monte Young and Toshi Ichiyanagi) and the compositions of Nam June Paik. Moreover she organized a dance evening for Merce Cunningham and Carolyne Brown (the wife of Earle Brown), with John Cage and David Tudor at two pianos.

Stockhausen knows a great many European and American painters personally and says that through the work of Mary Bauermeister he has gained a very precise insight into the problems and techniques of contemporary painting, and that he considers her most recent work to be amongst the most important that is being produced today. For long periods his composing has been influenced by close contact with her work and, among other works, he has dedicated *Momente* to her. In the presence of numerous composers taking part in Stockhausen's composition course in Darmstadt, the collaboration of Mary Bauermeister showed for the first time how his compositional procedures could be taken over into the field of painting and could be used for genuinely optical compositions, which in turn could prove stimulating for composers. On account of her excellent musical knowledge, Stockhausen has on several occasions asked her to take on the work of correcting his published scores.

Many sections of *Momente* constitute a 'portrait' of the effervescent and imaginative spirit of Mary Bauermeister; the score of *Plus/Minus* was formulated in Sicily in 1963 during a number of conversations in which her luminously intelligent way of seeing things made many ideas clearer; and in *Stimmung* some of Stockhausen's most beautiful poems are set to music which uses the human voice with great restraint.

Teacher and pupil

It is not by chance that as a composer Stockhausen was approached while still relatively young to take on the job of giving instruction to composers and composition students. The offer first came in 1957 from Dr. Wolfgang Steinecke, the founder and organizer of the International Summer School for New Music in Darmstadt, who died in 1961. However, Stockhausen refers back still further, dating the beginning of his 'pedagogical' activity as 1952, when he began to give introductory and analytical talks on the radio. From these beginnings he gradually evolved a technique of analysis of which there is further evidence in some of the *die reihe* articles. Subsequently the first Darmstadt course also took the form of a course of analysis, and here Stockhausen quickly realized that genuine instruction in composition would require a different form. Then in 1959 he first gave a composition course in Darmstadt. Participation was tied to a conditional clause: it was required that scores should first be submitted, and on the basis of these Stockhausen would decide whether the applicant should be admitted to the 'special course'; for he planned in advance for a restricted number of between ten and fifteen participants. Unlike the usual courses in which works were submitted and then discussed, each participant was to produce a composition within the course itself. However, this meant that the course would *a priori* have to last longer than usual. Already three weeks before the start of the Summer School proper a room was reserved in the hostel for each of the participating composers. It is worth recalling some of the names inscribed for the first course: Amy, Bussotti, Boehmer, Cerha, Goldmann, the Webern pupil Spira, Kaiser, Stiebler, Schwertsik, Tillmann, La Monte Young, Kelemen, Englert, Behrman—composers who had already become known through performances and were already experienced in their craft. The course began with Stockhausen propounding his plan to the participants: each was for once to attempt to make a clear formulation, regardless of the methods he usually employed, of the piece he proposed to write—in fact to produce a plan first. As it happened each also wrote a composition within the three weeks. Some of these were played in public at the end of the course and have since been performed a number of times. For this was Stockhausen's second underlying idea: direct contact was to be afforded between composer and interpreter. For this reason, Tudor, Caskel and Gazzelloni were already present during these three weeks. They could always be consulted, and it had been agreed that the compositions should be for these instruments alone—piano, percussion and flute. Every morning there was a three- to four-hour composition seminar in which individual work-plans were thoroughly discussed and developed. Then in the evening Stockhausen himself collected together what had meanwhile been worked out so as to prepare himself for the next day's discussion. The instrumentalists were already in a position to play certain pieces after only the first week.

Stockhausen sees this way of running a composition course as a model. Its three phases are constantly meshed together: 1) analysis; 2) practical composition with constant discussion and extremely close contact between participants both among themselves and with the director of the course; and 3) the cooperation of first-class artists as collaborators, advisers and interpreters. There should be opportunities for making corrections during rehearsals for the works' final performance, and particularly in the early stages: the actual sound must be the criterion. In this way the composer can learn his responsibilities towards the performer. All this is to take place *in camera*; the public is to be admitted only to the studio performance, the final concert. Thus the composition school, as Stockhausen conceives it, is nothing more nor less than a kind of laboratory, an uninterrupted collaboration over a period of a few weeks, a teacher–pupil work team. After these weeks of study the students go home and do further work on a completely specific task, not on theoretical exercises; in this way the impulse towards discovery remains strong and well stimulated, for it is directed to composition, regardless of the individual student's level of accomplishment.

A second possibility of instruction in composition as it might be understood by Stockhausen is founded on the idea of collective work, such as was developed in his collaboration with Cardew and of which his touring ensemble is the most notable example to date. The participants would be selected composers, in other words those who have previously presented themselves to Stockhausen by sending in their scores. The collective work would have to be pursued throughout a long period of time. The day would begin with a working discussion whose task would be to coordinate the work in accordance with a plan for which Stockhausen would be responsible, whereupon this plan could be continuously complemented by stimuli on the part of the collaborators. The idea would thus be one of equal participation on a single composition by all the composers in such a seminar—a group project, coordinated by the group leader. Alternatively, everyone might be equally responsible for the same parts; this would demand a very close participation, a very intimate contact, and a great deal of mutual respect. In this case Stockhausen himself would simply be a partner in the collaboration. To date, all experiments have fallen short of this conception. This possibility can be conceived as complementary to the usual form of instruction in composition, in which each writes his own piece and the participants come into contact with each other barely at all.

What considerations does Stockhausen have in mind when selecting his pupils? The students at Kranichstein were trained composers. His condition of acceptance is that they should have a 'completely spontaneous contact with contemporary music'. 'What is important is new thinking; that the student can cooperate fruitfully; that he understands why something is done in a particular way. Then he will also discover how it is done and how he himself can do it. If he has understood what essentially distinguishes present-day music from that of the past, then I have no doubt that he will learn to compose from instruction in composition; and by this I mean that he will *really* learn to compose—learn to invent and discover.' Hence it is not absolutely necessary to have already studied classical harmony, counterpoint and form. These can be learnt later. Insight into the rules of earlier systems will grow apace with a preoccupation with the rules of contemporary composition.

Profession and vocation

In specialist education the important emphasis is laid on the development of musical invention. The composer's idea (Stravinsky did not say this for nothing) is to a large extent brought into being by his work itself. Preoccupation with a single concern brings with it a concentration of invention that had previously been decentralized.

I think it important to bear in mind that these words, including the reference to Stravinsky, originate from Stockhausen himself. Stravinsky by no means sees inspiration as a precondition of the creative act, but rather as a manifestation of a secondary kind. In fact, creative activity is always linked with a gift for observation. That this view of Stravinsky's is only one among many is evident from history and from the differing opinions on intuition and inspiration that may be held either by artists themselves or by scientists, and in particular psychologists. On the other hand, Stockhausen has also spoken—and to this we shall come back later—of the 'inner voice', the 'call' and 'listening within oneself', hence of activities corresponding to attentiveness, listening and receptivity rather than to active and consciously directed work. One could further remark that both functions of the human mind, that of receptivity as a precondition and that of working out as a consequence, are naturally in no way mutually exclusive. Here in fact all we need do is to attend to the basic question as to which of the two activities the artist acknowledges at any time as the dominant function.

The question of technique is, to a certain extent, very important; each piece, in Stockhausen's view, demands its own technique. Each of his works poses radically new problems which cannot be approached from a common method or in accordance with any craft of composition, and still less as a matter of routine, but the method for each piece has to be worked out individually; everything must constantly be thought out afresh from first principles. It should go without saying that anyone aspiring to compose music ought to have an education that is not confined to music but traverses other fields as well. One has only to think of the impingence of music on other disciplines: for instance, its implications for acoustical engineering in broadcasting—and with what lessons the mechanical reproduction of music alone has enriched this field!— or its strong influence on visual artists, with Kandinsky and Klee at the forefront. Education should entail the development of a true understanding of all disciplines. Only by viewing his own horizons from such a broad plateau will the specialist be able to offer anything out of the ordinary. This should be an indispensable condition for all musical training, at least inasmuch as it aims at a comprehensive general education (and to the extent that the necessary intelligence is present in the first place).

A further and absolutely essential requisite for the budding composer is industriousness. There are, as Stockhausen has observed, many talented students with brilliant ideas but without the patience to work anything out to its conclusion. Composition—perhapes more than ever before, since works are very much more complex—requires boundless patience, for the composer has to spend a considerable time at work on each single composition. Moreover, one can hardly these days blithely present a copyist or a publisher with scores which introduce new notations; as a rule everything must be copied neatly by the composer himself, as well as being correctly paginated, supplied with clear illustrations of how the various symbols are to be printed, and so on. The process of composition is not today what it was in former times. No longer is it all wrapped up at the conceptual stage; nowadays the real work begins with writing the music down: one must think one's score through, justify every last detail, and pursue one's course consistently to the end, regardless of the fact that one may have new projects on one's mind. And then perhaps it may turn out at the performance that many details require still further improvement as their effect may not have been fully foreseen. One has to try things out and make corrections, for the realization in sound is more than the mere translation of what appears on the paper. In new scores there are more proposals than prescriptions.

About the process of creation itself Stockhausen has little to say; this makes his requirements for composers all the more significant. He has told how he will often leave off a score before the end and then feel an uncertainty about some passage or other. Counter-arguments will present themselves—the work is in order, it has all been thought through; and then the 'certain' will reappear. Stockhausen sees something of especial importance in this 'listening within oneself'. And equally important for him is the concentration needed to take up the inner voice that is like a call. It is as if one makes contact with oneself as with some unknown person, as if one wants to explore oneself, indeed has to explore and get to know oneself as something that mirrors itself and pays attention to itself. Stockhausen considers this attention to oneself the composer's alpha and omega: 'so that when something occurs to me, I can really hear, by listening, if a discovery is possible; in this way I can be open to things at exactly the right moment'.

Considerations of this kind also have their entailments in the pedagogical sphere. Obviously it is difficult to test out talents and to make assessments of character when one meets someone who wishes to study composition. Yet this self-critical attitude remains a criterion, even as early as the most elementary studies. 'If a composer is sharp enough in his judgment of himself, then he can also be sharp in his judgments of others; in just this way, outward criticism must have a corresponding counterbalance in inward criticism.'

In 1961 and 1962 the following students took part in the composition courses at the Darmstadt Summer School under Stockhausen's direction: Mary Bauermeister, François Bayle, Michael von Biel, Harald Bojé, Jacques Calonne, Aldo Clementi, Gertrud Meyer-Denkmann, Griffith Rose, Kurt Schwertsik and Makoto Shinohara; in 1967/68 the following took part: David Ahern, Jürgen Beurle, Boudewijn Buckinx, Gregory Biss, Junsang Bahk, Peter R. Farmer, Clare Franco, Johannes G. Fritsch, Rolf Gehlhaar, Nicolaus A. Huber, Mesias Maiguashca, Costin Miereanu, Tomàs Marco, John McGuire, Satoshi Nozaki, Jens-Peter Ostendorf, Jorge Peixinho, Avo Somer, Thomas Wells, Robert Wittinger, Fred van der Kooy and Jaroslav J. Wolf.

The students at the composition seminar at the University of California, Davis, in 1966/67 were: John Dinwiddie, Rolf Gehlhaar, Alden Jenks, William Johnson, Jonathan Kramer, Stanley Lunetta, John Mizelle and Gerald Shapiro.

Those who studied with Stockhausen at the University of Pennsylvania in Philadelphia in the Autumn of 1963 were: Stephen Albert, Thomas P. Aronis, Charles D. Gangemi, Charles A. Rudin, Maryanne T. Amacher and Michael Montgomery. In early 1964, they were: Allan L. Crossman, Richard J. Gross, Maryanne T. Amacher, Ronald E. Thomas, Carl R. Berky, Charles D. Gangemi, Joseph V. McDermott, Ellen Moore, Charles A. Rudin and David Saturen.

In the Summer term of 1963 Stockhausen taught at the Basle Academy of Music; here his students were: Salomon Fränkel, Hans Ulrich Lehmann, Pierre Mariétan, Paul-Lucien Méfano and Jorge Peixinho.

Musicology and new music

Musicology, as it is taught in Germany, is virtually exclusively an historical or systematic science. In the course of his visits to American universities Stockhausen got the impression that a salient feature there was a greater interest in contemporary music. Stockhausen sees nothing but advantages in the American conjugation of musicological research with musical practice and composition. It is precisely the musicologist who is best equipped to investigate with the necessary thoroughness the theoretical questions brought to light by the most recent developments in new music. Musicology would be in a position to offer assistance to musicians by providing examples and using analytical tools to examine the principles these embody. It is really among the tasks of musicology to see the present from its own special analytical point of view, so as thereby to make available an historical perspective, to clarify for the composer his place in his own world and to offer him fresh stimuli. One would hope in future times to see institutes of musicology, composition seminars and colleges for practical interpretation all housed together under one roof. The inclusion of facilities for studying acoustics and electroacoustics would be a necessary technical complement.

Such communal work might perhaps also do some good in an area which—at least in West Germany—suffers increasingly from qualitative deficiencies: music criticism. Should this in any case be any business of the newspapers, where it is deflected from specialist appraisal into an exercise in public relations? It is small wonder that Stockhausen cannot take criticism seriously, 'for it is hardly ever criticism of the matter in hand'.

Biographical notes

Karlheinz Stockhausen was born on 22 August 1928 in Mödrath, Cologne. His parents were of peasant stock; their marriage took place on 4 October 1927, and at the time of their son's birth the father, a teacher, was working at Reid, Cologne. Between 1935 and 1941 Stockhausen lived at Altenberg, Cologne. It was during this time that he attended the secondary school at Burscheid as far as the third form, after his first four years at primary school. At the beginning of 1941 he went as a boarder to the teachers' training college in Xanten (Lower Rhine). He took piano lessons from his sixth year onwards. In Xanten he received instruction on the violin, and he played the oboe in the 'symphony orchestra' and the piano in the 'salon orchestra' of the college.

Stockhausen's mother, who had been in a sanatorium since 1933, died in 1941. His father, who had joined the army in 1939, was reported missing in 1945 and according to a wartime comrade was killed in Hungary. Stockhausen remained at the teachers' training college until October 1944, when he worked at the front as a stretcher-bearer at a military hospital at Bedburg on the Erft. Here he remained until March 1945. The end of the war found him in Altenberg.

He took a job as a farm-hand to a peasant in the neighbourhood of Altenberg. At the end of 1945, he took evening work as a repetiteur at an amateur operetta theatre. At the same time he studied Latin up to the standard of the lower sixth form. On 5 February 1946 he enrolled as a student at the classical academy in Bergisch Gladbach, and here he took his school-leaving examination on 10 March 1947. During this time at the academy he worked as a pianist for a dancing instructor and he earned money by conducting operetta performances.

At Easter 1947 he began his studies at the Cologne Academy of Music. He enrolled in the piano class of Hans Otto Schmidt-Neuhaus, a pupil of Erdmann. At the same time he began studies in musicology, philosophy and philology at Cologne University. After 1948 he made a study of educational music, and was a student in musical theory under Hermann Schroeder. On 19 October 1951 he passed with distinction the civil service examination for art teaching in higher schools, his special subject having been piano teaching. His theoretical work for the examination was a study of Bartók's *Sonata for two pianos and percussion.*

All the time that he was a student he earned his living by playing the piano in jazz and light music. In his last year as a student he undertook a tour as an improviser with the conjurer Adrion.

His real studies in composition began in 1950 with Frank Martin at the Cologne Academy. It was here that he wrote the student works *Three songs* for alto and chamber orchestra and a Sonata for violin and piano which was strongly influenced by Schoenberg. At this time Stockhausen was familiar with almost every work of Schoenberg, Stravinsky and Bartók, but of Webern he knew only the *Five Movements* for string quartet, Op.5, of which he had a miniature score.

In 1951 Stockhausen chanced to become acquainted with Dr. Herbert Eimert, the critic on the *Kölnisches Rundschau*. The two immediately found common ground discussing the works of the Viennese school. Eimert invited the 22-year-old student to his house and suggested that he should give a broadcast talk on the theme of his examination work on Bartók's *Sonata for two pianos and percussion.* A little later Stockhausen showed him his own Sonata for violin and piano, and Eimert organized a radio recording of the work in which Wolfgang Marschner, then an orchestral leader, was the soloist with Stockhausen at the piano. Then Eimert gave him a number of assignments for the evening music talks he was organizing for West German Radio; amongst other things, Stockhausen analysed the Second Piano Sonata by Boulez.

In the Summer of 1951, on Eimert's recommendation, Stockhausen paid his first visit to the International Summer School at Darmstadt-Kranichstein. His most lasting impressions were records of the *Four Studies* for piano by Messiaen, above all the 4th *Etude*, Boulez's *Le Soleil des eaux*, and also the *Sonata for two pianos* by Goeyvaerts, which he and Goeyvaerts played in one of Adorno's composition seminars.

At the time of his civil service examination he composed *Kreuz-spiel* for oboe, bass clarinet, piano and 3 percussionists. At the beginning of December, through the good graces of Eimert, he was rehearsing it at West German Radio for its first broadcast.

On 29 December 1951 Stockhausen married Doris Andrae, who had been a fellow piano student in Cologne; *Kreuzspiel* is dedicated to her. There are four children by that marriage.

Stockhausen's stay in Paris began on 10 January 1952. With no knowledge of the French language, he took up residence at the Cité Universitaire, the students' quarters on the Boulevard Jourdan. Here he stayed until April 1953. He shared his room in the hostel with a Turk, and personally got to know students of all nations, spending his mealtimes in the company of people of the most varied tongues, customs and colours; he attended many concerts, hearing amongst other things the music of a native group from Bali, and attending the 1952 Festival of 20th-century music.

At the Conservatoire he was a regular participant in Messiaen's course in analysis and aesthetics, and he spent some hours at the home of Milhaud. He was vividly impressed by Messiaen's way of thinking, by his way of revealing the musical workings of compositions by Mozart, Stravinsky and Debussy, and by his analyses of his own works and his presentation of Indian rhythm and Gregorian notation: this was a mode of analytical observation which did not remain of the past, but related the past to the present in a practical manner. A personal contact with Pierre Boulez and Pierre Souvtchinsky began early in 1952. Parallel with his studies with Messiaen, Stockhausen worked at the studio for *musique concrète* that was affiliated to French Radio under the direction of Pierre Schaeffer. He got to know André Moles, Pierre Henri, Barraqué, Philippot, Hodeir, Fano, Yvonne Loriod and Yvette Grimaud. In the P.T.T. laboratory he analysed the sounds of speech, wood, glass, metal and so forth in respect of their acoustical properties, and conducted preliminary experiments in synthetic sound production on an electronic basis. In the studio for *musique concrète* he composed and realized an *Etude*.

The compositions dating from his time in Paris (all dedicated to his first wife, Doris Stockhausen) are as follows: the first commission of South-West German Radio for Donaueschingen, *Spiel* for orchestra, a *Percussion Quartet* for piano and six timpani, *Klavierstücke I–IV*, and the first versions of *Punkte* for orchestra and *Kontra-Punkte*.

During this time, too, Stockhausen and Eimert kept in touch through a lively exchange of letters on questions about electronic music. In May 1953 Eimert engaged Stockhausen as permanent collaborator at the West German Radio's electronic music studio, which was officially opened on the occasion of the International Music Festival during the same month.

Stockhausen complemented his work at the studio with a study of phonetics and communications under Professor Werner Meyer-Eppler at Bonn University (1954–56). Stockhausen's first compositions with electronically produced sounds were composed in the Cologne studio: *Studie I* in 1953, *Studie II* in early 1954, *Gesang der Jünglinge* in 1955/56; *Kontakte* was prepared as early as 1958, and was finally realized between September 1959 and June 1960.

In 1953 Stockhausen published his first Webern analysis (of the *Concerto* for nine instruments, Op.24) in the musical periodical *Melos*. During the same year he lectured on Webern at the Darmstadt International Summer School for New Music. Since 1957 he has directed courses in composition and analysis at Darmstadt, the only interruptions to this work having been in 1964 and 1965. In 1963, due to the initiative of Professor Hugo Wolfram Schmidt, the 'Cologne Courses for New Music' were inaugurated, of which Stockhausen was both founder and artistic director, since which time they have been conducted annually. In 1968 this institution gave birth to the 'Institute for New Music', which has thereafter functioned throughout the year, with Stockhausen in charge of the composition class. He directed a master class in composition at the Basle Conservatoire in 1963. In 1968 Stockhausen was awarded the Nordrhein-Westfalen Prize for Music.

For some years already Stockhausen had been making regular tours to give lectures and concerts of instrumental and electronic music. These concert- and lecture-tours have taken him round nearly all the countries of Europe, as well as the USA and Canada, several times. He has visited America in 1958, 1965 and 1966/67. In 1958 he performed new works, including electronic music, in 32 universities of the USA and Canada in the course of a concert- and lecture-tour. In 1965 he was Visiting Professor in Composition at the University of Pennsylvania, Philadelphia, and in 1966/67 he held a similar position at the University of California, Davis. In 1966 he spent several months in Tokyo working at the electronic music studio of NHK, while fulfilling two commissions there. But despite all these journeys Cologne has remained Stockhausen's permanent home ever since his appointment at the West German Radio electronic music studio there, where in 1962 he succeeded Herbert Eimert as director.

After composing *Mikrophonie I* (1964) Stockhausen founded an instrumental ensemble for live electronic music which gave performances of this work—with Stockhausen himself controlling the electronic transformation of sound with filters, potentiometers etc. —and for which he composed *Prozession*, the version of *Hymnen* with soloists, and *Kurzwellen*; this ensemble provided some of the determinant conditions for the compositions of *Aus den sieben Tagen*, and also created *Kurzwellen mit Beethoven* in December 1969. The players are Aloys Kontarsky, Fred Alings, Rolf Gehlhaar (previously Hugh Davies and Jaap Spek), Johannes Fritsch, Harald Bojé and—depending on the programme to be given— Christoph Caskel. Every year Stockhausen goes on tour with this ensemble for several months. Throughout Europe it has made a reputation as a model for the practice of live electronic performance, in which traditional instrumental playing is combined with electronic processes of transformation and modulation during performance. Several gramophone records have been produced which, in view of the increasing 'openness' of Stockhausen's scores, will take on a considerable importance in founding a new 'oral' tradition.

Stockhausen considers these tours and recordings to be of such importance that he prefers the scores of his recent works to remain unpublished until he has performed the work with his ensemble in most of the major European cities and brought out a recording of it. He has expressed the wish that other ensembles who are to play these new works should first listen to his performances, recordings and gramophone records and use them to provide criteria for the quality of their own interpretations.

An extended journey back from Japan by way of Hong Kong, Cambodia (Angkor), Thailand, and especially India, continuing through Persia, the Lebanon and Turkey, left a decisive impression on Stockhausen. In 1968 he paid quite extended visits to Hawaii and Mexico.

After Poland and Yugoslavia some time beforehand, Czechoslovakia has recently welcomed Stockhausen's work. Thus in April 1968 a seminar for new music was held in Smolenice (Bratislava), bringing lectures and performances of Stockhausen's works. In Bratislava and Prague he gave three concerts which included the compositions *Hymnen, Prozession, Zyklus, Kontakte* and *Klavierstück X*. Similarly a considerable number of young Russian musicians have shown an interest in Stockhausen's work in recent years, performing or playing tapes of his works in concerts and discussion evenings, and publishing some of his writings.

In 1970, in the spherical auditorium of the German Pavilion at the World Fair in Osaka, works by Stockhausen were performed live by 20 soloists from 5 different countries for $5\frac{1}{2}$ hours every day over a period of 183 days to a total audience of about a million listeners.

On 3 April 1967 Stockhausen married the painter Mary Bauermeister in San Francisco; she has borne him two children. *Momente, Plus/Minus* and *Stimmung* are dedicated to her.

Index of Stockhausen's works

(including collective compositions planned and supervised by Stockhausen)

Index of subjects

Index of names